# THE ENGLISH PRESBYTERIANS

# AN
# APOLOGY
### FOR THE
*English Presbyterians,*
## WITH A
# DEFENCE
### OF THE
## Heads of Agreement
Affented to by the *United Ministers,*
in the Year 91.

# LONDON,
Printed for *John Nutt*, near Stationers-
Hall, MDCXCIX.

# THE ENGLISH PRESBYTERIANS

## FROM ELIZABETHAN PURITANISM TO MODERN UNITARIANISM

BY

C. G. BOLAM
JEREMY GORING
H. L. SHORT
ROGER THOMAS

*London*
GEORGE ALLEN & UNWIN LTD
RUSKIN HOUSE  MUSEUM STREET

PRINTED IN GREAT BRITAIN
*in* 11 *point Ehrhardt type*
BY THE ABERDEEN UNIVERSITY PRESS
ABERDEEN

# PREFACE

This book was originally intended to be a contribution to the commemoration of the tercentenary of the Great Ejection—a history of the English Presbyterians from 1662 to the present day. When, however, it became apparent that the volume would not be ready for publication in time for the tercentenary celebrations it was decided to extend its scope by including a more detailed study of Presbyterian origins. It is hoped that this has made for a fuller and better work. Certainly the delay has had one beneficial result, in that the authors have been able to take cognizance of the large number of contributions to Dissenting history published in and after 1962.

In order to avoid repeating a tale that has often been told, in this book much of the general history of Dissent has been left on one side. No attempt has been made to describe the hardships which Presbyterians endured along with other Nonconformists, nor to catalogue the various efforts that were made to repeal repressive legislation. Instead the object has been to study the ideals, the stresses and strains, the changes of thought within Nonconformity as these affected the Presbyterians—and especially those amongst those who in times became the backbone of modern Unitarianism. But this is not a Unitarian history; other contributory streams in the making of later Unitarianism, such as that from the General Baptists, receive no close examination. Furthermore, since the focus is on England, little is said here about parallel developments in Scotland, Wales and Ireland.

The history that follows was designed as a composite work and the difficulties that attend such work are notorious. The conditions limiting the historical exertions of the four participants made these difficulties even greater, for the work has had to be prepared by people whose main preoccupations lie elsewhere. The editorial work has been shared by the two London contributors, Jeremy Goring and Roger Thomas, who have been fortunate in having the use of Dr Williams's Library as a place of meeting and as a centre for research. For this hospitality they wish to record their gratitude to the Trustees and staff of the Library.

The four collaborators would express a deep indebtedness to the Hibbert Trustees and to the Trust's Secretary, the late Dr H. Stewart Carter. The Trust has given support and encouragement throughout a long period of time and awarded a Hibbert Fellowship to Dr Goring to enable him to devote part of a year to research into eighteenth century Dissent. Grateful thanks are also due to the Council of the General Assembly of Unitarian and Free Christian Churches who made it possible for the authors to meet together regularly in London and Oxford.

A special word of thanks must go to Dr Patrick Collinson, Dr Geoffrey F. Nuttall and the late Dr Mortimer Rowe, who read parts of the work at early stages in its development and made most valuable comments and criticisms. Although they cannot of course be held responsible for its faults, any merits that the book may have owe much to their unstinted generosity in reading and comment. The authors are also greatly indebted to Mr Alastair K. Ross who read the whole work in the interests of its general intelligibility. The book is certainly a better book because of his wise and kindly advice.

*March* 1967

# ABBREVIATIONS
### *for works frequently referred to*

## BOOKS

Abernathy   G. R. Abernathy, Jr, *The English Presby-terians and the Stuart Restoration, 1648–1663* [*American Philosophical Society*, vol. lv, 1965]

Baillie   Robert Baillie, *Letters and Journals*, ed. David Laing, 3 vols., 1841–2.

Barlow   R. B. Barlow, *Citizenship and Conscience*, Philadelphia, 1962.

*Beginnings*   G. F. Nuttall and others, *The Beginnings of Nonconformity*, 1964.

Bennett   T. Bennett, *Laws against Nonconformity*, 1913.

Bosher   R. S. Bosher, *The Making of the Restoration Settlement*, 1951.

Bradshaw   William Bradshaw, *English Puritanisme* [Anon], ed. of 1660.

Brockett   A. Brockett, *Nonconformity in Exeter, 1650–1875*, 1962.

Calamy, *Abridgement*   Edmund Calamy, 1671–1731, *Abridgement of Mr. Baxter's history of his life and times*, 2nd ed., 1713, vol. 1.

Calamy, *Hist. Account*   Edmund Calamy, *Historical Account of my own Life*, ed. Rutt, 2nd ed. 1830.

Cal. Rev.   A. G. Matthews, *Calamy revised, being a revision of Edmund Calamy's Account of the ministers and others ejected and silenced, 1660–62*, 1934.

*CSPD*   *Calendar of State Papers Domestic.*

Caplan   Neil Caplan, 'The lean years of Sussex Nonconformity' in *CHST*, xix. 185–91.

*CL*   *The Christian Life.*

*CR*   *The Christian Reformer.*

Colligan, *Arian movement*   J. H. Colligan, *The Arian movement in England*, 1913.

Colligan, *Eighteenth cent. Nonconf.*   J. H. Colligan, *Eighteenth century Nonconformity*, 1915.

Collinson, 'Field'   P. Collinson, 'John Field and Elizabethan Puritanism' in J. E. Neale, *Elizabethan government and society: essays presented to Sir John Neale*, 1961.

| | |
|---|---|
| *CHST* | *Congregational Historical Society Transactions.* |
| *DNB* | *Dictionary of National Biography.* |
| Densham and Ogle | W. Densham and J. Ogle, *The Story of the Congregational churches of Dorset*, 1999 [*sic*]. |
| Doddridge, *Corresp.* | Philip Doddridge, *The correspondence and diary*, ed. Humphreys, 5 vols. 1829–31. |
| Drysdale | A. H. Drysdale, *History of the Presbyterians in England: their rise, decline and revival*, 1889. |
| *EHD* | *English Historical Documents*, ed. D. C. Douglas, 1953 etc. |
| *Enquiry* | *Enquiry into the state of the Dissenting Interest* [Anon.], 1730. |
| *Exeter Assembly: Minutes* | *The Exeter Assembly: the minutes ... as transcribed by ... Isaac Gilling*, ed. A. Brockett, 1963. |
| Every | G. Every, *The High Church Party*, 1956. |
| Gordon, *Cheshire Classis* | Alex. Gordon, *Cheshire Classis minutes 1691–1745*, 1919. |
| Gordon, *Freedom* | Alex. Gordon, *Freedom after Ejection*, 1917. |
| Gordon, *Heads* | Alex. Gordon, *Heads of Unitarian history*, 1895. |
| Gordon in *CL* 1888/9 | Alex. Gordon, 'English Presbyterianism' in *CL*, 1888, 597, 615; 1889, 2. |
| Halley | R. Halley, *Lancashire: its Puritanism and Nonconformity*, 2 vols. 1869. |
| *Heads of Agreement* | *Heads of Agreement assented to by the United Ministers in and about London: formerly called Presbyterian and Congregational*, 1691. (Reprinted in Gordon, *Cheshire Classis* and in D.W.L. *Occasional Paper*, no. 6, *An Essay of Accommodation*, 1957.) |
| Hunter | Joseph Hunter, *The Rise of the Old Dissent*, 1842. |
| James | T. S. James, *The History of the Litigation and Legislation respecting Presbyterian chapels ... 1816–1849*, 1867. |
| Jordan | W. K. Jordan, *The Development of Religious Toleration in England*, 4 vols. 1932–40. |
| *JEH* | *Journal of Ecclesiastical History.* |
| *JPHS* | *Journal of the Presbyterian Historical Society of England.* |

| | |
|---|---|
| *Jus divinum* | London Provincial Assembly, *Jus divinum ministerii, or the divine right of the Gospel-ministry* . . . 1654. |
| *LJ* | *Journal of the House of Lords.* |
| Lyon Turner | G. Lyon Turner, *Original records of early Nonconformity*, 3 vols. 1911–14. |
| McLachlan, *EETA* | H. McLachlan, *English education under the Test Acts*, 1931. |
| McLachlan, *Essays* | H. McLachlan, *Essays and Addresses*, 1950. |
| Martindale | Adam Martindale, *The Life of Adam Martindale written by himself*, ed. R. Parkinson (Chetham Soc., o.s., 4), 1845. |
| Merivale | Anna W. Merivale, *Family Memorials*, 1884. |
| Milton, *Works* | John Milton, *Complete Prose Works*, Yale U.P. and Oxford U.P., 1953 *etc.* |
| *MR* | *Monthly Repository.* |
| Murch | Jerom Murch, *A History of the Presbyterian and General Baptist churches in the West of England*, 1835. |
| Neale | J. E. Neale, *Elizabethan Government and Society: essays presented to Sir John Neale*, 1961. |
| Nuttall, *Visible Saints* | G. F. Nuttall, *Visible Saints: the Congregational Way, 1640–1660*, 1957. |
| Nuttall and Chadwick | G. F. Nuttall and O. Chadwick, eds. *From Uniformity to Unity, 1662–1962*, 1962. |
| Pearson | A. F. Scott Pearson, *Thomas Cartwright and Elizabethan Puritanism, 1535–1603*, 1925. |
| Powicke i | F. J. Powicke, *A Life of the Reverend Richard Baxter, 1615–1691*, 1924. |
| Powicke ii | F. J. Powicke, *The Reverend Richard Baxter under the Cross (1662–1691)*, 1927. |
| Powicke in *CHST* | F. J. Powicke, 'Arianism and the Exeter Assembly', 'The Salters' Hall controversy', 'The Salters' Hall Assembly and Advices for peace', in *CHST*, vii. 34–43, 110–24, 213–23. |
| Powicke in *UHST* | F. J. Powicke, 'Apology for the Nonconformist Arians of the 18th century', in *UHST*, i. 101–28. |

Powicke in *Essays Cong.*   F. J. Powicke, 'English Congregationalism in its greatness and decline (1592–1770)' in A. Peel, *Essays Congregational and catholic* [1931].

Puritan Manifestoes   W. H. Frere and C. E. Douglas, *Puritan Manifestoes* (Church Hist. Soc., 72), 1907.

Rel. Baxt.   *Reliquiae Baxterianae: or Mr. Richard Baxter's narrative of the most memorable passages of his life and times*, ed. Matthew Sylvester, 1696.

Savoy Declaration   *The Savoy Declaration of Faith and Order 1659*, ed. A. G. Matthews, 1959.

Shaw   W. A. Shaw, *A History of the English Church during the Civil Wars and under the Commonwealth*, 2 vols, 1900.

Studies, 1964   *Studies in the Puritan tradition* (Joint supplement, Congregational and Presbyterian Historical Societies), 1964.

Surman in *UHST*   C. E. Surman, 'The Presbyterian Classical System 1646–1660' in *UHST*, x. 193–202.

Thomas in *Beginnings*   R. Thomas, 'The Break-up of Nonconformity' in G. F. Nuttall and others, *The beginnings of Nonconformity*, 1964.

Thomas in *JEH*   R. Thomas, 'The Non-Subscription Controversy amongst Dissenters in 1719: the Salters' Hall Debate' in *JEH*, iv (1953), 162–86.

Tudur Jones   R. Tudur Jones, *Congregationalism in England, 1662–1962*, 1962.

UHST   *Unitarian Historical Society Transactions.*

Vindication   London Provincial Assembly, *A vindication of the presbyteriall government and ministry*, 1650.

Watts, *Post. Works*   Isaac Watts, *Posthumous Works*, 2 vols. 1779.

Whiting   C. E. Whiting, *Studies in English Puritanism from the Restoration to the Revolution, 1660–1688*, 1931.

Wilson, *Dissenting churches*   Walter Wilson, *The History of Dissenting churches . . . in London . . .* , 4 vols. 1808–14.

Wood, *Church Unity*   A. H. Wood, *Church Unity without Uniformity*, 1963.

# Abbreviations

# CONTENTS

# CHAPTER I

# INTRODUCTION

*by* JEREMY GORING

---

When by ancient privilege Protestant Dissenters present a loyal address to the Throne, those designated 'Presbyterian' appear twice over. They appear once as members of the General Body of London Ministers of the Three Denominations, Baptist, Congregational, Presbyterian. They appear again as the Body of London Ministers of the Presbyterian Denomination. Although the name is the same the denominational affiliations are different.[1] The first group belong to the Presbyterian Church of England, a nineteenth century foundation whose principal roots are in Scotland. The second group belong to the General Assembly of Unitarian and Free Christian Churches, a loose federation of congregations, many of which stem from the indigenous Presbyterianism of England, dating back to the sixteenth century.

Despite its four hundred years of continuous history English Presbyterianism has so far received little attention from historians. Much has been written about the early history of the movement up to the time of the Civil War, but its subsequent history in the three centuries following the Restoration has gone largely unrecorded. Some historians have appeared to suggest that there was no subsequent history worthy of record. Skeats and Miall stated that after 1689 'the denomination vanished as suddenly as it had arisen; and, excepting in literature, has left little visible trace of the greatness of its power'.[2] Others imply that, for a century or more, English Presbyterianism remained dormant like an ancient peerage, only to be brought out of abeyance with the creation of the 'Presbyterian Church in England' in 1836. This was the view put forward in

---

[1] On the last occasion that the privilege was exercised, on the accession of Elizabeth II in 1952, the 'Presbyterian Body' did so jointly with the Three Denominations, the 'Dissenting Deputies' and the Free Church Federal Council. On that occasion the deputation was (by a courtesy rota) led by Dr Mortimer Rowe, Secretary of the General Assembly of Unitarian and Free Christian Churches.

[2] H. S. Skeats and C. S. Miall, *History of the Free Churches of England*, 1891, 248.

B

A. H. Drysdale's *History of the Presbyterians in England* (1889), the last full-scale attempt to record the story of the English Presbyterians. In his later chapters Drysdale devoted a great deal of attention to the handful of old Presbyterian congregations that became affiliated to the nineteenth century 'Presbyterian Church' and all but ignored the far greater number that eventually became either Unitarian or Congregationalist.[1]

Although the Unitarians and Congregationalists may properly be regarded as the principal heirs of the English Presbyterians, no adequate account of this heritage can be found in any of their denominational histories.[2] Unitarian historians, being on the whole more interested in theological ideas than religious movements, have tended to focus their attention upon individual thinkers like John Bidle, Thomas Firmin and Samuel Clarke, who could by a little stretch of the imagination be counted as early exponents of Unitarian thought but who were not directly involved in the life of the congregations which came to be designated Unitarian. E. M. Wilbur's monumental *History of Unitarianism*, for example, only takes cognizance of Presbyterians in so far as they manifest definite anti-trinitarian symptoms. After a cursory glance at the Ejection of 1662 and the subsequent fate of the ejected, he comments: 'All that, however, is apart from the main current of the stream of history that we are following here.'[3] If the 'stream' that he was following appears to some observers to be more like a series of disconnected whirlpools, this is no criticism of his purpose nor any depreciation of his achievement. It merely means that there is a place alongside it for a more organic history.

If the Unitarians can be charged with neglecting their Presbyterian forebears, so also can the Congregationalists. The number of former Presbyterian congregations that are now affiliated to the

[1] For the congregations that became affiliated to the Presbyterian Church of England, see J. Goring, '1662 and the Unitarians' in *The Christian World*, November 23, 1961, 10.

[2] The Unitarian historian with the deepest understanding of English Presbyterianism was Alexander Gordon: unfortunately he never published anything more comprehensive than his excellent *Heads of Unitarian History*, 1895, and a number of valuable articles in learned journals. Another percipient writer was William Whitaker, whose *One line of the puritan tradition in Hull: Bowl Alley Lane Chapel*, 1910, serves as a model of what a chapel history should be.

[3] E. M. Wilbur, *A History of Unitarianism in Transylvania, England and America*, 1952, 210.

Congregational Union of England and Wales has never been calculated, but it is probable that it does not fall very far short of the
number joined to the General Assembly of Unitarian and Free
Christian Churches.[1] Congregationalist historians, however, have
tended to concentrate their attention upon those parts of their
tradition which stem either from seventeenth century Independency
or from eighteenth century Methodism. The most recent history
of Congregationalism gives no account of the way in which, in the
eighteenth century, some congregations that were Presbyterian in
origin parted company with their Rational Dissenting brethren and
aligned themselves with the evangelical Independents.[2] How and why
such congregations became Congregational rather than Unitarian
are among the questions which the present book will try to answer.

### English Presbyterianism not Scottish

Another aim of the book is to remove certain popular misconcep-
tions. The first and most persistent of these relates to the Presbyterians' failure, after the passing of the Toleration Act in 1689, to
establish some form of national ecclesiastical organization on the
Scottish model. Duncan Coomer remarked that after 1689, although
the Presbyterians occupied the premier position among Dissenters,
their 'Presbyterian' title was a misnomer, because 'they never
realized their dream of a land covered by a network of Synods,
Presbyteries and Church Sessions'.[3] Similarly Professor Tudur
Jones suggests that it was only the severe persecution which they
suffered after the Ejection which prevented the English Presbyterians from setting up 'that carefully articulated network of synods
and church courts which is Presbyterianism'.[4] The fact is that they
failed to set up such a network because they had no wish to do so.
The vast majority of them had no enthusiasm for that carefully

---

[1] There are about 100 Unitarian congregations in England which are Presbyterian
(or mixed Presbyterian-Congregational) in origin. They are mainly located in the larger
towns, whereas the Congregational chapels with a Presbyterian descent are generally
in more rural areas. A list of Unitarian congregations (with foundation dates, but with
no indication as to their original denomination—Presbyterian, Independent, General
Baptist, Methodist, etc.) is printed in the *Year Book* of the General Assembly of Unitarian and Free Christian Churches.

[2] R. Tudur Jones, *Congregationalism in England 1662-1962*, 1962.

[3] D. Coomer, *English Dissent under the Early Hanoverians*, 1946, 10.

[4] Tudur Jones, 110. Cf. G. R. Cragg, *The Church and the Age of Reason*, 1960, 136:
'The Presbyterians . . . believed in a national system of representative "church courts",
but they never succeeded in establishing it.'

articulated network of church courts which was characteristic of Scottish Presbyterianism and which had been introduced into England as part of the price of Scottish support for Parliament in the Civil War. To the average English Presbyterian of the second half of the seventeenth century Coomer's 'dream' might have seemed more like a nightmare.

Secondly, it has to be made plain that Scottish Presbyterianism is not the only Presbyterianism. The assertion that it is so might indeed be called one of the 'common errors of history'. As Alexander Gordon, himself of Scottish descent, observed many years ago, people have a strange tendency to 'run off to Edinburgh or Aberdeen' to find the model of what Presbyterian government ought to be.[1] But to do so is to forget that there are and always have been several distinct types of Presbyterianism, Continental, Scottish, English. Right from the beginning English Presbyterianism exhibited features which distinguished it sharply from the system established north of the Border. In England much greater importance was attached to the individual congregation: thus the 'presbytery' or prime unit of church government was not, as in Scotland, a meeting of delegates from different congregations; it was the governing body of a particular church, or what the Scots would call a 'kirk-session'.[2] Although there were English Presbyterians who did at times advocate a hierarchical Presbyterian system with higher courts exercising jurisdiction over churches, they generally insisted that a classis or synod should be purely consultative and should not interfere with the sovereign independence of the individual congregations.

The Scots, for their part, were insistent that the English system was not properly Presbyterian. Evidence of the strength of their feelings on this point comes from the pen of an English Presbyterian minister visiting Scotland in 1709, who had an amusing encounter with an old lady who denied that Englishmen had the Gospel. On going over the various aspects of the Gospel, he elicited from her the admission that there was no difference between them on these matters:

'Well then', said I . . . , 'if the belief of what God has revealed, and the fruits and effects of that belief where it is sincere and hearty, are the

[1] Gordon in *CL*, 1888, 597.          [2] Ibid.

same with us and you, how can it be that you should have the Gospel
with you and not we also among us?'—'Ah! Sir', said she, 'you have
with you no Kirk Sessions, Presbyteries, Synods and General Assemblies, and therefore have not the Gospel.'[1]

From this standpoint it would appear that Englishmen remained
without the Gospel until the nineteenth century, when, as a result
of Scottish missionary endeavours, a Presbyterian Church with a
complete hierarchy of ecclesiastical courts was eventually established in England.

But even if the English Presbyterians did differ fundamentally
from their Scottish brethren in matters of church government it
would be incorrect to conclude, as some have done, that they were
therefore virtually indistinguishable from the Independents or
Congregationals. To a casual observer a Presbyterian congregation
might seem to bear a very close resemblance to an Independent
one, but in fact there were significant dissimilarities reflecting essential differences in ecclesiastical theory. While Congregationals
thought in terms of the 'gathered church' of true believers, the
Presbyterians thought in terms of the parish and were prepared
to admit to Communion not just those who could give a satisfactory
account of their religious experience but all those in the neighbourhood who had some understanding of the Christian faith and had
not disqualified themselves by evil living. This Presbyterian attitude
was not changed by the upheaval of 1662 which drove the ministers
from their livings: though they were now without parishes they
continued to regard themselves as parish ministers, serving the
needs of everyone in their locality who wanted to attend their
services. Even today Unitarian churches still retain something of
this character: there is often on the one hand no clear demarcation
between members and non-members, and on the other a strong
tradition of service to the wider community.

*'Drifting into Arianism'*

The process by which in the eighteenth century many Presbyterians came to be Unitarian in theology has often received only superficial examination, the matter being dismissed with some such con-
temptuous phrase as 'drifting fast into Arianis'.[2] Such phraseology

[1] Calamy, *Hist. Account*, ii. 170.
[2] R. W. Dale, *History of English Congregationalism*, 1907, 541.

is doubly inaccurate. In the first place it is inexact historically to describe the heterodoxy of eighteenth century Presbyterians as 'Arianism'. While it is true that anti-trinitarian notions not altogether dissimilar to those of Arius were to be found among their ministers, it cannot be said that the Trinity was the major issue until Priestley and Lindsey began to preach a militant Unitarian doctrine in the last quarter of the century. What distinguished the 'new scheme preachers' from the old was not a doctrine about the person of Christ but one about the nature of man: the orthodoxy from which they were breaking away was not that of Athanasius but that of Calvin. With all due respect to J. H. Colligan, there was no 'Arian movement in England' (except perhaps in the Church of England).[1] In so far as there was a 'movement' among liberal Dissenters it was Arminian rather than Arian in complexion. One important piece of evidence for this comes from a document of 1732, in which an orthodox Independent inveighs against 'the spreading of Arminianism' among the Presbyterians. Their heterodoxy, he writes,

> is very often first manifested in their attacking the divine decrees by applauding the doctrine of universal redemption as a sentiment that is full of benevolence; from thence they appear fond of pleading the cause of the heathens, and of the possibility of salvation merely by the light of nature in a sincere improvement of the powers and faculties of men; and by degrees these charitable sentiments produce a small opinion of revelation and of the necessity of it in order to salvation . . . No wonder they become hereupon sceptics and amongst other truths the doctrine of the Trinity is with them a matter of jest and ridicule.[2]

Clearly the author regarded anti-trinitarianism as but one consequence of a fundamental Arminian attitude to the whole Christian scheme. It is wide of the mark to say that 'at this date the term Arminian connotes an Arian tendency',[3] because Arminianism connotes so much more than this.

The Arminianism of the English Presbyterians should not be confused with the Arminianism of the Wesleyan Methodists. Dr Geoffrey Nuttall distinguishes between these by describing the one as 'an Arminianism of the head' and the other as 'an Arminianism

[1] J. H. Colligan, *The Arian Movement in England*, 1913.
[2] 1732 MS. Report, 82/3–4.
[3] Coomer, op. cit. 78. He was referring to the document of 1732 quoted above, which he wrongly attributed to 1730.

of the heart'.[1] There is truth in this distinction, but the real difference between the two theologies is a historical one. Wesley's Arminianism was that of Arminius himself (as introduced into England before the Civil War by the Caroline divines), while the Presbyterians' Arminianism was that of a later generation of Remonstrants (as introduced into England by Limborch, Le Clerc and Locke, and reinforced by Baxter's dislike of Calvinism in its Antinomian form). Wesley might be described as a Calvinist who chose to contract out of the doctrine of Predestination, whereas the Presbyterians were thorough-going Arminians (in the contemporary Dutch sense of the term) who believed that 'it was only by relating revelation and reason that a workable theology could be formulated'.[2] This led them not just to be *against* particular election and redemption' but to be *for* justification by sincere obedience in the room of Christ's righteousness'.[3]

The Arminianism of the Presbyterians was no mere truncated or negative Calvinism into which men 'lapsed' or 'drifted', but a positive attempt to revive what they conceived to be 'primitive Christianity'. They were passionately concerned to lay before men 'the religion of Christ . . . in its original simplicity and native beauty, free from adulteration and mixture'.[4] As a distinguished Congregational historian pointed out, it is not true to say that the heterodox Presbyterians were necessarily less evangelical in fervour than their orthodox Independent contemporaries. They were critical of doctrines that took men's minds off the 'practical religion' found in the Gospels, for they 'had come to realize that if the Church preached a faith which had no vital relation to moral righteousness it was dead'.[5] Such a statement represents a corrective to the assessments of such writers as Drysdale, who likened eighteenth century theological liberalism to a poisonous fungus; McLaren, who compared it to dry-rot; Coomer, who called it a blight; or Bogue and Bennett, who spoke of it as a disease.[6]

[1] G. F. Nuttall, 'The Influence of Arminianism in England' in *Man's Faith and Freedom* (*ed.* G. O. McCulloh, 1962), 46–7.

[2] L. J. Van Holk, 'From Arminius to Arminianism in Dutch Theology' in ibid. 39.

[3] 1732 MS. Report, 87/8. (Editor's italics.)

[4] S. Bourn, *Religious education begun and carried on in three catechisms*, 1748, p. iii.

[5] Powicke in *Essays Cong.* 307.

[6] Drysdale, 508; *The Ejectment of 1662 and the Free Churches* (Nat. F.C. Council), 1912, 23; Coomer, op. cit. 28; D. Bogue and J. Bennett, *The History of Dissenters*, 1833, ii. 210.

Again, it has been alleged by many historians of Dissent that this 'doctrinal decay' led directly to the collapse of Presbyterianism as a significant religious movement.[1] The allegation is largely without foundation. While it is true that in the eighteenth century there was a considerable decline in the number of Presbyterian congregations, it cannot be said that heterodox theology was the primary cause. There was no such decline among the General Baptists, who, with an equally liberal theology, were at this period going from strength to strength.[2] Furthermore, where there was a decline in the Dissenting interest it was not only the heterodox congregations that were affected. It has been shown that of the thirty-odd Dissenting causes in and about London that became extinct in the 1720s more than half could be classified as orthodox. Orthodoxy could be much more lethal than heterodoxy: as F. J. Powicke said, 'Many an orthodox church died of its own orthodoxy —an orthodoxy so dry and sapless that it starved the highest impulses of the soul and only fed its self-righteousness, its malice and its pride'.[3]

Clearly then one must look elsewhere for the reason for the decline of the Presbyterians—and of the Independents too, for many of their congregations disappeared and many more were only saved from extinction by a last-minute transfusion of Methodist blood. One important factor in the situation was an economic one. The decline in trade badly affected the cloth-making districts of the West Country which had originally been strongholds of Presbyterianism: financial stringency, it should be noted, would have had a particularly serious effect upon a denomination which, with an ingrained antipathy to lay-preaching, looked upon the services of a paid, highly trained minister as a necessity.[4] Moreover, social considerations probably led numerous Presbyterians, both laymen and ministers, to conform to the Church of England: for the laymen it may have been a matter of social comfort and prestige, while for ministers conformity held out the added attraction of a parish ministry, with its wider opportunities for serving the community.[5]

[1] See. e.g. Wood, *Church Unity*, 290–2.     [2] Caplan, 188.
[3] Powicke in *Essays Cong.* 309.
[4] It is significant that the General Baptists generally did without paid ministers.
[5] Moreover, once the initial difficulty of the XXXIX Articles had been negotiated, there was probably more doctrinal latitude in the Church of England than anywhere else.

But perhaps the principal factor in the decline of the Presbyterians (and others) was simply the 'spirit of the age', which led the prosperous middle-classes (whose denominational allegiance might be Presbyterian, Independent or Anglican, but hardly ever Baptist or Methodist) to become pre-occupied with secular affairs. Religion, having ceased to be the master interest, dwindled into a mere department of life, and the warehouse replaced the meeting-house as the repository of men's highest hopes and aspirations.

## Why the Presbyterians 'lapsed'

The question is often asked: Why did the Presbyterians become 'tainted with heresy' while the Independents generally remained faithful to orthodox Christianity? Part of the answer seems to lie in the much more flexible constitutions of Presbyterian congregations. While the Independents adhered strictly to a system whereby such matters as the appointment of ministers, admission to communion and the exercise of discipline were the concern of the whole body of communicants assembled in church-meeting, the Presbyterians preferred a looser system by which spiritual matters were regarded as largely the concern of the minister. With them the appointment of ministers was made by an indeterminate body which might include all the 'hearers' and all the communicants, but which in practice more often than not consisted only of the trustees and principal subscribers. 'The Presbyterians', wrote R. W. Dale, 'trusted the management of their affairs to persons for whose religious life there was no guarantee—to trustees, subscribers and seatholders'.[1] This is not the place to ask whether there can be a 'guarantee' for anybody's religious life, even that of those who come forward with 'evidence' of the work of grace in their hearts. Dale, with his Congregational background, ignored the fact that at no period in their history had the Presbyterians adopted the practice of requiring 'testimonies' from prospective church members. Nevertheless, his point holds good: the Presbyterians preferred to trust the management of their affairs to a small number of people generally thought to be trustworthy rather than to a larger number who claimed to have had a particular religious experience. The Presbyterians with their more sceptical outlook were suspicious of people who claimed to have had spiritual experience. They tended to look down upon

[1] Dale, op. cit. 542; cf. Nuttall, *Visible Saints*, 112.

evangelicals as folk with 'a vast zeal, little knowledge and a violent attachment to a set of words and phrases which they have been used to look upon as orthodox'.[1] The Presbyterian leaders were an oligarchy who distrusted the sort of spiritual democracy associated with the Evangelical Revival.

It is not always realized that the 'oligarchy' which formed the hard core of the Presbyterian movement was composed not of ministers but of laymen. There has been a tendency to attribute the spread of heterodox views among the Presbyterians to their ministers who, having caught the infection at the academies, descended in their droves upon defenceless congregations of innocent unsuspecting Calvinists and proceeded to pass on the disease. But no germ, however deadly, can make any impact upon a body unless the body is ready to receive it; and in the eighteenth century the Presbyterian body was ready for Arminianism. The highly respectable merchants who were to be found among the trustees and principal seat-holders of Presbyterian meeting-houses in rich cities like Bristol, Leeds, Exeter and Norwich were generally out of sympathy with the type of 'enthusiasm' in which the colliers and weavers of less prosperous regions took such delight. A middle class for whom this seemed to be the best of all possible worlds found it difficult to accept the central idea of orthodox Christianity—that man was 'a weak and wretched creature in a doleful world, in dire need of being rescued and assured of a better world to come'.[2] To them Arminianism, with its optimistic view of human nature and its level-headed emphasis on practical morality, seemed to offer a truer scheme of salvation.

Perhaps because they tended to be better educated and of higher social standing, the Presbyterians were much more independent-minded than the Independents. In their approach to the Scriptures they were unwilling to be dependent upon the 'authoritative' interpretations of other men. They liked to think that their faith was rooted in the Bible and the Bible alone, but in this they were not quite accurate. Strictly speaking a man's faith is never rooted in the Bible, but in an interpretation of the Bible. The Independents' faith was rooted in the traditional Calvinistic interpretation— the Presbyterians' in what they took to be a more enlightened and therefore more authentic interpretation. For the one group ultimate

[1] Benson MSS. J. Smithson of Harleston to Benson, April 1755.
[2] R. N. Stromberg, *Religious Liberalism in Eighteenth Century England*, 1954, 120.

authority was vested in the tradition of the Church as enshrined in the Westminster or Savoy Confessions, for the other it was vested in free enquiry and reason. This emphasis on reason was to have far-reaching consequences. For that same reason which enabled the Presbyterians to maintain that such doctrines as Predestination, Original Guilt and the Trinity were non-scriptural was later to persuade them that even some scriptural beliefs could not be sustained, for Scripture is not always consistent with itself. Thus in the nineteenth century they were led, somewhat reluctantly, to conclude with Martineau that reason was 'the ultimate appeal, the supreme tribunal, to the test of which even Scripture must be brought'.[1]

## From Presbyterianism to Unitarianism

By 1800 the Presbyterians, who a century before had been the largest and most influential Dissenting denomination, were in a very much weakened state. Though still nominally the foremost of the Three Denominations, numerically they were now lagging a long way behind the Independents and the Baptists, whose ranks had been strengthened by the Evangelical Revival. Moreover, the balance of power had been further upset by the emergence of the Wesleyan Methodists, with more than seventy thousand members and many more unofficial adherents.

By resisting the Evangelical Revival the Presbyterians had cut themselves off from the main stream of the religious life of England. In choosing to ally themselves with the 'liberalizing' forces which were endeavouring to reconcile Christian faith and the new scientific outlook, they had separated themselves from the 'energizing' forces which were endeavouring to bring religion to the masses.[2] Furthermore, having taken the unpopular side in religion, they went on to do likewise in political thought: their championship of the cause of liberty first in America and later in France was another factor in the situation that led at the end of the eighteenth century to their near-extinction as a denomination.

By the second quarter of the nineteenth century, however, the fortunes of the English Presbyterians (or Unitarians, as they were

[1] J. Martineau, *Rationale of Religious Enquiry*, 3rd ed., 1845, 64.
[2] H. L. Short, *Dissent and the Community* (Essex Hall Lecture), 1962, 18 f.; Whitaker, 116 f.

now generally coming to be called) began to revive. This was partly due to the activities of enthusiastic anti-trinitarian propagandists who gave the movement a clearer doctrinal identity and attracted recruits from the Methodists and General Baptists.[1] Of deeper significance perhaps were the activities of less denominationally minded Unitarians who were inspired by the 'catholic' ideals of the old Dissent and who found for themselves 'a new way of belonging to the social order'.[2] The old Presbyterian concern for the wider community or 'parish' manifested itself in a new attempt at social usefulness. 'Domestic Missions' were established to give practical help to dwellers in the slums of great cities; 'undenominational' day schools were founded for the children of the industrial poor; congregations and individuals took a leading part in the work of creating new municipalities and reinvigorating old ones. In all this philanthropic activity there was a deliberate attempt to avoid proselytizing. The prevailing ecclesiastical spirit was comprehensive and catholic: some dreamed of a great federation of 'Free Christians' drawn from divers denominations, while others hoped for the evolution of a truly national Church of England in which all liberal-minded Dissenters could find a home. These hopes were not destined to be realized, and the denomination has continued its separate existence, though still cherishing the catholic ideal.

In describing the transition 'from Elizabethan Puritanism to Modern Unitarianism' this book tries to avoid making any extravagant claims. It does not seek to establish, as a narrowly denominational history might have done, the superiority of a particular spiritual lineage. It recognizes that there are several lines of the Puritan tradition in England—each with its own continuity from the past and each with its own contribution to the present. With comprehension in the air and a non-denominational (even a non-church) spirit abroad, this is no time for reviving ancient theological or ecclesiastical controversies. Rather is it a time for asking, after the manner of that earlier *Apology for the English Presbyterians*,[3] how denominational barriers arose in the past, why they have persisted into the present, and what can be done in the future to dissociate Christianity from sectarian bigotry and partisan zeal.

---

[1] H. McLachlan, *The Methodist Unitarian Movement*, 1919; the General Baptist wing of the Unitarian movement awaits its historian.

[2] H. L. Short, 23.          [3] Published 1699. See frontispiece of the present volume.

# CHAPTER II

# PRESBYTERIANS IN THE PARISH CHURCH

## ENGLISH PRESBYTERIAN BEGINNINGS

*by* C. G. BOLAM AND JEREMY GORING

According to the *Oxford English Dictionary* 'Presbyterian' was a new word in 1641.[1] This was a momentous year in which to make a début, one of the most tumultuous years in the history of England, the year that saw the trial and execution of Strafford, the imprisonment of the Twelve Bishops and the publication of the Grand Remonstrance. More significantly, from the presbyterian point of view, the year saw the beginning of a great debate, in and out of Parliament, on the subject of church government. For, late in 1640, 15,000 Londoners had presented a petition to the House of Commons praying

> That whereas the government of archbishops and lord bishops, deans and archdeacons, etc., with their courts and ministrations in them, have proved prejudicial and very dangerous both to the church and commonwealth . . . the said government with all its dependencies, roots and branches, may be abolished . . . and the government according to God's Word may be rightly placed amongst us.[2]

The subsequent debates on the 'Root and Branch' Bill, which occupied much Parliamentary time in the first half of 1641, form a watershed in ecclesiastical history, for they brought into the open and accentuated the divisions that had long existed in English religious life. One member who took a prominent part in the debates, Sir Edward Dering, said that he knew of three ways of church government: 'the Episcopal, the presbyterial, and that new-born bastard Independency'. Himself a moderate episcopal man, Dering

[1] We are indebted to Dr Patrick Collinson for pointing out that 'presbyterian' as an adjective was in use before 1641; Thomas Rogers used the word in *The Catholic Doctrine of the Church of England*, 1607 (see Parker Society reprint, 1854, p. 18). It may be that Rogers coined he word. 'Presbyterial' and 'presbytery' were current in Elizabeth I's reign.　　　[2] J. Rushworth, *Historical Collections*, 1692, pt. III, i, 93.

had no time whatever for Independency: 'I will be bold to brand it with the name of a new-minted seminary for all self-pride, heresy, schism, sedition and for all libertinism.' To such ecclesiastical anarchy the presbyterial way was, he believed, vastly preferable, being 'more orderly' and older established. Nevertheless, when compared with episcopacy, it too was a 'novelty'. 'It is enough for me that I can point out when it began: since my father was born, or I am sure at most in my grandfather's days.'[1]

## Early English Puritanism

Dering's chronology was correct. It was in 1558, the year of his father's birth and of Queen Elizabeth's accession to the throne, that those Protestant divines who, in Mary's reign, had fled to the Continent to escape Catholic persecution, began to return to England.[2] These divines, who had been deeply impressed by what they had seen of the reformed church of John Calvin at Geneva, formed the nucleus of a brotherhood of preachers who early earned for themselves the nickname 'puritans'; for they were dedicated to the task of purifying the work and worship of the Church of England. Unlike their Scottish counterparts, who had to contend with much more adverse political and social conditions, the English puritans were not primarily concerned about the reform of church government. They generally 'left the things of government alone and advanced their interests in the church by preaching within the established scheme of things'.[3] Representative of these Elizabethan puritans was Sir Edward Dering's great-uncle, another Edward Dering, who was a tireless and fearless preacher of the Word but who was not unduly distressed by the presence in the church of unscriptural ceremonial or polity.[4]

Among the Elizabethan puritans, however, there was a significant minority who did campaign for ecclesiastical reform. These men wanted to re-create the pattern of church life that they found in Scripture, which meant the removal not only of 'popish' vestments

[1] E. Dering, *A Collection of Speeches . . . in Matter of Religion*, 1642, 82. The speech was apparently never delivered.

[2] 1558 was the *probable* date of Sir Anthony Dering's birth. See E. Hasted, *History . . . of the county of Kent*, 1790, iii. 229.

[3] W. Haller, *Liberty and Reformation in the Puritan Revolution*, 1955, 106. Cf. ibid. 8.

[4] See P. Collinson, *A Mirror of Elizabethan Puritanism: the life and letters of 'Godly Master Dering'*, 1964.

and ceremonies but of 'prelatical' bishops and archbishops. In
the New Testament, they argued, there was no separate order of
bishops; there was only one order, that of presbyters. The leading
figures among these advocates of 'presbytery' or 'presbyterial discipline' were Thomas Cartwright, Walter Travers and John Field.
Cartwright, whose lectures on *Acts* delivered at Cambridge in 1570
are generally regarded as marking the genesis of English presbyterianism, was the 'theorist' of the movement.[1] He was possibly the
co-author of the 'Disciplina Ecclesiae' which was circulated widely
in manuscript form in 1584.[2] The principal author, however, was
Travers, who had been a younger colleague of Cartwright at Cambridge, had later gone to Antwerp as minister of the English congregation there and from 1581 to 1585 was deputy master of the
Temple in London, a position in which he 'at last found a place
where he had the liberty of building a second Geneva after the
manner of Calvin and Beza'.[3] Travers's move to London brought him
into close contact with Field, who, with Thomas Wilcox, was the
convenor of a group of ministers that constituted 'the nerve-centre
for a presbyterian movement extending into most of the English
counties south of the Trent'.[4] In 1572 the group appears to have
been responsible for launching the anonymous *Admonition to the
Parliament*, 'the first popular manifesto of English presbyterianism'[5]
and for setting up 'the first English presbytery' at Wandsworth.[6]
Later they were to be instrumental in the establishment of numerous
*classes* or conferences of ministers, meeting monthly to regulate the
affairs of their churches.[7] It was to these conferences that in 1584
Field and his associates distributed manuscript copies of the
'Disciplina Ecclesiae' in the hope that, after agreement had been
reached on any necessary modifications, it would become the blue-
print of a national presbyterial system.

[1] Collinson, 'Field', 132.
[2] Ibid. 156. The 'Disciplina' was first *printed* in 1644 as *A Directory of Church-
Government*. See below, p. 41.   [3] S. J. Knox, *Walter Travers*, 1962, 59.
[4] Collinson, 'Field', 131.   [5] Ibid.
[6] There is insufficient evidence to say whether the Wandsworth meeting was a 'presbytery' in the Scottish sense or a 'parochial consistory' after the English manner. It may
have been some kind of semi-separatist assembly. See A. F. Scott Pearson, *Thomas
Cartwright and Elizabethan Puritanism*, 1925, 74 ff.
[7] One of the best known conferences was that set up at Dedham. See *The presbyterian
movement in the reign of Queen Elizabeth as illustrated by the minute book of the Dedham
classis, 1582–1589* (ed. R. G. Usher, Camden Soc. 3rd. ser., vol. viii).

This stage, however, was never reached. The ministers were lukewarm in their support of Field's proposals for regular meetings of conferences and synods. The majority of English puritan parsons looked no further than their parish boundaries and could muster little enthusiasm for the 'classical' or hierarchical presbyterial system that was finding such favour in Scotland. Field, who was apparently influenced by his numerous friends north of the Border, may justly be accused of Scotticizing, or as contemporaries would have termed it, 'Scotizing'[1]. In furthering his ideal of a church as a commanding unity embracing and controlling individual congregations he was introducing a concept that was unfamiliar and probably unacceptable to most English puritans. He seems to have gone beyond the position of Cartwright and Travers who drew a distinction between 'the sacred discipline of the church described in the Word of God' (and therefore *jure divino*) and 'the synodical discipline gathered out of the synods and the use of the churches'.[2] While the 'sacred discipline', i.e. the government of each particular church by its own 'presbytery', was regarded as 'necessary, essential and common to all ages of the church', the 'synodical discipline' was merely 'profitable' and open to emendation 'as far as it is not expressly confirmed by the authority of Holy Scripture'.[3] Cartwright and Travers seem to have held that the essential unit of church government was the local presbytery, 'which is a consistory and, as it were, a senate of elders'.[4] Beyond the particular churches they certainly envisaged a graduated scale of *classes* or conferences (roughly the equivalent of the Scottish 'presbyteries'), synods and assemblies, but the obligation to adopt such a scheme appears to have been largely moral. Every particular church, they said, *ought* to consult its neighbours, but apparently it could not be compelled to do so; 'no particular church hath power over another'.[5]

Field, who had been behind several unsuccessful attempts to carry ecclesiastical reform bills through Parliament, died in the year of the Armada, 1588—the year which also saw the publication

---

[1] For Scottish influence on Field, see Collinson, 'Field', 154–6.

[2] *A Directory of Church-Government*, 1644, sig. A2. Those responsible for the edition of 1644 emphasized the distinction between the 'sacred discipline' (the first published translation of the 'Disciplina Ecclesiae') and the 'synodical discipline' by printing the section dealing with the former in black letter. cf. Gordon in *CL*, 1888, p. 597. cf. G. Yule, 'Some problems in the history of the English Presbyterians in the Seventeenth Century', in *JPHS*, xiii. 4.     [3] Ibid. sig. C4.     [4] Ibid. sig. A2 *verso*.     [5] Ibid. sig. A3.

of that swan-song of Elizabethan presbyterianism, John Udall's *Demonstration of the truth of that discipline which Christ hath prescribed for the government of his church.* Thereafter there would be no further attempts for more than half a century to set up a presbyterian Church of England on anything resembling the Scottish model. The conference movement, often driven underground by persecution, continued to provide ministers with the means of mutual encouragement and criticism, but it never represented a threat to the established ecclesiastical order. The majority of puritan ministers concentrated on the immediate tasks of preaching and of administering discipline in their own parishes. If pressed on the point they would doubtless have confessed themselves to be in favour of a modified episcopacy, but they were not fanatical opponents of bishops. Their views on church government probably corresponded fairly closely to those of William Bradshaw, whose *English Puritanisme*, first published in 1604 and reprinted several times during the next forty years, became virtually the textbook for the great majority of those English puritan divines who wished to avoid the two extremes of Brownist anarchy and Scottish rigidity.[1] Bradshaw reproduced the principles embodied in the 'Disciplina Ecclesiae', but the terms in which he expressed the autonomy of the individual church were more forcible and detailed. A congregation, he maintained, was 'a true visible church of Christ', and 'the same title is improperly attributed to any other convocations, synods, societies, combinations or assemblies whatsoever'.[2] A church or congregation owed allegiance to no ecclesiastical jurisdiction save 'that which is within itself'.[3] Hence, supposing that 'a whole church or congregation shall err in any matters of faith or religion', no other churches had any right to 'censure, punish or control the same', but are only 'to counsel and advise the same'.[4] It is possible that Bradshaw wrote his book to refute the pretensions of Scottish presbyterians who, with the accession of James I, might conceivably have begun to exert more influence in England: the title was perhaps chosen in order to distinguish *English* puritanism from the type that prevailed north of the Border.

---

[1] Cf. G. Yule 'Some problems in the history of the English Presbyterians' in *JPHS*, xiii. 4. 'Brownist' was the name given to those Congregationals who separated from the Church after the example of Robert Browne (d. *c.* 1633).
[2] Bradshaw, 36 (*sic*).     [3] Ibid. 37 (*sic*).     [4] Ibid.

In 1610 Bradshaw's book was published in a Latin translation by William Ames, who wrote an introduction in which he paid tribute to Dering, Acontius, Cartwright and other 'sweet lights which God was pleased should shine in our hemisphere'.[1] Ames, a saintly scholar whom both Presbyterians and Independents were later to look back to as one of their spiritual forebears, may be regarded as representative of the English puritans of the pre-Civil War period. He trod the narrow ridge between congregational democracy and presbyterial oligarchy. Not surprisingly some found it difficult to ascertain his precise ecclesiastical position. His vagueness on matters of church polity exasperated his friend John Paget, the author of a lengthy treatise in favour of the Scottish system. In the course of it he says of Ames:

> I may justly testify that I have found him wavering in his opinion touching the authority of synods. For through the inward familiarity which I had with him for a long time for more than twenty years together, having oftentimes had earnest conference with him touching this question, and much complaining of the wrong done to many ministers by that book *English Puritanisme*, which he had translated into Latin, wherein there is such a peremptory restraint of all ecclesiastical authority unto particular congregations; though he did never plainly retract that which he published, yet he shewed himself divers times inclining to a change of his judgment—yea, and sometimes acknowledged that synods had power to judge of causes.[2]

Paget's work was one of a vast number of books and pamphlets which burst upon England in 1641, urging men to think deeply about matters of church government and obliging many who had hitherto cared little for partisan labels to declare themselves episcopal or anti-episcopal in judgment. Among the numerous pamphlets of the time was *An Answer* to a work that had appeared the previous year, the *Humble Remonstrance* in which 'a dutiful son of the church' (Bishop Hall) had upheld the divine right of episcopacy.[3] The *Answer* to Hall was the work of 'Smectymnuus', the collective pseudonym—devised from their initials—of five leading puritan divines, Stephen Marshall, Edmund Calamy, Thomas Young, Matthew Newcomen and William Spurstowe, whose main purpose

---

[1] Bradshaw, 37 (*sic*). For Acontius, see below, 48 n.
[2] J. Paget, *A defence of church-government exercised in presbyteriall, classicall and synodall assemblies*, 1641, 106.
[3] *An humble remonstrance to the High Court of Parliament*, 1640.

was to point out the differences between the contemporary Church
of England (with its separate orders of bishops, priests and deacons)
and the church of New Testament times in which 'there were no
bishops distinct from presbyters'.[1] In their view the English diocesan
system was not so much episcopal as prelatical: it represented a
major obstacle to those who were endeavouring to restore the purity
of the primitive church. The Smectymnuans complained bitterly
of 'the practices of the prelates', who, 'from the beginning of Elizabeth
to this present day' had done all that they could to 'hinder all further
reformation'.[2]

This particular complaint occurred in the postscript to the
pamphlet which, it has now been established, was the work of John
Milton, formerly a pupil of Thomas Young, one of the Smectymnuans.[3] Milton may be regarded as typical of that great majority
of English puritans who had hitherto taken no part in controversies
over church government but who were now being drawn into the
battle about bishops. He saw himself presented with a choice
between two ways of ordering the church, the 'presbyterial' and the
'prelatical'.[4] Since the prelatical way, which he associated with the
hated ascendancy of Archbishop Laud, was anathema to him, he had
no alternative but to declare himself for 'presbytery, if it must be so
called'.[5] But if Milton, like so many English puritans, now ranked
as a Presbyterian, this did not mean that he favoured the ecclesiastical system that went by that name in Scotland.[6] He shared the
distinctively English emphasis of Bradshaw and Ames and regarded
the 'parochial consistory' as the essential unit of church government.[7] While it was advisable that parochial consistories should
associate to form councils, it was clear that such councils derived
their authority from below:

Of such a council as this every parochial consistory is a right homo-
geneous and constituting part, being in itself as it were a little synod,

[1] Smectymnuus, *An answer to . . . an humble remonstrance*, 1641, 16.
[2] Ibid. 103.          [3] Milton, *Works*, i. 79 f.
[4] Milton, *The Reason of Church Government*, 1641, in *Works*, i. 750.
[5] Milton, *Of Reformation*, 1641, in *Works*, i. 610.
[6] Milton was later to describe the Scottish system as 'not presbytery, but arch-presby-
tery, classical, provincial and diocesan presbytery, claiming to itself a lordly power and
superintendency both over flocks and pastors, over persons and congregations no way
their own'. Milton, *Eikonoklastes*, 1649, in *Works*, ii. 492. Cf. below, p. 42.
[7] Cf. A. E. Barker, *Milton and the Puritan Dilemma, 1641-1660*, 1942, 30.

and towards a general assembly moving upon her own basis in an even and firm progression, as those smaller squares in battle unite in one great cube, the main phalanx, an emblem of truth and steadfastness.[1]

This poetic vision of the ideal church symbolizes the essential vagueness of the conception of ecclesiastical government held by most English puritans. They all agreed that diocesan episcopacy ought to go, but they had no clear notion of what should be put in its place. They had little knowledge of the usages of reformed churches in other countries: even the Scottish presbyterian system was a 'stranger' to them.[2] Most of them would probably have been willing to settle for a scheme which represented a *via media* between ancient episcopacy and modern prelacy. Hence the enthusiasm with which many churchmen greeted the compromise formula put forward at this time by James Ussher, Archbishop of Armagh and Primate of Ireland. Ussher, the creator of the chronology that figures in the older editions of the Bible, was one of the foremost biblical and patristic scholars of his day and was widely respected by both prelatists and puritans. Bringing a great weight of historical learning to bear upon the contemporary ecclesiastical situation, he produced 'The Reduction of Episcopacy unto the form of synodical government received in the Ancient Church'. His proposals, which were exploratory in nature and tentative in tone, involved the establishment of deliberative assemblies at every ecclesiastical level. In each parish the incumbent would meet weekly with the church-wardens and sidesmen to administer discipline to scandalous livers. In each rural deanery there would be a monthly synod of parish ministers presided over by a 'suffragan': this meeting would deal with offenders referred to it by parochial consistories. In each diocese there would be a yearly or twice yearly synod, attended by the suffragans and by some or all of the parish clergy, and presided over by 'the bishop or superintendent, call him whether you will': this assembly would take cognizance of the proceedings of the monthly synods and, if need arose, amend their decisions. In each province there would be a triennial synod, consisting of all the bishops and suffragans and elected representatives of the parish clergy: the meeting would have the archbishop as its 'moderator' and would deal with matters referred to it by the diocesan synods.

[1] Milton, *The Reason of Church Government*, 1642, in *Works*, i. 789.
[2] Cf. below, p. 49.

Finally, the two provincial synods might come together during sittings of Parliament to form a national council.[1]

At one time it seemed that Ussher's proposals would prove to be almost universally acceptable; they went a long way towards meeting the puritans' objections to Anglican episcopacy, because the bishop's power was to be limited by his need to have the concurrence of his clergy to his acts. On December 28, 1640 Robert Baillie, a Scottish observer in London, reported that 'a great faction' were supporting the Irish Primate in his advocacy of limited episcopacy.[2] This 'faction' clearly represented a formidable obstacle to those who supported the city of London's petition for the total abolition of all the 'roots and branches' of episcopacy. Ussher himself was in a key position, for he was a member of the committee set up by the House of Lords in March 1641 to consider the city's petition and the much milder 'remonstrance' subscribed by 700 or 800 of the more moderate puritan clergy from all over England.[3] To this committee, of which Bishop Williams of Lincoln was chairman and at least two of the Smectymnuans (Marshall and Calamy) were members, Ussher submitted his 'Reduction of Episcopacy' on March 12th.[4] Although the puritan representatives were apparently in favour of accepting Ussher's scheme, other members of the committee, including the chairman, wanted to see a less radical reform.[5]

Ussher's scheme also had the support of puritan laymen in Parliament. Sir Edward Dering, who in May 1641 agreed rather reluctantly to move the first reading of the Root and Branch Bill, clearly had many members behind him when he declared his preference for a reformed, primitive episcopacy. On June 21st he even went so far as to put forward a scheme of his own for an 'episcopal presidency' which in many important respects bore a close resemblance to Ussher's proposals: in each shire there would be a 'presbytery' of twelve or more able and grave divines, presided over by 'a

[1] For the full text of Ussher's 'Reduction', see R. B. Knox, 'Archbishop Ussher and English presbyterianism' in *JPHS*, xiii. 26–35. See below, p. 61.

[2] Baillie, i. 286–7.     [3] Shaw, i. 23, 66.

[4] J. C. Spalding and M. F. Brass, 'Reduction of episcopacy as a means to unity in England, 1640–1662' in *Church History*, xxx. 417.

[5] A. Gordon in *DNB*, s.v. Stephen Marshall. Doubtless the Smectymnuans would have liked to strengthen the provisions in Ussher's scheme regarding lay elders. See their *Answer*, 61 f. and their *Vindication of the Answer*, 1641, 183 f. The *Answer* was probably written while Bishop Williams's committee was in session.

bishop, or an overseer, or a president, or a moderator, or a superintendent, or a ruling elder, call him what you will'. Dering relates
that his speech lost him the prayers of thousands in the city, but it
won him some allies in the House.[1] The majority of the Commons,
it seems, were moderate men who would have been satisfied with
what has been described as a 'programme of purely Anglican
puritanism', which meant in practice a modified form of episcopacy.[2]
There was little or no demand for the extreme measures advocated
by either Independents or Scottish Presbyterians. As Dering put it
in a speech of November 20, 1641:

> Mr. Speaker, there is a certain new-born, unseen, ignorant, dangerous,
> desperate way of Independency. Are we, Sir, for this Independent
> way? Nay, Sir, are we for the elder brother of it, the Presbyterial
> form? I have not yet heard any one Gentleman within these walls
> stand up and assert his thoughts here for either of these ways.[3]

But in another assembly shortly to be convened at Westminster
both 'ways' were to find eloquent champions.

*The Westminster Assembly of Divines.*

On November 22, 1641 the Commons, by a narrow majority,
passed the Grand Remonstrance. This called for

> a General Synod of the most grave, pious, learned and judicious
> divines of this island, assisted with some from foreign parts professing
> the same religion with us, who may consider of all things necessary for
> the peace and good government of the Church, and represent the results
> of their consultations unto the Parliament, to be there allowed of and
> confirmed, and receive the stamp of authority, thereby to find passage
> and obedience throughout the kingdom.[4]

After considerable delays, occasioned by the outbreak of the Civil
War in August 1642 and the consequent national disruption, the
Assembly of Divines eventually met at Westminster on July 1,
1643. Apart from lay assessors one hundred and twenty-one English
divines were appointed to attend. Among these were a number of
moderate episcopal men, including Ussher who refused to attend
because the King had not given his sanction to the Assembly.[5]

---

[1] Dering, 27 f.; Shaw, i. 93.     [2] Shaw, i. 100.       [3] Dering, 47.
[4] Rushworth, pt. III, i. 428, 450.     [5] Spalding and Brass, 420.

The course of the Assembly's proceedings was greatly influenced by the events of the war. In September, Parliament, desperately anxious to obtain the support of the Scots in the struggle against Charles, yielded to pressure from Edinburgh and adopted the Solemn League and Covenant. The Covenant, which obliged those taking it to uphold the reformed religion as established in the three kingdoms of England, Scotland and Ireland, and to root out popery and prelacy, was promptly passed to the Assembly for its consideration.[1] The Assembly, which had hitherto been engaged in a discussion of the proposed alterations to the XXXIX Articles, then turned its attention to the more controversial matter of church government. The series of heated debates that ensued, which continued intermittently for nearly two years, revealed the extent of the ecclesiastical differences that divided the members. At one extreme were those who favoured a hierarchical presbyterian system on the Scottish model: this group looked for leadership to the five Scottish clerical commissioners (Alexander Henderson, Robert Douglas, Samuel Rutherford, Robert Baillie and George Gillespie) who, though not strictly members of the Assembly, took a prominent part in its debates. At the other extreme there were the Independents who would allow no interference with the sovereignty of the local church: foremost among them were Thomas Goodwin, Philip Nye, William Bridge, Jeremiah Burroughes and Sidrach Simpson, later known as the Dissenting Brethren. In the middle there was a large number who were not committed to any particular ecclesiastical blue-print but who wanted some kind of compromise solution. In this central party came some of the most learned and influential divines: William Twisse, a peace-loving man whose appointment as the first prolocutor of the Assembly earned the strong disapproval of Baillie and the Scots; Cornelius Burges, who deputized for Twisse in his illness and whose championship of a modified episcopacy led him to oppose the original form of the Covenant; and Thomas Gataker, who also had scruples about the Covenant and declared himself in favour of 'a duly bounded and well regulated prelacy joined with presbytery'. To them should be added the five Smectymnuans, although, with the passage of

[1] The full text of the Covenant is printed in *Rel. Baxt.* ii. 391–2. It was ordered to be taken by all Englishmen over the age of 18. They were not sworn to abolish the monarchy.

time and the pressure of the Scots, they veered towards a more rigid Presbyterianism.[1]

In the absence of any clearly-defined or consistent ecclesiastical policy among the English divines, it was perhaps inevitable that the Scots, with their very definite views, should have had a dominant influence on the thinking of the Assembly. From the outset they seem to have been determined to foist upon the English church a full-blown presbyterianism with a hierarchy of courts each ruling the court below. They started with the initial advantage that the English had accepted the Covenant as the price of Scottish aid against Charles. Baillie unashamedly counted upon the success of Scottish arms 'to assist our arguments'.[2] He acknowledged the reluctance of the English to fall in with Scottish ideas: 'As yet a presbytery [i.e. synodical authority] to this people is conceived to be a strange monster.'[3] But he and his fellow commissioners missed no opportunity, by enlisting the powerful influence of the city of London, by soliciting letters from reformed churches abroad in support of their cause, by propaganda and indeed by all available means, to exert pressure on the Assembly. In the process they not only encountered but provoked opposition and, what in the long run was more devastating, half-hearted and reluctant support. The most determined opposition came from the Independents, whose emergence as a consolidated party may almost be called the consequence of Scottish ineptitude. Initially the Independents had no unified ecclesiastical programme. They merely proposed that the church 'should go on in the manner and direction which the puritan brotherhood had been following all along'.[4] There is a very real sense in which it may be said that the Independents, in the early days of the Assembly, were upholding the ideals of a distinctively English presbyterianism. It was therefore with a good deal of truth that Sidrach Simpson could declare that the term Independent originally applied 'to those who stood for presbyterial government'.[5]

[1] For Twisse, Burges and Gataker, see A. Gordon in *DNB*. Cf. E. W. Kirby, 'The English Presbyterians in the Westminster Assembly' in *Church History*, xxxiii. 418–28, seen too late to be quoted. This supports the findings of this chapter in essentials with additional detail and a careful examination of the debates on separate items of church government, e.g. ordination and ruling elders. Cf. *An apology for the English Presbyterians*, 1699, 29 ff.

[2] Baillie, ii. 111. Cf. ii. 122, 201. Cf. G. Yule, 'Some problems in the history of the English Presbyterians' in *JPHS*, xiii. 9.      [3] Baillie, ii. 117.

[4] Haller, 115. Cf. Gordon in *DNB*, s.v. Philip Nye.      [5] Gordon in *CL*, 1888, 597.

The views of those who 'stood for presbyterial government' (in the English sense of the term) were most clearly expressed in the *Apologeticall Narration* which the five Dissenting Brethren published in 1643. The authors enlisted 'Master Cartwright, holy Baynes and other old Nonconformists' in support of their arguments for the primacy of particular churches and made an eloquent plea for a middle way between extremes.

> We believe the truth to lie and consist in a middle way betwixt that which is falsely charged on us, Brownism, and that which is the contention of these times, the authoritative presbyterial government in all the subordinations and proceedings of it.[1]

In the following year, as a reminder to contemporaries of the historic character of the 'middle way' of the English puritans, there came the first printed edition of Travers's and Cartwright's Elizabethan 'Disciplina Ecclesiae'. Translated into English and published as the *Directory of Church Government*, it had a profound influence upon the debates of the Westminster Assembly and helped to 'stay the movement of the Scotticizers'.[2]

In their effort to halt the onward march of Scottish presbyterianism the Dissenting Brethren were being driven to an ever more extreme intransigeance that perhaps went beyond their own better judgment; moderate men, as well as the Scottish commissioners, might well feel that the English church had need of some authority, some established government, in the regulating of its affairs. Independency, in its extreme demands for toleration, could be made to look like anarchy.

As matters developed, the Smectymnuans, who initially had wanted no more than the riddance of prelatical episcopacy and the substitution of any scheme of church government that would secure essentials and be free from tyranny, found themselves in a cleft stick. On the one hand they were endeavouring to accommodate the Scottish point of view, which had some measure of support from the city of London. On the other hand they were

---

[1] T. Goodwin *et al.*, *An Apologeticall Narration*, 1643, 12–13, 24. 'Holy Baynes' refers to Paul Baynes (d. 1617), whose *Diocesans Tryall* upheld the authority of 'parishional' against diocesan or provincial churches; this book, with a preface by Ames in which he likened the author's writings to those of Dering, Cartwright, Bradshaw and other puritan leaders, was published posthumously in 1621 and reprinted, significantly enough, in 1644.     [2] Gordon in *CL*, 1888, 597.

trying to conciliate the Independents, while avoiding the elements of anarchy of which they suspected them. Calamy, at one time a disciple of Ussher, seems to have taken up a more rigid presbyterian position through fear of the disintegrating tendency of congregationalism.[1] Marshall, however, seems throughout to have sought every means to find a way of satisfying the Dissenting Brethren and winning them over to a compromise solution of the ecclesiastical problem; certainly on a number of occasions he exasperated Baillie by so doing, and as late as 1646 Baillie was complaining that 'Mr. Marshall, our chairman, has been their [the Independents'] most diligent agent, to draw too many of us to grant them much more than my heart can yield to, and which to my power I oppose'.[2] But even Marshall had to succumb to Scottish pressure.

What those less involved in these ineluctable negotiations were thinking it is not hard to guess. Perhaps Milton was their most eloquent voice when he addressed his Smectymnuan friends and other English Presbyterians with the words:

> Because you have thrown off your prelate lords
> . . .
> Dare ye for this adjure the civil sword
> To force our consciences that Christ set free
> And ride us with a classic hierarchy,
> Taught ye by mere A. S. and Rutherford.
>
> Men whose life, learning, faith and pure intent,
> Would have been held in high esteem with Paul,
> Must now be named and printed heretics
> By shallow Edwards and Scotch What d'ye call.

No wonder he came to the conclusion that

> New PRESBYTER is but old PRIEST writ large.[3]

---

[1] See below, p. 50.                    [2] Baillie, ii. 343.

[3] D. Masson, *The Life of John Milton*, iii. 187, 468–71. 'A.S.' refers to Adam Steuart, who wrote two of the severest attacks on the *Apollogetical Narration* in 1643 and 1644; Rutherford was one of the Scots commissioners; Edwards was the notorious author of *Gangraena*, 1646, a bitter attack on the Independents; 'Scotch What d'ye call' apparently refers to Baillie.

## The Presbyterian Establishment

The occasion of Milton's outburst was almost certainly the publication in March 1646 of the first of a series of Parliamentary ordinances enforcing the scheme of church government which, after prolonged debate, had been agreed on by the Westminster Assembly.[1] This ordinance provided for the establishment of a network of church assemblies. In every parish there was to be a 'congregational assembly' consisting of ruling elders elected by the minister and members of the congregation and meeting weekly. Every county was to be divided into a number of 'classical presbyteries' consisting of ministers and lay elders elected by a body of Parliamentary nominees: meetings were to be held monthly. Each classical presbytery was to appoint at least six of its members (two ministers and four laymen) to attend the twice-yearly meetings of the provincial assembly, and each provincial assembly was to choose a similar number of delegates to any national assembly that Parliament might summon.[2]

Although on the surface it might appear that England had adopted the Scottish presbyterian system with all its ramifications, in fact this was not the case. Classical assemblies were declared to be lawful but no attempt was made to prove the special postulate of the Scottish system that individual congregations were bound to submit themselves to superior jurisdiction.[3] Baillie, comparing the new order with that which obtained in his own country, dubbed it 'a lame Erastian Presbytery'.[4] Another advocate of the Scottish system, John Bastwick, described the new scheme as 'Presbyterian Government Independent' in contrast to the genuine article north of the Border, which was 'Presbyterian Government Dependent'. The English system, he complained, upheld the independence of the local congregation and restricted the classical and provincial assemblies to a merely advisory role.[5]

[1] The scheme was finally agreed upon by the Assembly in July 1645. It was then passed to Parliament, where it underwent some modification before its eventual publication and enforcement.

[2] *LJ*, vii. 544–5.     [3] Gordon in *CL*, 1888, 615.

[4] Baillie, ii. 362. 'Erastian' was a word coined at this time to designate those who advocated the supremacy of the State in ecclesiastical affairs. Baillie regarded the English presbyterian system as Erastian because it left too much ecclesiastical discipline in the hands of the lay authority.

[5] J. Bastwick, *Independency not God's Ordinance*. Bastwick's book was published in 1645, when the scheme of church government was still being debated in the Assembly.

Baillie and Bastwick criticized the presbyterian order created in England because it failed to satisfy what they regarded as fundamental concepts, but these defects in themselves need not have prevented a presbyterian state system from functioning. That it was as lame in operation as Baillie contended it was in theory was soon quite obvious, for in many counties the system was never erected. Provincial assemblies were achieved only in Lancashire and London. The provision for a national assembly remained but a paper scheme never to be implemented. Parliament, which contained a small but vocal Erastian element, strongly opposed to a theocracy on the Scottish model, never showed any willingness to surrender its final authority to a religious assembly.

Failure at the national level was matched by failure at the local level. One factor essential to the effective running of presbyterianism (in both Scottish and English theory) was the co-operation of lay-elders. But here a very real difficulty soon manifested itself, for even in those 'classes' which showed vitality the surviving minutes record the strain, and then the impossibility, of finding laymen willing to serve.[1] In London there seems at first to have been no shortage of 'gracious and able elders',[2] but there too the problem of lay participation could become acute. One minister later confessed to Lewis du Moulin

> that being pastor of the greatest parish in London, he was never able to establish in it a consistory, nor find any that would be of it but a pitiful Scotch tailor.[3]

One gets the impression, moreover, that the pastor himself had not tried very hard to implement the scheme. English puritan divines generally had no great love for lay-elders, as Baillie had discovered to his sorrow in the course of the Westminster Assembly debates. The most that the Assembly could be got to formulate was that the office of the elder was scripturally warrantable, not that it had been expressly instituted as an office to be of perpetual and individual obligation in the church, as was the ministry.[4]

---

[1] See, e.g. *The register-booke of the fourth classis of the province of London 1646-59* (ed. C. E. Surman, Harleian Soc. 82/83), pp. xvi-xvii.

[2] Baillie, ii. 390; cf. 388.

[3] L. Du Moulin, *The Conformity of the Government . . .* , 1680, 36.

[4] Baillie, ii. 116 f.

Any hopes that a Scottish type of Presbyterianism might be established in England were finally dashed by the overthrow of the Presbyterian majority in Parliament. In December 1648, the Army, growing impatient with the lack of a decisive policy, 'secluded' some 140 M.P.s and obliged the remaining 'rump' to bring the King to trial. The execution of Charles, which followed on January 30, 1649, horrified the Presbyterians and led to a serious rupture between them and the Independents. Never a party of extremes, Presbyterians came to be representative of those puritans who still cherished further reformation in church order but were definite in their fundamental loyalty to the Crown. They were upholders of an established government which could restore order and control the elements threatening to disrupt the stability of law and the economic structure.

## The Commonwealth

From 1654 to 1660 there was no recognizable pattern of ecclesiastical organization, though presbyterianism still remained on the statute book. Against the advice of the advanced thinkers among his own supporters who wanted a purely voluntary system, Cromwell still favoured a national church and set up a body of 'Triers'. The Triers' task was to bring some order out of the confusion: they did not control the ordination of ministers but they did assess the fitness of preachers to receive their statutory maintenance. In outlook they were 'ecumenical': if a candidate presented were godly and able to teach it did not matter whether he were Presbyterian or Congregational or Baptist. Modes of worship, moreover, were matters for individual ministers: in one parish a rigid Presbyterian might follow the form laid down in the *Directory*, which had taken the place of the Prayer Book, while in another an Independent might be using no liturgy at all. Even the old forbidden liturgy was used clandestinely.

Presbyterian order was gradually being submerged in the prevailing variety of practice. Where, as with the Wirksworth classis, everything was done to maintain a functioning presbyterianism under whose operation fifty-four ministers received ordination between 1653 and 1658, the minutes do not disguise the fact that difficulties mounted with the passing years. Ministers received ordination but, once settled in their parishes, failed to participate in fellowship. In the classis that had been erected at Nottingham in 1654 every ministerial member was asked to engage personally in a special recruiting campaign, but the results were meagre.[1]

At this time there was no adequate central authority or unifying force in the national church system. Although most of the really recalcitrant royalist clergy were sequestered, a careful survey of parish records shows that many sympathizers with the old order continued to discharge their pastoral duties without molestation either in their former livings or elsewhere. Such men could scarcely be regarded as ardent supporters of any ecclesiastical regime other than a restored episcopal church. Many ministers had entered their office accepting presbyterian ordination without entertaining any particular opinions in its favour: to them it was merely the legal machinery and its loss would not occasion serious heart-searching. A small number, under two hundred, had entered the state system as Independents in judgment and constituted a group which can best be described as non-separating congregationals: many of them conducted worship for their particular gathered churches within the established order. It was in these circumstances, as we shall see, that the famous Richard Baxter, stormy petrel of later puritanism, was able to move into one of the key positions by advocating 'mere' Catholicism or Christianity—and offering a hope of reconciliation to the divided brotherhood of English puritans.

# THE RISE OF THE RECONCILERS

### by ROGER THOMAS

*Who were the Presbyterians?*

'The vulgar called them by the name of Presbyterians.' So Richard Baxter reported of 'a great number of ministers and people who had', as he put it, 'addicted themselves to no sect or party at all'.[2] Elsewhere he spoke of the same group (which included himself) as Reconcilers and coupled them with the Presbyterians, saying that 'of these two . . . sorts (if I be not taken for a partial witness) are the soberest, the most judicious, unanimous, peaceable, faithful, able,

[1] Cf. Surman in *UHST*, x. 195 ff.     [2] *Rel. Baxt.* ii. 146 (§3).

constant ministers in the land'.[1] The vulgar may perhaps be for-given for not observing nice distinctions between Presbyterians and Reconcilers where so much solid worth (whether they saw it as such, or not) was had in common. We too may perhaps be forgiven if we employ the term Presbyterian and follow what has, after all, become common usage and one that Baxter, for all his niceties, was powerless to prevent. That he should have wished to avoid the name Presbyterian is understandable. The reason was partly that he wanted to avoid all party names in the interests of church concord. But his reason was partly that he wished to dissociate himself from the 'Parliamentary Presbyterianism' which had been thrust upon Englishmen by the Scots as the price of military support in the Civil War and which was far from the presbyterial ideal that had animated many, indeed most, English Puritans since the days of Elizabeth.

Had the term been in use, these English Presbyterians might well have been called Church Puritans, or better, Parish Puritans to distinguish them from such Puritans as objected to, or broke through, the parish system as the Independents did. For until the luckless and generally unwanted experiment of Parliamentary Presbyterianism, English Presbyterianism never had any clear definition, for the good and sufficient reason that until the Civil War it never had the semblance of any sort of formulated system as the established practice of any church in England; and even after the imposition of Parliamentary Presbyterianism it was at best a halting and imperfect approximation to the Scottish system. Hitherto in England it had in fact never been more than a name for numerous earnest ministers and laymen inside the Church of England who looked for a further reformation of their Church in a Puritan direction. It would be quite improper to distinguish between Presbyterians and Anglicans at this period, for Presbyterians *were* Anglicans and few of them would have been opposed to moderate episcopacy. They might be vocal critics within the Church but they hated separatism and sectarianism; they were wedded to the parish system, and, as they were never able to effect the reformation that they desired, it is not surprising if their reforming zeal ranged the whole way from pale pink to vivid red. They were agreed that Puritan discipline should be based on the parish and that the parish clergy should be autonomous rulers in their several parishes, but beyond

[1] *Rel. Baxt.* ii. 387 (§285).

that it is not easy to find any clear lines of agreement, unless it lay in the institution of Ruling Elders who were to exercise discipline in the parish, but who did not teach or administer the sacraments.

## Baxter on the Presbyterians

When Baxter came to relate his own position to Presbyterianism the one thing that is clear is that he was not dealing with any one clearly defined system. He records four dislikes, but in every case he has to qualify his dislike. The first thing that he disliked was the Presbyterian order of Ruling Elders (lay-elders he usually calls them, because that is what they were and because therein lay his objection to them) 'who had no ordination nor power to preach nor to administer sacraments'. His second dislike is directed against the 'more rigid' Presbyterians because they 'drew too near to prelacy, by grasping at a kind of secular power'; or by bringing in the magistrate to enforce their ecclesiastical authority. 'Till magistrates keep the sword themselves', he wound up, 'and learn to deny it to every angry clergyman that would do his work by it and leave them to their own weapons, the Word and Spiritual Keys . . . the Church shall never have unity and peace'.[1] In the third place he 'disliked some Presbyterians that they were not tender enough to dissenting brethren; but too much against liberty as others were too much for it; and thought by votes and numbers to do that which love and reason should have done'. His fourth objection was that, in practice, instead of leaving government at the parish level in the hands of the officers of a single worshipping church, the Presbyterians tended to group ten or a dozen neighbouring churches together for the purposes of government.[2] It is remarkable that in three of his dislikes his complaint is only against 'some Presbyterians' or against a tendency. In each case we find Baxter very far from Scottish Presbyterianism and very near to the English Puritanism of, for example, William Bradshaw. Only in one matter, that of lay-elders, does he differ from Bradshaw or other typically English Presbyterians; and even here there are occasions when he exonerates the Presbyterians

[1] This is virtually the same complaint as Milton's against new presbyter being old priest writ large. The passage might almost have been lifted from Acontius' *Stratagemata*. Cf. G. Bonet-Maury, *Early sources of English Unitarian Christianity*, 1884, 176 f.

[2] *Rel. Baxt.* ii. 142-3 (§13). Cf. Martindale, 68, 69. Baxter held that one minister alone in a parish could be, so to speak, the body of elders, or presbytery, for that parish (R. Baxter, *Church Concord*, 1691, 21).

on that score also, saying 'that church-elders are not accounted laymen but sacred officers by those that are for them'.[1] Baxter insisted that discipline, preaching and administration of the sacraments were the professional work of the minister just as much as prescribing and treatment of the sick were the professional work of the physician, and that there was no place in such matters for the layman without professional training and responsibility.

## A Change of Mood

While Baxter's reaction against Presbyterianism was in part a reaction against the imported hierarchical system (which was 'but a stranger' in England) and a reversion in favour of a more indigenous English Presbyterianism, it was also in part a protest against the belligerency of certain Presbyterians during the Laudian régime. He sometimes refers to them as the more 'rigid' Presbyterians and sometimes as 'the ancient Presbyterians', a term that suggests that they or their belligerency were passing away by the 1650s and that a more conciliatory mood had supervened.[2] There had indeed been a change of outlook and it is possible to date it fairly closely to the years following the rise to power of the Independents when they took over the Government, threw over the Solemn League and Covenant with its upholding of the monarchy, executed Charles I, replaced the Covenant by the Engagement and turned the kingdom into a commonwealth.[3] Not very surprisingly the first reaction of the Presbyterians, as the party in possession, was not so much an effort

[1] *Rel. Baxt.* ii. 403 (§333). Cf. J. M. Ross, 'The Elizabethan elder' in *JPHS*, x. 126–39, xi. 59–70; A. F. Mitchell, *Westminster Assembly*, 1883, 490; *Rel. Baxt.* ii. 150 (§31); S. Neill and H.-R. Weber, *The Layman in Christian History*, 1963, 201. The Nottingham Presbyterian Classis, which did not convene until 1655 or 1656, subjected its ruling elders to a formidable theological examination, a practice that may have been a response to such criticisms as those of Baxter disparaging ruling elders as mere lay elders (C. E. Surman, 'The Presbyterian Classical system, 1646–1660' in *UHST*, x. 195).

[2] *Rel. Baxt.* ii. 146 (§23). Cf. W. K. Jordan, *The Development of Religious Toleration in England*, iii (1938) 273. Jordan distinguishes between an older group, the irreconcileables, who 'had grown to maturity during the Laudian régime' with an average age at the outbreak of the Civil War of about forty-two, and a younger group, Reconcilers, who 'attained maturity during the troubled and uncertain days of the civil war'. This distinction is suggestive, but should not be pressed too far, for there are cases that do not fit the theory, e.g. Edmund Calamy, who was born in 1600.

[3] The Engagement was a declaration ordered by an Act of 2 January 1650 to be taken by all men aged 18: 'I do declare and promise that I will be true and faithful to the Commonwealth of England as it is now established, without a King or House of Lords' (*Cal. Rev.* lxxi).

D

for peace as a howl of dismay and horror at the proliferation of
strange sects encouraged by the intrepidity of the Congregationals
in breaking through the parish system and setting up 'anti-churches',
as the Presbyterians called the Congregational gathered churches,
separated out of the general community. As we have seen, in 1646
Edmund Calamy was exclaiming that 'the famous City of London
is become an Amsterdam, separation from our churches is countenanced, toleration is cried up, authority lieth asleep'.[1] At the end
of 1647 the London Provincial Assembly issued a manifesto in the
form of *A testimony to the truth of Jesus Christ and to our Solemn
League and Covenant* and proclaimed that it was a protest 'against
the errors, heresies and blasphemies of these times, and the toleration of them'. It is some indication of the feeling in the country
amongst parish ministers that the next six months saw the publication of numerous supporting *Testimonies* (from five counties),
*Attestations* (from three counties), a *Joint-testimonie* (from Devon),
a *Concurrent Testimony* (from Wiltshire), a *Vindiciae Veritatis* (from
the West Riding of Yorkshire), and a *Harmonious Consent* (from
Lancashire).[2] These protests did little to stem the increasing
influence of the Independents, and the following year saw the
seismic upheaval of the execution of the king. Thereafter the growing anxiety of the Presbyterians was to find some road to concord
amidst the confusions and conflicts and to come to terms with their
opponents. As Calamy was to write in 1654, 'the Lord hath strangely
made way for the long-desired union by the bitter, woeful and
unutterable fruits of our divisions, which have almost destroyed not
only the ministry, but even the very heart and life of religion and
godliness'.[3] Under this sense of threatening calamity the London
ministers first tried to present Presbyterianism in a favourable

[1] Edmund Calamy (1600–66), *The Great Danger of Covenant-refusing and Covenant-
breaking*, 1646, 3. Cf. Spinoza, *Tractatus theol. pol.*, 1670, ch. xx, ed. A. G. Wernham
(in *Political Works*), 1958, 241: 'Take the city of Amsterdam whose enjoyment of this
freedom [of judgment] has made it great and admired by the whole world. In this
flourishing state, this city without peer, men of every race and sect live in the greatest
harmony, and before they entrust their goods to anyone there are only two things they
want to know: whether he is rich or poor, and whether he is honest or dishonest. His
religion or sect does not matter, for it has no influence on the decision of lawsuits;
and no sect whatsoever is so detested that its members (provided that they harm no one,
give every man his own, and live decent lives) are refused the protection of the civil
authorities.'                                        [2] *Cal. Rev.* 553–8.
[3] London Provincial Assembly, *Jus divinum ministerii evangelici*, 1654, 'To the Reader'
sig. B.3.

light, and as something that could be made acceptable to moderate Independents, in their *Vindication of the Prebyteriall-government* of 1650, which stresses on its title page that it is 'an exhortation to all ministers, elders and people . . . whether joining with us, or separating from us'. A further attempt by the London ministers was the publication, in 1654, of the *Jus divinum ministerii evangelici, or the divine right of the Gospel-ministry*.[1] This time the appeal seems to have been even more to the Episcopalians than to the Independents. In any case the spirit of accommodation behind these somewhat novel efforts towards reconciliation can be well seen in the 'Epistle' before the *Jus divinum* where specific reference is made to both these parties and the possibility of coming to terms with them. To 'our Reverend Brethren of *New* and *Old-England* of the Congregational way', they say

> We have been necessitated to fall upon some things, wherein they and we disagree, and have represented the reasons of our dissent. But yet we here profess that this disagreement shall not hinder us from any Christian accord with them in affection. . . . And that we shall be willing to entertain any sincere motion (as we have also formerly declared in our printed Vindication) that shall further a happy accommodation between us.

To 'the moderate, godly Episcopal men that hold ordination by presbyters to be lawful and valid, that a bishop and a presbyter are one and the same order of ministry . . . and yet hold that the government of the Church by a perpetual moderator is most agreeable to Scripture-pattern', they say,

> Though herein we differ from them, yet we are far from thinking that this difference should hinder a happy union between them and us. Nay, we crave leave to profess to the world that it will never (as we humbly conceive) be well with England till there be an union endeavoured and effected between all those that are orthodox in doctrine, though differing among themselves in some circumstances about church-government.[2]

---

[1] The leading mind in both books seems to have been Edmund Calamy (1600–66) who on each occasion received the thanks of the Assembly for his part in the preparation of the book (Provincial Assembly minutes (Sion College MS.) September 14, 1652, March 10, 1653, November 1, 1653, in transcript by C. E. Surman (D.W.L. MS. 201.12), fos. 118, 123, 130).

[2] *Jus divinum*, 'To the Reader', sig. B.2 verso.

## The Worcestershire Association

Meanwhile, and at the very time when the *Jus divinum* was under preparation by the London Assembly, a movement for reconciliation was taking place in Worcestershire, whose importance lies in the fact that it led to union in practice and that it led to, if indeed it was not anticipated by, like movements in other counties.[1] It was the Voluntary Association movement heralded by the formation, under Baxter's guiding hand, of the Worcestershire Association in 1653, which was a clear break with Parliamentary Presbyterianism. The aim was 'to unite in the practice of so much of discipline as the Episcopal, Presbyterians and Independents' were 'agreed in, and as crosseth none of their principles'.[2] In fact, as it turned out, the Worcestershire Association was composed almost entirely of ministers of parishes who inclined either towards episcopal government or to presbyterial government. It is unlikely that the Independents would have shown much interest in a purely ministerial association, especially one where the ministers were first and foremost parish ministers with no great love for rival 'gathered' churches in their midst; but in any case, Baxter reports, there were not above five or six Independents in the county, and of these only one joined the Association.[3] It was doubtless this absence of

[1] G. F. Nuttall, 'The First Nonconformists' in Nuttall and Chadwick, 172; G. F. Nuttall, *Richard Baxter and Philip Doddridge*, 1951, 7; Nuttall, *Visible Saints*, 122–3; Brockett, 7–10; Martindale, 112. The Worcestershire Association was a clear break with Parliamentary Presbyterianism such as Bastwick had advocated. Baxter says that 'some few of the ancient Presbyterians were against it' (*Rel. Baxt.* ii. 167 (§35)). Elsewhere he defends himself from such criticism (*Christian Concord*, 'Explication', 1653, 31): 'We did in this county seek Authority from the Parliament many years ago for the establishment of the Presbyterian Government; and all our endeavours were frustrate.'

[2] *Rel. Baxt.* ii. 167 (§36). Writing at the time to Edward Harley, September 15, 1656 (D.W.L. MS. 59, i. 226) Baxter said, 'The Worcestershire Agreement, the Presbyterians ordinarily subscribe to, as not inconsistent with their principles in any necessary thing. Learned and godly Congregational men offer to do the like. And so have some Episcopal men' (R. Schlatter, *Richard Baxter and Puritan Politics*, 1957, 5–7). Writing at a later time (*c.* 1670) he said (*Rel. Baxt.* i. 97 (§140), 'In our Association in this county, though we made out terms large enough for all, Episcopal, Presbyterians and Independents, there was not one Presbyterian joined with us that I know of (for I knew but one in all the county, Mr. Tho. Hall) nor one Independent, nor one of the New Prelatical way (Dr Hammond's) and all the rest were mere Catholics.' Baxter's change of terminology, pre- and post-Restoration, is striking *and* instructive.

[3] *Rel. Baxt.* ii. 148 (§28). In a careful analysis of the various lists of those who joined the Worcestershire Association Dr G. F. Nuttall (*JEH*, ii. 204), reckons four who could probably be counted as Independents out of seventy-two.

Independents that to some extent made for the success of the Worcestershire Association and allowed it to function readily as an association of parish ministers.[1] Those who joined the Association who cannot be classed as Presbyterians (or Independents), and perhaps not even as Puritans, were men who had no quarrel with episcopacy or the proscribed Book of Common Prayer, who 'thought both Common-Prayer and the Directory, Episcopacy and Presbytery tolerable'. Baxter spoke of them as 'disengaged' or as men who had 'engaged in no faction, nor studied much in such kinds of controversies'. They were men primarily concerned to carry on their pastoral duties unmolested. Without being 'Vicars of Bray' they were glad enough in 1653 to associate with Presbyterians to their mutual benefit; in 1662 they were equally glad to conform. 'And these in 1660', as Baxter said, 'did conform but most of the rest were ejected and silenced'.[2]

## Baxter on the Independents

Evidence of the new mood of growing efforts towards reconciliation is to be found in the rapid spread of the Voluntary Association movement which Baxter did so much to foster.[3] In some counties also, especially in the north, there would seem to have been a greater readiness on the part both of Presbyterians and Independents to make some concession to opposing points of view. Nevertheless the shock of the rise to power of the Independents, culminating in the execution of the king, could hardly do otherwise than make parish ministers, whether Episcopal or Presbyterian, more willing to make common cause against a common foe. What Baxter and Presbyterian ministers generally had in common with other parish ministers loomed larger than the Puritanism that the Presbyterians shared with the Independents. Puritanism had little to fear from co-operative Episcopal ministers while the parish

[1] Baxter notes, *Rel. Baxt.* ii. 167 (§35): 'The Wiltshire ministers were so strictly held to it by the Independent party, that they could get them but to the following preparatory articles' which he then sets out. Other Associations (e.g. Cheshire) seem to have been more successful in assimilating the Independents. This may well have been the case with the Norfolk Association with above eighty associated ministers. (*The agreement of the associated ministers in the county of Norfolk*, 1659.)

[2] R. Baxter, *Church Concord*, 1691, Preface, p. 3; *Rel. Baxt.* ii. 143 (§14). Cf. 'Episcopall, Presbyterians, Independents and the disengaged' (D.W.L. MS. Baxter Treatises, ii. 892, printed in *MR*, xx. 287). Cf. C. E. Surman, *UHST*, x. 198.

[3] G. F. Nuttall, 'The First Nonconformists' in Nuttall and Chadwick, 172.

system, which both Presbyterian and Episcopal ministers cherished, was constantly threatened by the Congregationals and the break-away congregations that they fostered. Whatever else Baxter might be, or not be, he was not a Congregational; a united undivided parish was the solid basis of all his churchmanship.[1] In a number of places he lays down his objections to Independency. On one occasion he enumerates eight things that he disliked; on another, in a paper of 1655 with a view to conciliating the disagreement, he enumerates ten differences.[2] Numerous as these differences are they can most of them be reduced to the one root difference of adherence or opposition to the parish system. It can be conveniently summed up in the terms of a modern distinction, applied to certain trade-union legislation, between 'contracting-in' and 'contracting-out'. For membership of an Independent church it was necessary to contract-in by giving proofs of adequate and supposedly high qualifications and by entering into the church covenant of the particular church to which a member became attached. In the case of a parish church, on the other hand, whether the government was Pres-byterian or Episcopal, all were eligible for membership unless they disqualified themselves—and so contracted-out—by scandalous living, manifest unbelief or gross ignorance of the Christian faith, refusal of discipline, incapacity to acknowledge their baptismal covenant or mere negligence. This was the meaning of Baxter's insistence, and the insistence of other Presbyterians, that no more should be required for admission to communion than a 'credible profession of faith' such as any normal person could compass who had been well schooled in the catechism. To Congregationals this seemed a superficial test for admission and was one of the grounds on which some of them condemned the parish churches as no churches.[3] As Baxter put it, their complaint was 'that we take those for godly

[1] *Rel. Baxt.* iii. 67.

[2] *Rel. Baxt.* ii. 193 (§47) Matthew Sylvester, the editor of the *Reliquiae Baxterianae*, noted in the margin that 'This writing, being some how or other mislaid, cannot yet be found'. The reason was that Baxter had himself published it in *Church Concord*, 1691, just before he died. The frequent references to the Presbyterian point of view in this writing of *c.* 1655 suggests that before the Restoration Baxter was less loath to use the term Presbyterian in a wide inclusive sense than he was at a later date. Cf. p. 52 above, n. 2.

[3] G. F. Nuttall, *Visible Saints*, 51, 58 ff.; R. Baxter, *Church Concord*, 41–2. Cf. *Rel. Baxt.* ii. 143 (§14), 233 (sect. 3). But cf. also R. Baxter, *Certain disputations of right to sacraments*, 1657. Cf. Baillie, ii. 236.

that they take not for such'.[1] Since Congregationals were not satisfied with a mere statement of faith and acknowledgment of baptismal covenants but required also a claim to an experience of the saving work of grace in the heart, it followed that an Independent church was a 'gathered' church, separating the godly out of the parish (or out of several parishes) into a separate community, so creating what the parish minister might strongly object to as an anti-church, a sort of local *praemunire*—an *imperium in imperio*.[2] Philip Henry, in Shropshire, complained of the Independents 'that they unchurched the nation' and 'that they plucked up the hedge of parish order'.[3] So too Adam Martindale, in Cheshire, complained that 'the congregational way of gathering churches was the way to spoil many churches for the new making of one'.[4]

It followed from Congregational principles that the distance between pastor and flock, between teacher and taught, was vastly reduced; and from this followed a characteristic which Baxter particularly disliked, that the people by a majority of votes governed the church, adjudicated on the discipline of members and not only chose their ministers but ordained them. Thus, as he put it, they made 'too light of ordination', taking it out of the hands of presbyters, who were the proper people to make ministers and the best qualified to determine a candidate's suitability.[5] Another difference, arising from the same source, was that not only did they make the minister no more than one of the members of a particular church, but also they refused him authority to exercise his ministry in any other church or in conjunction with other ministers.[6] In addition any member who had the gift was as much entitled to be a preacher as duly ordained ministers. 'Gifted brethren', as such lay-preachers were called, were a constant source of irritation because of their missionary preaching in neighbouring parishes where the incumbent might well resent their intrusion.[7]

[1] R. Baxter, *Church Concord*, 15.

[2] Nuttall, *Visible Saints*, 110–14; *Rel. Baxt.* ii. 143 (§14, sect. 3); R. Baxter, *Church Concord*, 42; *Rel. Baxt.* iii. 67.

[3] P. Henry, *Diaries and Letters*, ed. M. H. Lee, 1882, p. 277; Nuttall, *Visible Saints*, 108.

[4] Martindale, *Life*, 66, where are also a number of other criticisms of Independency closely similar to Baxter's.

[5] *Rel. Baxt.* ii. 143 (§14, sect. 1); R. Baxter, *Church Concord*, 23.

[6] R. Baxter, *Church Concord*, 32, 33.

[7] Op. cit. 38.

## Reconciliation with the Independents

The sixteenth-fifties were times when attempts at church concord were being made and many of these differences might have been composed but for the root difference of separatism and the setting up of gathered churches. On this Baxter told the Independents bluntly, 'You know that this is the great point which you must yield in, or you cannot have union with the contrary minded'.[1] Doubtless it was because of this root difference that he had little success in coming to terms with those of the Congregational persuasion, but it was not for want of trying. He made a serious attempt to come to an agreement with Philip Nye, the eminent Independent who had been one of the five Dissenting Brethren in the Westminster Assembly. His discussions with Nye are instructive. They show how anxious Baxter was for agreement that he was willing to make concessions even on the question of setting up gathered churches within the parish, but, having gone so far, he hedged the concession round with such conditions that Nye exclaimed 'that it would cast a slur on [the Congregationals] to be, as it were, excommunicated by [the Presbyterians] that were the greater number'. Baxter's stipulations were that the Congregationals should join in the Voluntary Associations or synods of ministers on a constant basis. Although these assemblies were to be consultative only, yet agreements made were to be accepted; and the grounds for setting up a gathered church (such as the insufficiency of the existing incumbent of a parish) were to be deliberated in these assemblies. No wonder that Nye thought that his ideal of a gathered church was being turned into an inferior, if not reprehensible, stop-gap. They disagreed also on the ordination of ministers, since Nye would not concede that other ministers should always play some part in ordinations.[2] It is easy to see that incompatible principles were in conflict. For Nye the gathered church was the norm; for Baxter the parish church was the norm and the gathered church was an inferior alternative, to be discouraged as much as possible and to be permitted only under stringent conditions for the sake of unity and to keep dissident elements within the framework of the one national church.

[1] R. Baxter, *Christian Concord*, 1653, pt. II, *Explications*, 35.
[2] *Rel. Baxt.* ii. 188 (§46).

*Presbyterians and a Toleration*

There was and in fact could be no middle way or compromise between these conflicting religious ideals. If the Presbyterians or the Episcopalians had had the power they would have done their best to discourage the setting up of churches in rivalry with the parish church; hence their reputation for intolerance. Indeed in these years 'a toleration' (with the indefinite article) almost has the technical meaning of a tolerated separation. In this sense it was also a major plank in the platform of the Independents. The *Testimonies* and *Attestations* and the rest in 1648 were appeals against a toleration in this sense; it was of one of them, the *Harmonious consent* from Lancashire, that Robert Halley could declare that 'nothing more horrible was ever put upon paper by religionists of any sort'.[1] As a specimen of what Alexander Gordon called its 'implacable verbal virulence' we need only quote such a sentiment as that 'a toleration would be the putting of a sword into a madman's hand, a cup of poison into the hands of a child'.[2] But such sentiments should be read in their historical context. To understand the dismay that the idea of 'a toleration' had for Baxter and others we need only to consider a few parallels from the present day. Who would not say that freedom for children to play truant from school with impunity was intolerable?—And parish ministers regarded their flocks as *in statu pupillari*. Again, what would be our reaction if Her Majesty's Opposition, Labour or Conservative, decided to withdraw from the unitary State and set up independent parliaments of their own for their own followers? Imagination boggles at the consequences of such a disruption of the community. Baxter's reactions towards those who proposed to separate from the church was the same. Indeed Baxter is just as definite as the *Harmonious consent* and in one passage at least he not only asserts his dislike of 'a toleration' but characteristically gives pungent reasons for this dislike. He pleads that since 'Scripture is the sacred Perfect Law of the most high God' magistrates

> should restrain men that would bring God's Word into contempt
> under the pretence of preaching it, that every ignorant fellow whose

[1] Robert Halley, *Lancashire: its Puritanism and Nonconformity*, 1869, i. 468.
[2] *Harmonious Consent*, 1648, 12; R. Halley, op. cit. 470. Cf. Gordon *Cheshire Classis*, 104; Drysdale, 349–53.

tongue hath catcht a lax, may not run up into the pulpit to ease himself; nor every one have leave to disgorge himself in the holy assemblies,
that hath got a surfeit of pride and self-conceit. O if you knew the
weakness of poor people and how apt they are to be deceived, you
would not give deceivers liberty to do their worst. You, that will not
give men leave to persuade your wives to adultery, your children to
lewdness, your soldiers or subjects to rebellion and treachery, would
sure be as regardful of men's souls and the honour of Christ.[1]

The church is regarded in the same light as other moral and legal
institutions of an undivided community. When Baxter speaks of
the aptness of people to be deceived he expresses a sentiment that
could receive some cogent support from the success of television
advertising at the present day. When he protests against 'deceivers'
liberty to do their worst' he was thinking of the duty of the community in its religious aspect and through the church to save
people from themselves. He believed that liberty to separate off into
sects opened the door to every folly, every licence, every heresy; it
was one of his most serious complaints against the Independents
that their way did just that.[2] The church had its duty in this respect
to the whole community and its teachers had as much right to
withstand the interference of deceivers as physicians, in a parallel
profession, had to withstand quacks. The *Harmonious Consent*
claimed no more. Without accepting this view of the matter it is
not hard to understand and even to sympathize with the horror that
was felt at granting a toleration that made inroads on the community's organized system for restraining excess and inculcating
moral observance.

If we take toleration in the wider sense of the toleration of differences of opinion and conduct, the Presbyterians might well be able
to show as good a record as others in their day. Few at that date,
whether Presbyterians or Independents, were prepared to tolerate
Papists or Socinians. When Parliament in 1654 set up a committee
to determine what was tolerable in doctrine and to draw up a list
of fundamentals, John Owen and Francis Cheynell, who dominated
the proceedings, were for laying down a hard and fast list of doctrines
which it was obligatory to believe, while it was Baxter who pleaded

---

[1] R. Baxter, *Saints Everlasting Rest*, 2nd ed., 1651, pt. II, Preface, last page.
[2] *Rel. Baxt.* ii. 143 (§14, sect. 4): 'And I disliked also the lamentable tendency of
their way to divisions and sub-divisions, and the nourishing of heresies and sects.'

for reducing fundamentals to a minimum and exacting no more than adherence to 'the Creed, Lord's Prayer and Decalogue'.[1] When it was objected that 'a Socinian or a Papist will subscribe all this', Baxter's retort was, 'So much the better'. Doubtless he would have had his own methods of reducing heresies by means of reason and Scripture and also by Puritan discipline if need be, but on these more general questions of doctrine it was Owen the Congregational and Cheynell the doctrinaire Presbyterian who provide examples of intolerance rather than Baxter and like-minded Presbyterians.[2]

It could be argued that, where heresy was concerned, Owen had to favour intolerant legislation just because he favoured a toleration of separation from the parish churches and that Baxter could afford to exercise considerable charity so long as control resided securely in the hands of a unified national church in which the pressure of 'Love and Reason' might succeed where legislative repression would fail.[3] Be that as it may, given the comprehension of men of different schools of thought within the one national church, the Presbyterians were prepared to be, for their day and age, remarkably tolerant. Thus in the 1650 *Vindication of Presbyteriall-government*, published by the London Provincial Assembly and largely written by Edmund Calamy, we find such liberal sentiments as this, 'We abhor an over rigid urging of uniformity in circumstantial things.' Or again they held that it was 'their duty to hold communion together, as one church, in what they agree; and in this way of union mutually to tolerate and bear with one another in lesser differences.'[4] Sentiments as laudable, and similarly restricted to a Christian dogmatic framework, could be quoted from Independents writing during the 1650s.[5] Thus the question of tolerance was not one that separated Presbyterians and Independents but one that cut across both communions, with the one exception already mentioned that, in the eyes of the Presbyterians, the one thing that could not be tolerated was separatism and sectarianism. The church had its part to play

---

[1] *Rel. Baxt.* ii. 198 (§52). The fundamentals as set out by the Committee were published and a copy is in the British Museum under 'England: Churches and Religious Bodies: Committee of Divines, 1654'. This was also given in Daniel Neal, *History of the Puritans*, ed. J. Toulmin, 1793–7, iv. 98–100.

[2] Cheynell was a fanatic and a Presbyterian of the sort that might make Baxter and many others dislike the Presbyterian name. Cf. Gordon in *CL*, 1889, p. 2. Cf. above, p. 48.                    [3] Gordon, *Heads*, 92.

[4] London Provincial Assembly, *Vindication*, 1650, 119–20. Cf. A. F. M. Mitchell, *The Westminster Assembly*, 1883, 204–9.                    [5] Nuttall, *Visible Saints*, 117.

in the spiritual well-being and education of the community and for this it felt obliged to be a national institution. Possibly one of the effects of a toleration when it came in 1689 was that much of the work traditionally the province of the church had ultimately to be taken over by the State.[1]

## Reconciliation with Episcopalians

No such major question of 'a toleration' hindered agreement between the Episcopal and Presbyterian parties in the national church, at least amongst parish ministers. Moreover parish ministers of differing outlooks had become painfully aware of their common danger from the separatist threat and the incentive to sink their mutual differences was thereby increased. Concord here should have been a comparatively simple matter. So Baxter found it in his first two tentatives to reach accord with other Episcopal ministers. The first was the striking success of the Worcestershire Association in 1653 and of the other Voluntary Associations that it inspired. The second was the happy chance that brought him into personal relation with Archbishop Ussher in the Autumn of 1654, when Baxter was in London conferring with John Owen and others in drawing up for Parliament a list of fundamentals in doctrine.[2] But it was not so much fundamentals in doctrine that Baxter and Ussher discussed when they met as a basis of concord to be found in a modified episcopacy. For Ussher was the author of a piece of scholarship that afforded a rare example of the impress of academic learning on the course of events. This was his *Polycarpi et Ignatii Epistolae* (1644) in which he had distinguished the genuine from the spurious in the works handed down as the epistles of Ignatius. He had thereby elicited an unexceptionable picture of episcopacy as it had been practised in the earliest days of the Church, with the result that in the late 1640s those involved in disputes over episcopacy had to take the measure of Ussher's work.[3] For men who had suffered from the suppression of episcopacy following the Solemn League and Covenant Ussher's work became the warranty of the justice of their

---

[1] It is not too much to claim that the Welfare State is the outcome of the breakdown of a unified national church. The essence of it is that it is centralized and unified in a way that was impossible for the churches after 1689; it may be admitted that a unified church might have developed on lines less liberal than the State has in fact done.

[2] Powicke, i. 121; *Rel. Baxt.* ii. 197 (§50).

[3] N. Sykes, *From Sheldon to Secker*, 1959, 107–11.

cause. For such men as John Owen, opposed to episcopacy in any shape or form, it became obligatory to do what they could (with the aid of certain Huguenot writers) to discredit Ussher's scholarship— to the ultimate damage of their own reputations as scholars. For men of the stamp of Baxter and Ussher the history exhibited the gap that lay between the primitive and later forms of episcopacy. For them a return to the more primitive forms of the institution might afford a heaven-sent opportunity to reconcile the conflict between Presbyterians and Episcopalians. The distinction between primitive episcopacy and later prelacy was not new; what was new was a firm basis in history for the distinction. Beza had distinguished between *episcopus divinus*, *episcopus humanus* and *episcopus diabolicus*. His divine bishop was the presbyter, his human bishop was the bishop chosen by the presbyters to be president over them, while his diabolical bishop was the diocesan with sole power of ordination and jurisdiction, 'lording it over God's heritage and governing by his own will and authority'.[1] To Ussher and Baxter it might seem that a reduction of the familiar English diocesan bishop to the *episcopus humanus* as a superintendent or permanent moderator could afford a basis of compromise between contending parties. Ussher admitted to Baxter that he was the author of what has been called 'one of the most important ecclesiastical documents of the time'. This was 'The Reduction of Episcopacy to the Form of Synodical Government received by the Ancient Church'.[2] Ussher not only admitted that he was the author of this document but he also told Baxter that he had offered it to the king in 1641 and that then 'the King had refused it, but at the Isle of Wight [in 1648] he accepted it, and as *he* would not when *others* would, so *others* would not when *he* would'.[3] As Baxter later reported his interview with Ussher, he and the archbishop 'had in an hour's time agreed on the necessary terms' for an agreement that could have settled the age-old conflict between Episcopal and Presbyterian parties in England.[4]

In summing up his discussion with Ussher Baxter set out the

---

[1] *Jus divinum*, 1654, Appendix, 121.

[2] Text: *Rel. Baxt.* ii. 238–40. For the history of the text see *D.N.B.* under J. Ussher. Cf. N. Sykes, *Old Priest New Presbyter*, 1956, 134–5. Cf. above, p. 36.

[3] *Rel. Baxt.* i. 62. (§93, sect. 2); F. Peck, *Desiderata curiosa*, 1779, p. 407 (§3)—November, 27, 1648.

[4] D.W.L. MS. Baxter Treatises, ii. item 28, printed in *MR*, xx. 288; J. C. Spalding and M. F. Brass, 'Reduction of Episcopacy' in *Church History*, xxx (1961), 421–3.

points of agreement about church synods and assemblies in terms
very similar to those already quoted from Ussher's *Reduction of
Episcopacy*, but he is careful to add that they also agreed on the
validity of ordination by presbyters without a bishop and that
'Synods are not properly for government, but for agreement among
the pastors; and a synod of bishops are not the governors of any one
bishop there present'.[1]

When Baxter speaks of moderate episcopal men and when he
applies this term to himself, it is Ussher's 'Reduction of Episcopacy'
or some closely related scheme such as that outlined above that he
has in mind. But his calling himself an episcopal man on terms so
tenuous is only equalled for temerity by his denial of Presbyterianism
on similarly tenuous terms. For Ussher's scheme is a very much
presbyterianized form of episcopacy and, as Ussher himself put it,
'in our church this kind of Presbyterian government hath been long
disused'.[2] It was with a note of despondency that writing at a later
date Baxter recalled that Ussher had agreed that such a scheme
'might suffice for peace and unity among moderate men', but that
with 'intemperate men' Baxter was not likely to have any better
success than Ussher himself had had.[3] When all is said Ussher was
no more a typical Episcopalian than Baxter. For that matter neither
he nor Baxter could have qualified as thoroughgoing Presbyterians
as the term was understood in Scotland. But Baxter could claim,
and with reason, that the Presbyterian London Provincial Assembly
would have accepted episcopacy on Ussher's terms.

In 1655 Baxter put his plea for accord to a man who was far
more representative of traditional episcopacy than Ussher. This
was Ralph Brownrigg, the deprived bishop of Exeter.[4] If he could
have come to terms with such a man as Brownrigg the cause of
reconciliation would have made solid progress, but Brownrigg's
response was not sufficiently forthcoming to make Baxter think it
worth pursuing matters with him further, though afterwards he
regretted that he had not done so. At a later time, on the eve of the

---

[1] *Rel. Baxt.* ii. 206 (§62).

[2] J. Ussher, *Reduction*, 1656, 6; *Rel. Baxt.* ii. 239; *JPHS*, xiii. 339. Cf. R. B.
Whitehorn, 'Richard Baxter—Meer Nonconformist' in *The Beginnings of Noncon-
formity* (Hibbert Lects.), 1964, 73–4; H. A. Jukes, 'Gunning and the Worcestershire
Agreement' in *The Modern Churchman*, vii (1963/4), 185.

[3] *Rel. Baxt.* ii. 206 (§62).

[4] *Rel. Baxt.* ii. 172–9. Cf. N. Sykes, *Old Priest New Presbyter*, 68.

Restoration, he fared little better with Henry Hammond who, though glad enough to avail himself of Ussher's proof of the primitive character of episcopacy against John Owen, was not similarly willing to follow him in reducing the Laudian conception of episcopacy to a more primitive and presbyterian form.

## Puritan Parish Discipline

The difficulty in coming to terms with episcopacy as practised in England was that under it had been sacrificed what both Baxter and Ussher regarded as central. This was the right and duty of the parish minister to exercise what Ussher called the 'discipline of Christ' and what we should describe as Puritan discipline. Ussher regarded this as something that had at one time been exercised in the Church of England, which had fallen into disuse but which could be restored by the law of the land. Seeing that our Church, he said,

> still professeth that every pastor hath a right to rule the Church (from whence the name of rector also was given at first unto him) and to administer the discipline of Christ, as well as to dispense the doctrine and sacraments, and the restraint of the exercise of that right proceedeth only from the custom now received in this realm; no man can doubt, but by the law of the land, this hindrance may be removed.[1]

Baxter's complaint against what he variously called prelacy or diocesan episcopacy was that it 'altered the ancient species of presbyters, to whose office the spiritual government of their proper folks as truly belonged, as the power of preaching and worshipping God did' and that in place of discipline at the parish level had been set up 'courts [under the control of the bishops] that were more secular than spiritual, in the manner of other secular courts; and that the government of the Church by excommunications, suspensions, absolutions, &c, was exercised by a chancellor, who was a civil lawyer and a layman even against ministers themselves, unless for a blind some priest did formally pronounce the sentence'.[2] This transfer of government to the bishops was the root of the trouble. With the huge English dioceses the bishops were too few and too remote to cope with the needs; they could not have the intimate personal knowledge of the people that was necessary if

[1] J. Ussher, *Reduction*, 6; *Rel. Baxt.* ii. 239.
[2] *Rel. Baxt.* ii. 142. In D.W.L. MS. Treatises, iv. fo. 303 (3rd part of 'Gildas Salvianus') Baxter seems to allow for a distinction between diocesan episcopacy and prelacy.

right decisions were to be taken on such questions as who should be admitted to communion and how the sins of various wrongdoers should be treated. Only the local minister had the intimate knowledge required and was competent to take wise decisions. In place of parish discipline the bishops had set up ecclesiastical courts that dealt with the wrong cases in the wrong way. The machinery was too cumbersome to deal with local cases of minor shortcomings; it was also out of all proportion to the offence—a steam hammer to crack a nut. Worse still the cases commonly dealt with were apt to be concerned with the non-payment of fines, contempt of court and the like—matters remote from the Puritan interest in sin. Worst of all perhaps jurisdiction in these courts was handed over to chancellors who as lay officers were objectionable on that account and whose procedure was secular, imposing fines instead of labouring for that well-being and reform of the wrongdoer which was the aim of discipline as the better Puritans understood it. As Baxter put it,

> It is not with holy seriousness and patience as may tend to the melting of a sinner's heart into contrition . . . nor is it at all fitted to work upon the conscience. (Who can expect that lay-men, and such men, in a public court, and such a court, should do it?). Nor do I believe that any subscribing conscionable minister will say that he ever heard a chancellor convert a sinner. . . . But on the contrary they work on them by terror of corporal penalties and mulcts and harden them into a hatred of those that vex them . . . whereas Christ's discipline is paternal, by love and convincing reason.[1]

One may be forgiven for thinking that it should not have been beyond the wit of man to adjust the differences between right-wing Episcopalians and the Presbyterian Reconcilers; there were at least no such insuperable differences of fundamental principle here as separated Presbyterians from Independents. But reconciliation failed, for time was running short and the mood was unfavourable. It may have been in part that being dispossessed by a Presbyterian Parliament rankled with the Laudian Episcopalians. They doubtless

[1] *Rel. Baxt.* ii. 403 (§335). Cf. Wm. Bradshaw, *English Puritanisme*, 1641, 15–16; H. L. Short, 'The importance of the seventeenth century in Unitarian history' in *UHST*, ix. 193. In *Rel. Baxt.* ii. 150 (§31) Baxter explains his own practice in some detail, which makes it plain that the whole purpose was as privately as possible to bring home to the sinner a sense of his wrongdoing and to secure his voluntary repentance—not to administer punishment.

also resented the treatment subsequently meted out to them under Cromwell. Baxter alludes to treatment of this sort in ordinances of Cromwell in 1654. He expressed satisfaction with them in ejecting ministers 'who were notoriously insufficient or scandalous', but when the ordinance went on to eject those who had taken 'part with the King against Parliament' he complained that this action against old-time Episcopalians, 'by offending them, hindered our agreement with them'.[1] But the trouble went deeper than Baxter was always willing to admit. The numerous sequestrations as a whole created a growing resentment for which later a price would have to be paid. Many of the clergy may well have deserved the disciplinary action taken against them, but as Dr Anne Whiteman has pointed out, 'the truth (so far as it can be recovered) about the ejections was probably less important than what was widely believed about them'. A martyrology was created 'more potent than the facts, and did much to breed up Anglican resentment and hatred'. 'Particularly important', she points out, 'was the influence exerted in favour of "Laudianism" by the ejected or dispossessed clergy who found their way into households of the nobility and gentry, as tutors or unofficial chaplains; how well they imparted their lesson was to be seen in the temper of the young cavaliers in Charles II's Long Parliament.'[2] She is right; it was not merely the misapplication of discipline that caused the mischief, but the discipline itself. It was not so much Presbyterianism as its very Puritanism that was hated. The same was true not only of discipline exerted against insufficient ministers but also of Puritan discipline in general—it bred resentment and had damaging consequences especially when exercised against the gentry and others of influence. Baxter was doubtless more conscientious, understanding and charitable in this respect than some other Presbyterians, but an example of the trouble caused may be drawn from his own parish of Kidderminster in his dealings with Sir Ralph Clare. The knight wished to take communion in the parish church kneeling, contrary to the custom established under Baxter of taking it in the Puritan fashion, seated; he wished too to have it administered at another time than that of the regular celebration

[1] *Rel. Baxt.* 179 (§39). Cf. Bennett, 110-11, where the offence is defined as public and frequent use of the Book of Common Prayer 'since the first of January last' (Ordinance of August 28, 1654). Cf. Bosher, 7-8.

[2] Anne Whiteman, 'The Restoration of the Church of England' in Nuttall and Chadwick, 33-4, 41.

E

of communion. Baxter sent him a lengthy paper of arguments against taking it kneeling, but so far consented to his humour as to allow him to take it in the posture he wished provided that he communicated at the same time as other parishioners at the regular administration. According to his lights Baxter was more indulgent than other Puritans might have been, but it is not hard to understand that Baxter's determination to rule his parish was resented by Sir Ralph—so that when the Restoration came he used all his influence to see to it that Baxter never returned to Kidderminster.[1]

Baxter was so sure of the rightness of Puritan discipline and the obligation upon all parties to maintain it that he hardly does justice to the resentment caused by it and the extent to which it undermined whatever goodwill Presbyterianism had once enjoyed. More than once he alludes to Presbyterian as an 'odious name', but he seems to imply that the odium was caused by the excesses of the 'ancient' irreconcileable Presbyterians who had striven against the Laudian regime and who, with Parliamentary backing, had foisted an alien type of Presbyterianism on to an unwilling country. But there are also times when he lets slip an awareness that it was much more than this and that it was Puritan discipline itself that was hated and that made the Presbyterian name odious. In arguing against a free Parliament he can admit that 'the far greater part of the people hate practical godliness' and that 'more of them are slaves to their malignant landlords that hate it worse'.[2] That was in 1659. Elsewhere one of his complaints against 'the diocesan party' was their 'gratifying the multitude of the ungodly'. And he evidently saw the danger signal when he further recorded that 'hereby it came to pass that the multitude of the ignorant and ungodly people were become the zealous pleaders for prelacy, and made it the breastwork to exercise their enmity against the serious practice of religion'.[3] So it proved. When the Restoration came it was greeted by many as a release from burdens long endured, often dreaded, always hated; it thereby cast a gloom upon reforming ministers who saw their efforts to create a godly England being laid in the dust. Soon after

[1] Powicke i. 180–1, 185; *Rel. Baxt.* ii. 157–62, iii. 71 (§150): Sir Ralph Clare 'was my applauder, but remover.' A typical reaction of a congregation to attempts to discipline gentry is to be found in J. Rastrick, *Account*, 1705, 10.

[2] D.W.L. MS. Baxter letters, vi, fo. 233—printed in R. Schlatter, *Richard Baxter and Puritan Politics*, 1957, 63.

[3] *Rel. Baxt.* ii. 142 (§12, sects. 6–7). Cf. Bosher, 175.

the Restoration Henry Newcome, minister at Manchester, was travelling through Rutland and reports,

> We found maypoles in abundance as we came and at Oakham I saw a morris-dance, which I had not seen of twenty years before. It is a sad sign the hearts of the people are poorly employed when they can make a business of playing the fool as they do. This I found, that in most places they either have bad ministers to rejoice in or else good ones whom they hate.[1]

It was not this or that form of Presbyterianism so much as the Puritanism it enshrined that proved its undoing.

### Richard Cromwell

But we anticipate. When Oliver Cromwell died on September 3, 1658 and his son Richard succeeded him as Protector, time's laggard step may have been hurrying on towards the restoration of the monarchy, but all was quiet and it could hardly have been seen at the time that the return of the monarchy was so near at hand.[2] Indeed at the time there was real hope for the Reconcilers that their cause was making solid progress. Adam Martindale in Cheshire could speak of the year 1659 as one 'when moderation was grown in fashion'.[3] Richard Cromwell seemed 'to favour the sober people of the land, to honour Parliaments'. Baxter had hopes of him 'because he never meddled' in the processes that brought him to the protectorship 'nor sought the government' and 'because he was against all . . . fanatic turbulent men'.[4] There is little doubt that he was a Reconciler on the Presbyterian model.

At the very moment of Richard Cromwell's elevation the Independents were on the point of meeting in conference at the Savoy to settle their faith and order. According to a report that Baxter received it was their intention to do so in a way that 'tended much to healing'.[5] But when the resulting Savoy Declaration was published

---

[1] Henry Newcome, *Autobiography*, ed. R. Parkinson, 1852 (Chetham Soc. o.s. 26) 121 (June 11–16, 1660).

[2] *Calendar of the Clarendon State Papers*, iv. ed. F. J. Routledge, 1932, 131.

[3] Martindale, 70.

[4] D.W.L. MS. Baxter Treatises, iii, item 62, fo. 110 (deleted paragraph 44); *Rel. Baxt.* i. 101.

[5] A. G. Matthews, *The Savoy Declaration*, 1959, 11–12 (Goodwin's address to R. Cromwell).

he found that his 'expectations upon that report were frustrate' and 'the work of peace began to seem so much more hopeless than it was before'.[1] He had some years earlier prepared a work to show how by mutual concessions the position of the Independents and Presbyterians might be reconciled or at least 'proving that the differences were not such as should hinder concord and communion'.[2] With the accession of Richard Cromwell to power the moment may well have seemed ripe for the publication of this work, but Baxter's olive branch did not appear; he felt that the Savoy Declaration had spiked his guns. Yet there were Independents who assured him 'that many good and peaceable men that were there present [at the Savoy] intended not the dividing distant sense which many words in the Declaration do openly import'.[3] This curious ambivalence of the Declaration may have owed something to the accession of Richard Cromwell and to the fact that John Owen, who took a leading part in the conference, was neither in favour with the new Protector nor any admirer of the Presbyterian reconciliation that the new Cromwell was likely to support.[4] Whether that was so or not, Baxter determined to make the best of the ambiguous document and embarked on a postscript to the volume that he had ready for publication in the interests of concord. But he never finished his postscript and his olive branch was cast aside.[5] The book was not published until many years after, in 1691.

No such untoward circumstances interfered with the publication of another olive branch that he had to offer, this time to the Episcopalians. This was his *Five Disputations* 'on purpose to carry on the business of reconciliation'.[6] These may have been the fruits of debates held in the Worcestershire Association, in which he nailed his colours to the mast and in a wealth of detail expounded such necessary terms of concord as he believed all moderate men would accept. Amongst other things he claimed that the London Presbyterians had accepted moderate episcopacy, as well they might,

---

[1] D.W.L. MS. Baxter Treatises, vi, fo. 203 (item 201).

[2] *Rel. Baxt.* ii. 193 (§47). The paper referred to was published in Baxter's *Church Concord*, 1691.          [3] D.W.L. MS. Baxter Treatises, vi, item 201.

[4] A. G. Matthews, *The Savoy Declaration*, 10, 41–45. Baxter denounced also the Antinomianism of the Savoy Declaration (*Rel. Baxt.* i. 104 (§194)).

[5] Doubtless the fall of Richard Cromwell overtook him while writing the postscript. This postscript (D.W.L. MS. Baxter Treatises, vi, item 201) was not published when the papers to which they were a postscript were printed at long last in his *Church Concord*, 1691.          [6] D.W.L. MS. Baxter Treatises, iii, fo. 110 verso.

seeing that it was Ussher's version of episcopacy that earned the description of moderate.[1] Most of the points that would come up for debate after the Restoration in attempts to reach an agreed settlement were discussed here on temperate lines, with the permissive acceptance of a liturgy, but stipulating against the imposition of unscriptural tests and unscriptural ceremonies. It was an impressive platform but events were hastening on and we shall never know whether Baxter's proposals would have had the success that their moderation deserved in the situation under the protectorate for which they were designed. The only good that his manifesto could do him was to demonstrate after the Restoration that his concessions to the Episcopalians had been made before the Restoration and were not dictated by any subsequent spirit of time-serving. The *Five Disputations* was published by the beginning of March 1659 with a dedication to Richard Cromwell, from whom Baxter evidently had great hopes.[2] But in May 1659 Richard was driven from power. This was a calamity for the Reconcilers and Baxter was so sure of John Owen's complicity in it that his resentment knew no bounds.[3] It was soon after this that Sir Ralph Clare in Kidderminster instigated Baxter to make the move for unity with Henry Hammond which we have already mentioned. It was in July that he was in communication with Hammond. Away in Lancashire at almost the same moment, on the initiative of the Independents, an agreement was reached between them and the Presbyterians in which considerable concessions (without precedent in the Savoy Declaration) were made to the Presbyterian point of view.[4] Hopes raised by the agreement were swiftly dashed, however, because the royalist rising of Sir George Booth, in which many Lancashire Presbyterians were involved, followed soon afterwards and caused estrangement once more with the Independents who were naturally opposed to all royalist aspirations.[5] The rising failed and the confusion increased until General Monk entered London in 1660 and proclaimed a free Parliament. But there was still no certainty of the outcome. Baxter had been let into the secret

---

[1] R. Baxter, *Five Disputations*, 1659, 346 (12); *Jus divinum*, Appendix, 122.

[2] G. Thomason (British Museum *Catalogue* of his pamphlets) had a copy of the *Five Disputations* by March 2, 1659.

[3] *Rel. Baxt.* i. 101 (§145); iii. 42 (95); G. F. Nuttall, 'Manuscript of the Reliquiae Baxterianae (1696)' in *J.E.H.* vi. 73-79.

[4] Martindale, 126-31.          [5] Martindale, 131. Cf. Abernathy, 26-32.

of the royalist rising of Sir George Booth but had held aloof; his reason may have been prudential, but he may have had other reasons, for there can be little doubt that he would have preferred the restoration of Richard Cromwell to the restoration of Charles II. London Presbyterians would seem to have made up their minds (or had their minds made up for them) in favour of Charles and a restoration of the monarchy. At the end of March William Bates was writing to Baxter from London to enlist him in the royal cause.[1] On April 13th Baxter was in London to confer with the Earl of Lauderdale, whose purpose in seeking consultations with him was likewise to make sure of his support for the royalist cause.[2] On April 15th the Convention Parliament met. On May 1st Parliament 'did unanimously vote home the King'.

## Platform for the Restoration

On the previous day Parliament had observed a fast and Baxter was one of the three ministers called upon by the House of Commons to preach on the occasion.[3] He was the only one of the three to depart from generalities and to lay down succinctly a programme for an ecclesiastical settlement.[4] After alluding specifically to his earlier agreement with Archbishop Ussher 'in less than half an hour's debate', he went on to lay down a four-point programme,

These are the sum of our requests: 1. That holiness may be encouraged, and the overspreading profaneness of this nation effectually kept down. 2. That an able diligent ministry may be encouraged, and not corrupted by temporal power. 3. That discipline may be seriously promoted and ministers no more hindered by magistrates in the exercise of their office than physicians and schoolmasters are in theirs; seeing it is but a government like theirs, consisting in the liberty of conscionable managing the works of our own office that we expect. Give us but leave to labour in Christ's vineyard with such encouragement as the necessity of obstinate souls requireth and we will ask no more. You have less cause to restrain us from discipline than from preaching: for it is a more flesh-displeasing work that we are hardlier brought to. I foretell you that you shut out me and all that are of my mind if you force us to

[1] D.W.L. MS. Baxter Letters, vi, fo. 155 (W[illiam] B[ates] to Baxter, March 30[1660]).
[2] Powicke, i. 189. Cf. Abernathy, 44 f.          [3] Rel. Baxt. ii. 217–18 (§§76,78).
[4] The other two were Edmund Calamy and John Gauden. Calamy's sermon was not printed, but Dr G. F. Nuttall has located a manuscript copy in the Congregational Library, London.

administer sacraments without discipline and without the conduct of our own discretion, to whom the magistrate appoints it; as if a physician must give no physic but by your prescript. . . . The question is not, Whether bishops or no? but Whether discipline or none? and Whether enough to use it? 4. We earnestly request that Scripture sufficiency as the test of our religion and only universal law of Christ may be maintained; and that nothing unnecessary may be imposed as necessary nor the Church's unity laid on that which will not bear it nor ever did. . . .[1]

It will be noticed what an emphasis Baxter places upon discipline; in subsequent negotiations it will be noticed that this was almost the only point on which the restored churchmen made some, if rather grudging, concessions to the Puritan point of view.

Baxter's activities during the previous ten years made him a key figure at the Restoration. He had a clear programme which with goodwill could have been the basis of a lasting settlement. In the short time that there had been he had made considerable strides towards winning acceptance for it in practice. It had had its greatest success with ministers inclining to the episcopal side; and it would be Episcopalians who, when the king was restored, would have the main responsibility for the success or failure of any subsequent settlement. Remarkable too was the fact that the Presbyterians found in Baxter their acknowledged leader. Doubtless they regarded him as one of themselves, whatever distaste he may then and subsequently have had for the Presbyterian name. In the negotiations that followed the Restoration, if Baxter did not speak for the London Provincial Assembly he spoke for most of the men who composed it and he spoke for many more beyond the confines of the metropolis. He had remarkable success too in placating the more rigid Presbyterians, less willing than himself to make concessions to the Episcopalian point of view.

It may well have been the activities of this remnant of rigid Presbyterians that made Baxter desire to avoid the entanglements of the name Presbyterian, which could be made to imply more than he and many other Presbyterians wished to insist upon. In the event

[1] R. Baxter, *A Sermon of Repentance . . . April 30, 1660*, 42–3. Cf. Baxter's MS. letter to John Swinfen, February 17, [1659] (D.W.L. MS. Baxter letters, vi, fo. 233) quoted by R. Schlatter, *Richard Baxter and Puritan Politics*, 66: 'The Pastors be forced to exercise discipline—the non-exercise of it continueth the Independents' withdrawing more than any distance in principles.' Cf. Every, 9.

the reverse was to be the actual history; the Presbyterian name came to mean what Baxter approved and those ministers and churches that employed the term did so in the old English traditional sense of Cartwright, Travers and Bradshaw, but with such modifications as Baxter's Voluntary Associations had made in the older conception. To this there would be two exceptions. After the ejection such Presbyterians could no longer be parish ministers though the parish conception continued to dominate their relations with their congregations. The failure of the Restoration settlement meant ultimately the failure of Puritan discipline because for practical purposes the power of enforcement was gone. It would have to be 'love and reason' or nothing.

# CHAPTER III

# PRESBYTERIANS IN SEPARATION

## THE CATACLYSM

*by* C. G. BOLAM AND JEREMY GORING

---

## The King Returns

The Presbyterian divines who assembled before St Paul's on May 29, 1660, to present a gold-clasp Bible to the returning King were probably under no illusions as to what his return would mean. It would mean the restoration not only of the monarchy but also of episcopacy and liturgy and many other features of the ecclesiastical *status quo ante bellum*.[1] But they were also under the impression that there would be room in the restored Church for those with Puritan scruples. Charles's 'Declaration from Breda', issued on April 4, 1660, had promised 'a liberty to tender consciences' and had affirmed 'that no man shall be disquieted or called in question for differences of opinion in matters of religion which do not disturb the peace of the kingdom'.[2] Moreover the Presbyterian ministers who had later waited on the King at the Hague had been well pleased with their reception: they had been unable to persuade Charles to make Puritanism the rule of religion in his own household but their hopes had been raised by his 'encouraging promises of peace'.[3] Whether the King's suggestions of mutual concessions were honestly meant or whether they were a mere *ruse de guerre* is hard to say and need not detain us in this discussion. It is likely enough that his policy of conciliation was genuine, though he may have been more concerned for his Roman Catholic, than for his Protestant, dissenting subjects. But when it came to the point he was clearly more afraid of offending the Episcopal than the Presbyterian party.

[1] For the negotiations between the Presbyterians and the episcopal party directly preceding the King's return, see Bosher, 105 f.
[2] *EHD*, viii. 58.     [3] Bosher, 130.

At this date, however, the King's favour was not as important as it was later to become, because the Presbyterians enjoyed considerable support in the Convention Parliament.[1] Here apparently their cause continued to prosper. A Bill for Settling Ministers passed its second reading on July 30th and received the royal assent on September 13th: this measure, though it reinstated the sequestered clergy and displaced 695 Puritan 'intruders', had the effect of confirming the great majority of Presbyterians in their livings. This modest success, nevertheless, owed much to the defection during the summer season of the young royalist squires who returned to their estates and their country employments, leaving the Commons with a preponderance of Presbyterian sympathizers.

## The Turning Tide

The turn of events was soon to show that the Presbyterians were enjoying less and less popular support. All over the country sequestered clergy, in defiance of a royal proclamation of June 1st that expressly forbade them, were proceeding, almost without opposition, to eject their Puritan successors from their livings. The maypoles returned to the village greens and the prospect of an end to the hated Presbyterian discipline caused universal rejoicing. Moreover in London, where the greatest strength of the Presbyterians lay, their cause was weakened by divisions within their own ranks. Early in June the old Covenanting Presbyterians in and about the city petitioned the King 'that the things of God and religion, which have been so solemnly covenanted for, may be owned and confirmed by your royal authority'.[2] This petition, which apparently never reached the King, caused a great deal of consternation. It was widely rumoured that it had been 'set on foot and influenced by the Scots'.[3] Certainly the majority of English Presbyterians would have nothing to do with it, fearing that it would sabotage their attempts to reach a compromise settlement with the bishops. Soon afterwards a number of the leading moderates, including Calamy, Reynolds, Baxter and others among those recently appointed royal chaplains, had an audience with Charles, in the course of which they disavowed the factiousness and disloyalty of 'some fanatics'

---

[1] G. F. Trevallyn Jones, 'The composition and leadership of the Presbyterian party in the Convention' in *EHR*, lxxix. 307–54. Cf. Abernathy, 50 ff.
[2] Z. Crofton, *Berith Anti-Baal*, 1661, p. xiii.          [3] Bosher, 152.

and declared their desire for collaboration with the episcopal party. The King responded favourably to the idea of collaboration, insisting that 'it must not be by bringing one party over to the other, but by abating somewhat on both sides and meeting in the midway'. More practically, Charles suggested that the ministers should draw up proposals regarding church government and at the same time agreed to their request that the bishops should be asked to do likewise.[1]

The ministers duly conferred at Sion College with sundry of their city and provincial brethren, and two or three week later, on July 10th, laid their proposals before the King. In the main what they offered was Ussher's scheme for a modified episcopacy: they wished to see the appointment of suffragan bishops, to be chosen by local associations of ministers, and were particularly insistent that these associations should not be so large as to 'make the discipline impossible'.[2] Baxter, looking back on the negotiations, emphasized the point that they did not plead for what he called 'Presbytery' (by which he doubtless meant the hierarchical Scottish system), 'unless a Moderate Episcopacy be Presbytery'.[3]

In this country and at that date it would probably have been true to say that Moderate Episcopacy *was* Presbytery. For, as Baxter expressed it in a memorable passage:

Any man that was for a spiritual serious way of worship (though he were for moderate Episcopacy and Liturgy), and that lived according to his profession, was called commonly a Presbyterian, as formerly he was called a Puritan, unless he joined himself to Independents, Anabaptists, or some other sect which might afford him a more odious name. . . . And of the ministers, he was called a Presbyterian that was for Episcopacy and Liturgy, if he conformed not so far as to subscribe or swear to the English diocesan frame and all their impositions.[4]

But if the Presbyterians disliked the English diocesan frame they were for the most part equally hostile to the Scottish hierarchical structure. Baxter's friend John Corbet put the matter in a nutshell:

The form of ecclesiastical government by parochial and classical presbyteries, provincial and national assemblies is remote enough from their [the Presbyterians'] main cause, and . . . many that approve

[1] *Rel. Baxt.* ii. 230–1.    [2] Ibid. 232–8.
[3] Ibid. 232.    [4] Ibid. 278.

a regulated episcopacy will be found of their number. For there is a vast difference between the ancient episcopacy and the height of prelacy or hierarchy of the latter times. This latter is the true opposite of Presbytery. And so they may not abhor to be named in several respects both Presbyterian and Episcopal, yet not Prelatical. Some of them commend, and I think most of them allow in order to peace, *Episcopum Praesidem non Principem*.[1]

Even Zachary Crofton, one of the most militant of the old Covenanting Presbyterians, insisted that he was not opposed to the kind of episcopacy advocated by Ussher, for whose memory he professed the highest regard, but only against what he called *Despoticum Tyrranicum Regimen*.[2]

Baxter and the Reconcilers hoped that by taking their stand on Ussher's scheme they would be able to reach a solution acceptable to all. They expected also that the attitude of the episcopal party would be equally conciliatory. In this they were disappointed. The bishops' reply to the Sion College proposals was courteous but unhelpful. Knowing that time was on their side, they were loath to be drawn into any negotiations. Meanwhile the restoration progressed apace. The cathedral chapters were filled up in preparation for the elections to vacant sees due to take place in the autumn and winter. Attempts were made to buy off the leading Presbyterians with offers of preferment. Baxter was offered the see of Hereford, Calamy that of Lichfield and Coventry, and Reynolds that of Norwich, while Manton and Bates were offered deaneries. All except Reynolds declined.

## The Worcester House Declaration

Baxter's ostensible reasons for declining preferment were his doubts about the reliability of the King's recently published Declaration on Ecclesiastical Affairs. The first draft of this Declaration had been circulated among the Presbyterian leaders early in September. Whatever the motives which led Charles and Clarendon to issue this document, it appeared on the surface to be a conciliatory gesture to the Presbyterians. Baxter, however, was not satisfied with the draft and petitioned the King for a scheme of church government more closely akin to that of Archbishop Ussher. His

[1] J. Corbet, *Interest of England*, c. 1660, 29–30.
[2] Z. Crofton, *Analepsis*, 1660, 3.

petition was ignored and on October 22nd Charles called a joint
conference of bishops and Presbyterian ministers at Worcester
House, Clarendon's residence. Here the ministers presented their
proposed 'Alterations' to the draft, the most important of which
was intended to guarantee the parson's freedom of action in his
own parish. But neither the King nor the bishops were in any mood
for making concessions and the meeting came to an end without
anything material having been achieved. However, when the Declaration was published on October 25th Baxter was pleased to find that
some of the 'Alterations', including the all-important one regarding
parish discipline, had in fact been embodied in it. The London
ministers promptly drew up an address of thanks to Charles,
which was signed by all but the most rigid of the ancient Presbyterians.[1]

The Worcester House Declaration as it came to be called was to
be the high water mark of mutual concessions. It embodied a
workable scheme for a State Church that would not have looked so
very different from the traditional Church of England, yet would
have brought in a vast number of those subsequently ejected. It
did little or nothing for the Independents, but it is hard to see
how any national church settlement could have suited them. At
Worcester House Clarendon had proposed a measure of toleration
for those outside the Church, who presumably included Papists as
well as Independents and Anabaptists: the long silence which
greeted this proposal was eventually broken by Baxter, who, to
the regret of his colleagues, burst out with a protest that there
ought to be a distinction between 'tolerable parties' and 'the intolerable'.[2] The outburst was a comparatively mild one, but it was
to have an adverse effect upon relations between Presbyterians and
Independents.

The Presbyterians' failure to reach a seriously tenable *modus
vivendi* with the Independents, in spite of Baxter's earlier efforts
to find one, was now to have unfortunate consequences at Westminster. When the Commons reconvened in November the Presbyterians, who were doubtful about the legal status of the Worcester
House Declaration, sought to have it confirmed by Act of Parliament. This proposal, however, met with opposition from more than

[1] Bosher, 188–90; *Rel. Baxt.* ii. 279, 284. Cf. Abernathy, 74–7.
[2] *Rel. Baxt.* ii. 277.

one quarter. It was opposed by the Church party, many of whom tried to argue, with Sir John Masham, that they had been confronted with 'an excellent Declaration metamorphosed into a very ugly Bill'.[1] It was also opposed by the representatives of the Court, who were anxious lest a temporary expedient should be given the force of a permanent regulation. Less to be expected was the opposition of the Independents, who had little interest in comprehension and who were irritated by the Presbyterians' indifference to their case for toleration. Though the Independent members were few in number their influence was probably decisive in securing the Bill's defeat by 183 votes to 157.[2] November 28th was a black day for the Presbyterians; 'their failure to retain control of their last stronghold, the House of Commons, left them, as Andrew Marvell observed, "henceforth [to] rely only upon his Majesty's goodness" '.[3]

## The Savoy Conference

Unfortunately, however, his Majesty's goodness, whether reliable or not, was powerless to stem the growing anti-Presbyterian tide. During the winter and spring the vacant sees were filled with new bishops, most of them right wing episcopalians or 'Laudians', who promptly proceeded to restore the old order in their dioceses. The Quarter Sessions records show that all over England incumbents were being presented for non-reading of the Prayer Book. The force of revived episcopal authority was felt in London, where Sheldon ejected ministers who would not be re-ordained and obliged others against their wills to read the Common Prayers. This regimentation of London churches produced such a strong reaction in the city that at the Parliamentary elections in March 1661 the Presbyterians gained in London an overwhelming victory. Unfortunately for them it was a success limited to London.

While the Parliamentary elections were in progress the King, in accordance with the promise made in the Worcester House Declaration, commissioned twelve bishops and twelve Presbyterian divines to meet at the Savoy and 'to advise upon and review' the Book of Common Prayer.[4] Even at the first meeting on April 15th it became apparent that the bishops were in no mood to make

[1] Bosher, 197.          [2] Ibid. 146, 198.          [3] Ibid. 198.
[4] See E. C. Ratcliff, 'The Savoy Conference' in Nuttall and Chadwick, 105 f.

concessions. Sheldon, who was their effective leader, wasted no
time in pointing out that

> it was not they, but we [i.e. the Presbyterians] that had been the
> seekers of this conference, and that desired alterations in the liturgy;
> and therefore they had nothing to say or do.[1]

From this tactical vantage-point the bishops compelled the Presbyterians into the weak position of offering suggestions and emenda-
tions to the Prayer Book, and these were used as a broad target for
minute criticisms that led inevitably to stalemate. Faced with this
situation it is difficult to see what the Presbyterians could have done
but fight for the whole of the programme which they had drawn up
at a time when their hopes had not been so bleak. To add to their
difficulties they were under pressure from their own side not to
make concessions: an eye-witness account of one of the meetings
of the Presbyterian representatives records that Baxter and Calamy
'stumbled at' some of their fellow-commissioners' suggestions.[2]
In view of these circumstances it is not surprising that the bishops
saw fit to dismiss almost without discussion a Reformed Liturgy
which Baxter had prepared as an alternative to the Book of Common
Prayer and upon which he had expended much labour.[3] However,
they did accept some of the alterations to the Prayer Book which the
Presbyterians had suggested: perhaps the most significant of these
was the adoption of the Authorized Version of the Bible for the passages from the Gospels and Epistles included in the liturgy. Moreover, as will be seen later, further concessions were to be made
before the new Prayer Book was eventually published.[4]

## What the Ejected Could Not Swallow

Early in May, while the Savoy Conference was still in progress,
the new Parliament met. So ultra-royalist was its complexion that
it earned the name of the 'Cavalier Parliament'. Immediately it
set to work to put the clock back to 1642. The Covenant was ordered
to be publicly burned by the common hangman. All members of
the Commons were required to receive the Sacrament according

[1] *Rel. Baxt.* ii. 305.
[2] Letter from John Collinges to Philip, Lord Wharton in Bodl. MS. Carte 77, fo. 635.
[3] The 'Savoy Liturgy', which was entirely the work of Baxter, was couched in scriptural language and was intended as an alternative form of service for those with scruples
about the Prayer Book. See Ratcliff, op. cit. 112–13, 119 f.          [4] See below, p. 81.

to the Prayer Book rite. Ignoring the fact that the Savoy Conference was then meeting to discuss the liturgy, the Commons introduced a Uniformity Bill enforcing the Prayer Book of 1604: this passed its third reading on July 9th, but its progress through the Lords was held up by Government intervention. After the summer recess there was a fresh spate of anti-Presbyterian legislation. In December the Act for Settling Ministers was amended in such a way as to reverse its effects and the Corporation Act was passed, obliging all members of corporations to renounce the Covenant and receive the Sacrament 'according to the rites of the Church of England'. From now onwards the Commons set the pace and the King and Clarendon, fearful of the consequences of a too severe treatment of the Presbyterians, did their best to apply a brake. The measure of their failure is to be seen in the Act of Uniformity which, after lengthy debates in the Lords and some final amendments in the Commons, eventually became law on May 19th, 1662.[1]

The Act was to come into force on St Bartholomew's Day, August 24th, 1662—a date that had been chosen deliberately in order to deprive non-conforming ministers of the half-yearly tithes due at Michaelmas. Baxter, however, gave over preaching forthwith in order to make clear to the Government his intention to obey them in all that was lawful, and to his fellow-ministers his intention not to conform.[2] Clarendon resented his action, accusing him of being 'proud and factious' and wishing to 'occasion confusion'.[3] But Baxter was not alone in silencing himself; a considerable number of ministers withdrew from their places before the end of May. Others decided to remain to the last, hoping perhaps that some last-minute indulgence would save them from the painful necessity of resigning their livings. But in spite of a number of Presbyterian petitions to the King, no indulgence was forthcoming.[4] Charles and Clarendon were probably sympathetic but they would not or could not undo what Parliament had done. And so Sunday, August 17th saw hundreds of Presbyterian pastors bidding farewell to their flocks. At St Dunstan's in the West in Fleet Street Samuel Pepys stood in the hot overcrowded gallery to hear the 'silver-tongued' William Bates speak his parting words to his parishioners:

[1] Bosher, 248 f.; Bennett, 119.
[2] G. F. Nuttall, 'The First Nonconformists' in Nuttall and Chadwick, 155 f.
[3] Bosher, 258, n. 3.                [4] Ibid. 258 f.

You know it is not my manner to speak anything in the pulpit that is extraneous to my text and business; yet this I shall say, that it is not my opinion, fashion or humour that keeps me from complying with what is required of us; but something after much prayer, discourse and study yet remains unsatisfied.[1]

What was this something that remained unsatisfied? What was it in the terms of the Act of Uniformity that Bates and his fellow-Presbyterians found unacceptable? Most of the accounts of the Ejection single out two of the Act's provisions as being the major stumbling-blocks: one was the compulsory re-ordination of all those who had not been ordained by a bishop;[2] the other was the requirement of 'assent and consent' to everything in the Prayer Book. While it is true that both these issues were very real ones, it is also true that they tended to loom largest in the minds of that small minority of the ejected who, being Independent in judgment, were opposed to episcopacy and liturgy in any form. Most Presbyterians were certainly not opposed to a liturgy as such and many of them would probably not have found so much to object to in the Book of Common Prayer as to make conformity impossible. Between the close of the Savoy Conference in July 1661 and the passing of the Act nine months later a number of substantial improvements had been made in the Prayer Book, including the re-instatement of the celebrated rubric on kneeling that had disappeared in 1559;[3] so that Baxter was hardly justified in complaining that the new Book 'made things far harder and heavier than before'.[4] But he was on firmer ground when he declared that the demand for assent and consent to the Book's entire contents constituted a new and intolerable interference with men's liberty; for the Puritans were now required not merely to adopt practices which were repellent to them but also to express positive approval of them. This requirement was an imposition which Baxter and his associates believed that no Government had the right to make.

---

[1] *Diary of Samuel Pepys* (ed. H. B. Wheatley), 1904–5, ii. 288–9. Cf. S. K. Jones, *Dr. Williams and his Library*, 1948, 3, 30.

[2] At least 420 of the ejected had been in episcopal orders before the Civil War and a further 45 had received episcopal ordination between May 1660 and August 1662. *Cal. Rev.* lxi.

[3] This explained that kneeling at Communion did not represent any adoration of the elements.                    [4] *Rel. Baxt.* ii. 369.

F

There were, however, two other aspects of the Act which, although they had no significance for the Independents, had profound consequences for the Presbyterians.[1] The first of these, which might be described as the 'hidden factor' in the Ejection, was the old question of parish discipline. Before the King's return Baxter had affirmed that if ministers were forced 'to administer the sacraments without discipline' he and those of like mind with him would be 'shut out' of the Church. During the ensuing negotiations with the bishops the Presbyterians had not ceased to emphasize the same point. Their efforts had not been altogether fruitless. Although the new Prayer Book was a long way from meeting all their requirements in this respect, it did contain a rubric authorizing parish clergy to refuse communion to scandalous livers. The value of this, however, was largely nullified by a provision that ultimate responsibility for disciplining the wrongdoers lay not with the local incumbent but with the bishop by whom suspension from communion was subject to review; the bishop moreover would almost invariably delegate such duties to his chancellor, an official whom the Presbyterians, with their intense dislike of lay interference in ecclesiastical affairs, regarded as unfitted for the work. 'The utter neglect of discipline by the over-hot prelates', wrote Baxter, 'had caused all our perplexities', and he went on to affirm that it was this issue and not that regarding ceremonies which constituted 'the chiefest part of our differences with them'.[2]

Another almost equally important 'difference' was over the Solemn League and Covenant.[3] The Act of Uniformity obliged all clergy not merely to abjure the Covenant for themselves but also to declare that it was an unlawful oath and therefore not binding upon anyone who had taken it. This clause was repugnant not just to the old Covenanting Presbyterians like Crofton but also to moderates like Baxter, who had no great liking for oaths but had a profound distaste for perjury. Baxter, who, contrary to what has often been stated, had himself taken the oath, devoted thirty-nine paragraphs of his memoirs to this 'controversy', as compared with ten to 'assent and consent' and one to re-ordination.[4] More than

[1] For a fuller treatment, see J. Goring, 'Some neglected aspects of the Ejection of 1662' in *UHST*, xiii. 1–8.          [2] *Rel. Baxt.* ii. 233.
[3] For the terms of the Solemn League and Covenant, see above, p. 39.
[4] *Rel. Baxt.* ii. 408–28.

once he castigated the Independents for regarding the Covenant as 'an almanac out of date'.[1] A London Independent minister, in March 1663, said of the Presbyterians: 'Had not the Covenant 'pinched them, very many of them would not have stuck at submitting to the Common prayers, as it is generally believed'.[2] Confirmation of the strength of Presbyterian feelings about the renunciation of the Covenant comes from a speech of Bishop Morley in a House of Lords debate in October 1665. Referring to the ejected ministers he said:

> Many of them have been with me and with others of my brethren. I have asked them, 'Can you read the Book of Common Prayer?' 'Yes.' 'Can you use the ceremonies?' 'Yes.' 'Why do you not then subscribe to the assent and consent, since it is only to the use of it?' 'I can.' 'Can you subscribe that which concerns the Covenant?' 'No.' Here they stick. They will not say they will renounce the last war and they will forestall another.[3]

### For Conscience' Sake

In the absence of personal testimonies from more than a handful of the ejected it is impossible to say with certainty what part of the Act of Uniformity 'pinched' them most. What is certain, however, is that all of them came out 'for conscience' sake'. John Barrett, ejected from St Peter's, Nottingham, knowing that the issues which seemed paramount to himself and his colleagues were liable to misinterpretation and might have been dismissed as pernickerty, spoke thus to his parishioners on the eve of his departure:

> I know some think, and will not spare to say, that we wilfully bring this obscurity on ourselves. But the Lord the Searcher of all hearts knows and will manifest to the world one day whether it was a mere humour or whether indeed it was not conscience that would not suffer us to comply with the things now imposed.[4]

In all about 1,000 ministers refused to comply with the demands of the Act and therefore resigned their livings. When to this figure is added the number ejected in Wales (who have often been overlooked), those deprived as a result of the Act of 1660 and those

---

[1] *Rel. Baxt.* ii. 421, 439. Cf. Z. Crofton, *St. Peter's Bonds Abide*, 1660, 9.
[2] A. G. Matthews, 'A censored letter' in *CHST*, ix. 266, 273.
[3] Bodl. MS. Carte 80, fo. 757, ed. Caroline Robbins in *Bull. Inst. Hist. Res.* xxi. 223–4.    [4] *England's Remembrancer: being a collection of farewell sermons*, 1663, 65.

removed from their benefices by unofficial procedures at sundry times, the number of the ejected comes near the legendary 2,000. It is difficult to know what proportion of the total body of clergy this represented, but it probably amounted to about one-fifth. Among them were many of the most scholarly and capable men in the Church: of the fifty-three ministers silenced in the cities of London and Westminster in 1662, forty-eight were graduates of Oxford or Cambridge, five of them being D.D.s. In London, as elsewhere, the great majority of the ejected were Presbyterian in judgment: it has been estimated that only 172 of those deprived of their livings in 1660-2 were Congregationals.[1]

What of those Presbyterians who remained in the Church? Among them, it is certain, there was a not inconsiderable number of moderate men who believed that they could best serve God and men by staying where they were. It was easy for contemporaries to be satirical about these men, as was Edward Browne, when in a memorable passage he pictured John Rowlandson of Bakewell, formerly a zealous anti-royalist, heading the column of Derbyshire conformists who went to subscribe at Chesterfield[2]—but to do so was to misunderstand the dilemma in which so many sincere men found themselves at this time. More sympathetic was William Bagshaw, ejected from Glossop and later known as the 'Apostle of the Peak': while admitting that Rowlandson's conduct might be regarded as that of a turn-coat, he asked his brethren to 'retain due charity for the grave divine'.[3] Rowlandson was an insignificant figure, but there were among the Presbyterian conformists men of the calibre of Edward Reynolds, John Tillotson and John Wallis, who became the progenitors of a Low Church party, remaining loyal to Puritan ideals and favouring the comprehension of Dissenters within the Church.

## Presbyterian Separatists

The Presbyterians ejected in 1662 found difficulty in reconciling themselves to the idea of being separatists. Many of them still regarded themselves as members of the Church of England and

[1] For a full analytical study of the ejected, see *Cal. Rev.* For the number of Congregationals, see Nuttall, *Visible Saints*, 23, n. 1 and 'Congregational Commonwealth Incumbents' in *CHST*, xiv. 155–67.

[2] 'Extracts from the common-place book of Edward Browne' in *The Reliquary*, xi. 73–8.    [3] W. Bagshaw, *De spiritualibus pecci*, 1702.

continued to attend parish worship. Such men were reluctant to
set up conventicles and, when they did so, took care to hold them
outside the hours appointed for mattins and evensong.[1] A number
believed with John Whitlock, ejected vicar of St Mary's, Nottingham, in a policy of 'preaching by silence'. In bidding his congregation farewell Whitlock had declared:

> God now calls us and many others to preach to you by silence. And
> the very silence of so many ministers, if blessed by the Lord, may
> prove the most powerful and effectual sermon to people that they have
> had.[2]

In some parts of the country this Presbyterian silence was to
remain unbroken for a decade, but in others a somewhat different
spirit prevailed. In Devonshire, for example, the county with the
highest number of ejected ministers, Presbyterians continued to
serve those of their former parishioners that were prepared to
follow them. The 1665 episcopal returns for the county revealed
that a considerable number of deprived clergy continued to reside
in their old localities and some were known to preach.[3] George
Hughes and Thomas Martyn, former vicar and lecturer respectively
at St Andrew's, Plymouth, were described in the returns as 'private
perverters' and were later arrested for preaching in the town.[4]
Their friend John Quick, ejected from nearby Brixton, had already
been imprisoned for a similar offence. The bishop's report, sent to
Sheldon in December 1663, throws light on the dilemma which
led Quick to break his silence:

> He saith that after his removal he stayed some months to see whether
> any other would supply his place, but at length finding that no man
> was put in his stead and that the people went off, some to Atheism and
> debauchery, others to Sectarism (for he is a Presbyterian) he resolved
> to adventure to gather his flock again.[5]

The Conventicle Act passed in May 1664, with its harsh penalties
for those attending nonconformist worship, was clearly aimed not
only at the more militant separatists but also, ironically enough, at
staid and respectable Presbyterians who were known to have a deep
distaste for 'Sectarism'.

[1] Whiting, 60–1     [2] *England's Remembrancer*, 42.     [3] Lyon Turner, iii. 66–8.
[4] *Cal. Rev.* 282.     [5] Ibid. 402.

The Conventicle Act was followed in October 1665 by an 'Act for restraining Nonconformists from in-habiting Corporations': this Act, commonly called the 'Oxford Act' or the 'Five Mile Act', was occasioned by the receipt of the bishops' information regarding the whereabouts of the ejected clergy. Under its terms every Dissenting minister was obliged to take an oath not to 'endeavour any alteration of government in church or state'; those refusing were forbidden to reside within five miles of any corporate town or of any place where they had formerly ministered. The Act, which was designed to weaken the power of the Dissenters in the places where they were strongest, had one unforseen result: it led new preachers to come forward to fill the gaps left by the banished ministers. It even led Presbyterians to take a step which they had been most loath to take, viz. to ordain ministers outside the established church. It has often been stated that the first Presbyterian ordination after the ejection took place in 1672, but it is clear that a number had taken place some years before that. George Trosse, a native of Exeter and an Oxford man, left this account of his ordination in 1666:

> At first I found myself not much inclined to it [ordination]: But at length, when the Corporation Act [=Five Mile Act] came abroad, the design of which was to drive all nonconforming ministers from all corporations and their benefices so that those of the City [Exeter] would be forced to depart. . . . I consented to an ordination, that so, in the absence of these ministers, I might both preach and administer other ordinances freely.[1]

In London the emergence of Presbyterians as avowed separatists took a slightly different course. It was the Plague that brought them into the open as unashamed schismatics. Altogether eight Presbyterians, all but two of whom were provincial ministers who had come to the city after ejection, are known to have remained in London during the Plague, braving both pestilence and prosecution in order to serve the stricken inhabitants.[2] Their immediate reward, it was noted, was the Five Mile Act, passed by a Parliament that

[1] *Life of . . . Trosse . . . by himself*, 1714, 90; I. Gilling, *The life of . . . Trosse*, 1715, 21. There were 22 ejected ministers resident in Exeter in 1664. Brockett, 23-4.

[2] The eight were William Carslake, Robert Chambers, John Chester, Robert Franklyn, James Janeway, John Mortimer, John Turner and Thomas Vincent. See *Rel. Baxt.* iii. 2 and *Cal. Rev.* s.v. There were also a number of parish ministers who remained in the stricken city.

had taken refuge from the Plague in Oxford. Their delayed reward
was a new respect that brought the makers of that Act no small
measure of obloquy. Many shared the feelings of the Earl of
Devonshire, Lord Lieutenant of Derbyshire, who, when ordered to
remove Thomas Stanley, the ejected rector, from the Plague-stricken
village of Eyam, replied

> that it was more reasonable that the whole country should in more than
> words testify their thankfulness to him, who together with his care of
> the town had taken such care, as none else did, to prevent the infection
> of the towns adjacent.[1]

## Presbyterians under Persecution

At the same time the Five Mile Act brought to light new differences among the Presbyterians, particularly in London. Some
older ministers, among them Bates, Jacomb and Manton, thinking
that the oath required by the Act meant no more than a promise
not to endeavour to change the Government by unlawful means,
subscribed to the Act and earned the name 'Five Mile Men'.[2]
On the other hand, some of the younger men, among whom were
Annesley, Vincent, Watson and Janeway, refused to take the oath.
These two groups later came to be known as 'Dons' and 'Ducklings':
the former was a natural term for those who tended to lord it over
the others; the latter was a fitting description of those who, it was
said, 'did not fear the water', i.e. those who were ready to take the
plunge in breaking the law and setting up conventicles.[3] The existence of these two parties was to have a significant effect upon the
Presbyterians' hopes of comprehension within the established
church.[4]

Fleeting hopes of comprehension continued to illumine the dark-
ened sky of nonconformity in the years following 1665. Hopes rose
too with the prospect of a relaxation in the penal code, particularly
because the Conventicle Act, which had been moribund for some
time, finally expired in March 1669.[5] When, later that year, an

---

[1] *Cal. Rev.* 459.

[2] *CSPD*, 1671–2, 27–9. Cf. *Rel. Baxt.* iii. 13. Baxter's list of 'Five Mile Men' is
incomplete.

[3] Lyon Turner, iii. 201–2. The term 'Don' was also applied to Baxter by Judge
Jeffreys in the question 'What will become of their mighty Don?' (Sir James Stephen,
*Essays in Ecclesiastical Biography*, 1848, 234.)

[4] See below, p. 95.                    [5] Tudur Jones, 69.

episcopal survey was undertaken to provide factual evidence in
support of the Act's renewal, the Derbyshire return set out four
reasons why nonconformists maintained their integrity:

1. The expiration of the Act of Parliament.
2. The hopes of its being dissolved.
3. The King's Allowance
4. And friends at Court.[1]

To this might have been added a fifth reason, viz. the strength of
local lay supporters. The Derbyshire returns give some idea of
the number and quality of these supporters. At Stenson it was
reported that about 160 people, 'divers of them considerable
persons', sat under a nonconformist preacher at the house of John
Stone.[2] Not far away at Little Ireton between two and four hundred
people gathered 'every Lord's day at the house of Colonel Saunders',
which was 'within a mile of Sir John Carson's dwelling-house, who
(though a justice of the peace) never went about to restrain them':
they were served by no less than seven ejected ministers, of whom
six ranked as Presbyterians.[3]

The 1669 returns, incomplete and unreliable though they un-
doubtedly were, were more than sufficient to prove that Dissent was
too large an element in the country to be ignored.[4] In consequence
there came the second Conventicle Act of 1670, more burdensome
in many respects than that which it replaced; now field-meetings
came under the same embargo as house-meetings and magistrates
were to be fined for failing to harry nonconformists. The latter
provision was particularly relevant in London, where the leniency
of the magistrates had encouraged many Dissenting ministers to
take up residence in the city.[5]

[1] Lyon Turner, i. 54.

[2] Ibid. 51. The preacher was Thomas Ford, an ordained Presbyterian minister.

[3] Ibid. 49–50. The six were Samuel Beresford, John Hieron, Samuel Ogden, Robert
Seddon, Daniel Shelmerdine and Timothy Staniforth. They had all been ejected from
Derbyshire livings and five of them had been educated at Christ's College, Cambridge.
See *Cal. Rev.* s.v.

[4] It is probable that the number of Dissenters was minimized. See Lyon Turner, iii.
73.

[5] Mr Ian Philip, Secretary of the Bodleian Library, has kindly supplied us with a
copy of 'Memorandums and hints how a justice of the peace, more especially in London,
may demean himself in case of an informer's pressing upon him the Bill of Conventicles
as not to disturb them, and yet not to be liable to any forfeiture': Bodl. MS. Carte 77,
fos. 578–9.

*The Declaration of Indulgence*

A lenient attitude to London Dissenters, however, was part of the policy of the King, and especially at this time when the prospect of war with Holland made urgent the problem of money. Through an intermediary, Nicholas Butler, he decided to sound the leading ministers in the city. Sir Joseph Williamson, clerk to the Council, recorded under date, November 11, 1671:

> The meeting-house men have been viewed by the Doctor [Nicholas Butler] from house to house. They are a stout, sturdy, dissatisfied people. [He] fears they have still more heart and indignation towards the Government than some seem to tell us.

He therefore wondered 'whether [it would] not [be] better for the King now of himself to offer what is capable to content them'.[1] Charles took the hint and in March 1672 issued his Declaration of Indulgence, which, in making concessions to nonconformists, also helped Roman Catholics—whose emancipation was the object of one of the clauses of the Secret Treaty of Dover (1670).

The Dissenters, though sharing the lawyers' doubts about so wide an extension of the royal prerogative as was contained in the King's Declaration, felt that this offer of relief from persecution was too great an opportunity to be missed. Several Presbyterians now for the first time openly engaged in public preaching: even Whitlock broke his sacramental silence and took out licences at Mansfield and Nottingham. Their willingness to take out licences caused some Churchmen to jeer at the Presbyterians: 'How like to Independent-Apes your new congregations will make you look.' This addition of insult to injury was too much for Baxter:

> If you will take my spoon and knife from me, and then say that I eat like an ape or a beast, I will not be so prated and fooled out of my meat.[2]

But no matter how vehemently Baxter insisted that the ugly role of separatist had been forced upon him by his opponents, he could hardly deny that this in fact was now his role. Unwilling though they were to admit it, the action of taking out licences made the

[1] *CSPD*, 1671, 563.
[2] R. Baxter, *Sacrilegious desertion of the holy ministry rebuked, and tolerated preaching of the gospel vindicated*, 1672, 53.

Presbyterians *ipso facto* schismatics. Stillingfleet was right to date the 'presbyterian separation' from 1672.[1]

In all 1339 English ministers were licensed, 923 being Presbyterians and 416 Congregationals: of the Presbyterians by far the greatest number (89) were in Devonshire, with London (62) taking second place.[2] The apparent indifference to nomenclature which resulted in the same minister being licensed in one place as a Presbyterian and in another as a Congregational suggests that in some parts of the country denominational differences had lost some of their importance. Common sufferings had made them ready to co-operate in the practical work of maintaining the ministry and serving conventicles. One of the few points of difference between the two denominations related to the office of minister and this is reflected in the returns: almost all those designated Presbyterian, as compared with a much smaller proportion of those designated Congregational, were ejected ministers.[3] While the Presbyterians restricted the ministerial office to those who had been formally ordained by their fellow-ministers, the Independents tended to open it to 'gifted brethren', as they were called, who felt called to preach.

The freedom of worship which the Dissenters acquired under the Indulgence was not, however, to last for long. Under stiff pressure from the House of Commons Charles wavered and then capitulated by withdrawing the Declaration in March 1673. This was not the end of the matter, for the Commons, anxious lest the King should betray liberty and religion to the Papists, proceeded to pass the Test Act. This required everyone in the civil and military service of the State not only to take the oaths of allegiance and supremacy but also to receive the Sacrament according to Anglican rites. The King detested this measure but his financial needs were desperate and he gave way.

---

[1] E. Stillingfleet, *Unreasonableness of Separation*, 1681, p. xxiii.

[2] Lyon Turner, iii. 733-5. About 200 Baptists were also licensed.

[3] In Kent, for example, of the 19 'teachers' licensed as Presbyterians 17 were ejected ministers; of the remainder one, Robert Traill, was an Edinburgh graduate ordained in London in 1670, while the other, a Mr Bright of Goudhurst, was probably a near relative of the ejected vicar of that parish. (Lyon Turner, ii. 991-8; Gordon, *Freedom*, 370; *Cal. Rev.* 74-5.) On the other hand of the 14 licensed as Independents only 8 were ejected ministers; the remainder included a hatter, an attorney and a local squire. (Lyon Turner, ii. 998-1002.)

*From Persecution to Toleration*

The decade and a half that elapsed between Charles II's capitulation and William III's accession was a period of great uncertainty for the Dissenters. Initially they were uncertain about the validity of their licences, which were subject to no time limit and were not formally cancelled until 1675.[1] In that year, however, their hopes rose somewhat in the expectation of measures of relief. But their hopes were soon to be dashed to the ground again; in 1676 Archbishop Sheldon, anxious to prove that nonconformists were an insignificant minority undeserving of either comprehension or toleration, ordered the bishops to make a return of the numbers of Dissenters in their dioceses.[2] The numbers returned were probably smaller than the true figures, partly perhaps because the bishops deliberately kept the numbers down and partly because they were uncertain as to what constituted a Dissenter. Thus the Canterbury return stated that 'the Presbyterians are divided; some of them come sometimes to church—therefore such . . . are not returned as wholly Dissenters'. The same return also included the rather ominous entry: 'The sending forth of these inquiries has caused many to frequent the church.'[3] Fear of persecution was clearly a strong motive for occasional conformity.

Severe persecution, however, was not to break out until 1682, when Dissenters were widely accused of plotting to overthrow the Government. At Norwich one of the leaders of the 'violent Whigs' was reported to be Dr John Collinges, 'a man of some learning, which he employs in promoting Presbytery'.[4] At Taunton members of the 'great meeting of Presbyterians', now held at the same time as the parish church service, were alleged to worship with pistols in their pockets.[5] At Bristol matters were much more serious: fifty-two Presbyterians were committed to the Newgate prison there, which in consequence became so overcrowded that twenty-six prisoners were confined in one small room.[6] In London the situation was not much better, as Edmund Calamy, the grandson of Baxter's colleague, records in his account of this unhappy time, when he himself was but a boy of ten or eleven:

[1] Lyon Turner, iii. 57.
[2] Sheldon made it clear to the bishops that he wanted the numbers kept low. See T. Richards, 'The Religious Census of 1676' in *Trans. of the Soc. of Cymmrodorion*, session 1925–6, 4–5.      [3] Lyon Turner, i. 27.
[4] *CSPD*, 1682, 54.      [5] Ibid. 36–7.      [6] Ibid. 128.

Often was I . . . sent in those days to Newgate, New Prison, and other places of confinement with small presents of money to such Dissenting ministers as were clapped up, such as Mr. Richard Stretton, Mr. Robert Franklin, &c. . . . My own father was never cast into prison, but often had warrants out against him, and was forced to disguise himself and skulk in private holes and corners, and frequently change his lodgings.[1]

Towards the end of 1682, however, saner counsels began to prevail. In October the King's Fishmonger was fined £40 'for saying in two coffee-houses in St Bartholomew Lane that the Presbyterians had murdered Sir E. B. Godfrey and put it on the Papists'.[2] After this the rumours of plots, Presbyterian or Popish, gradually died down, but persecution of Dissenters continued until after the accession of the Roman Catholic James II in February 1685.

A new situation was created in October 1685 by Louis XIV's revocation of the Edict of Nantes, which caused thousands of Huguenots to seek shelter in England and brought the word 'refugee' into the English language. This had the immediate effect of bringing Churchmen and Dissenters closer together in a common fear of Roman Catholic domination. Even James's own 'Edict of Nantes', the 'irrevocable' Declaration of Liberty of 1687, though it brought the longed-for relief from persecution, was regarded with widespread suspicion. A degree of certainty came into the situation only with the arrival of Dutch William in November 1688 and the passing of the Toleration Act in the following May. Happily for nonconformists as a whole there was now the certainty of a large measure of legal security. Unhappily for Presbyterians as a denomination there was also the near-certainty that, effectually excluded from the Church to which spiritually they still belonged, they would remain a denomination for ever.

[1] Calamy, *Hist. Account*, i. 88.  [2] *CSPD*, 1682, 475.

# PARTIES IN NONCONFORMITY

## *by* ROGER THOMAS

### ECCLESIASTICAL DIFFERENCES

With the Ejection Nonconformity took on a new and less concise meaning. Of old, Nonconformists (indeed they were sometimes spoken of as the 'Old Nonconformists'), had been those of Puritan outlook who sought to remain as parish ministers within the Church while refusing to conform in certain matters of conscience. When the Ejection came many of those with this outlook found themselves willy nilly outside the Church and its parish ministry if they were to hold to their conscientious scruples. They thus came to be lumped together with separatists who had always operated outside the Church. Both types were now outside the Church, and Nonconformity took on the somewhat novel sense of exclusion. But their common fate brought them no nearer together except in so far as both groups suffered under the same penal laws. The Presbyterians had as little liking for Quakers as ever, and Baxter, conservative in this as in so much else, endeavoured to perpetuate the older meaning of Nonconformist by insisting that his was 'mere nonconformity'—'the question', as he put it, 'not extending to Quakers, Seekers, Papists, Antinomians or any sect which was more than mere Nonconformists'.[1]

However, even among 'mere Nonconformists' there was no real community of interest; old differences persisted and the aftermath of the Ejection sowed the seeds of new differences. The former differences between Presbyterians and Independents persisted. The chief of these was that the Presbyterians believed in a State Establishment on a parochial basis with everyone eligible for communion unless he had to be excluded as unfit; while the Congregationals believed in gathered churches separated out from the general community, with no one eligible for communion until he had proved himself fit by bringing evidence of the work of the Holy Spirit in his soul. In the second place, while the Presbyterians

[1] R. Baxter, *Judgment of ... Reason*, 1676, 2. Cf. R. D. Whitehorn in *Beginnings of Nonconformity*, 68.

thought in terms of the Church Universal, the Congregationals regarded the particular local church as the supreme unit, each church having sovereign power in determining all matters concerned with its conduct and membership, and for some of them, at least, this meant 'that everything done in a church must be by the majority of the votes of the brethren'—ministers had no power of the keys. As a consequence, while for Presbyterians the ordination of ministers was the work of fellow ministers and was admission to the ministerial office in the church at large, for the Congregationals, though there might be fellowship between churches, and other ministers might assist at an ordination, the final responsibility lay with the particular church and admission was to office in that church alone. Similarly, although there was no room for synods and perhaps little desire for them amongst the Presbyterians, the Independents continued to suspect the Presbyterians of synodical ambitions, whether, as with Baxter, synods were supposed to have only moral authority, or, as with the Scots, they were to have stated jurisdiction and authority. Perhaps the fact that persecution made any meetings of a synodical character dangerous if not impossible rendered it all the harder to know what the Presbyterians would want to do in this direction if they ever had the opportunity.[1]

## Emphasis on Independency

After the Ejection whatever differences there may have been amongst the Independents, there was little change in their outlook; indeed they may have been more united, for there was now no longer the temptation that had formerly existed to compromise with the parochial system and hold parochial ministries in addition to organizing gathered churches. With the Presbyterians it was quite otherwise. They had always thought of themselves as parish ministers first and foremost. But parish ministers they could no longer be, unless some agreement and reconciliation could be reached with the Established Anglican Church. Attempts were at various times made to heal the breach so that ejected Presbyterian ministers could return and serve the State Church, but it soon became apparent to some at least of the Presbyterians that there was little hope of

[1] R. Thomas in *Studies*, 1964, 28–40. Cf. Nuttall, *Visible Saints*, 86, 112; *Exeter Assembly: Minutes*, 7; Calamy, *Hist. Account*, 341 ff.; Gordon in *CL*, 1888, 597, 615; John Rastrick, *An Account of the Nonconformity of John Rastrick*, 1705, 45.

success for any such efforts and that, if they were to serve at all as ministers, it must be outside the established Church. In retrospect it cannot be denied that these latter had rightly assessed the irreconcilable temper of the restored Church. In consequence their alienation from the Church grew, and they saw their only hope of continuing a gospel ministry as lying in gathering congregations outside the Church and in separation from it like the Independents, 'so that', as Baxter put it, 'their congregations were through necessity just of independent and separating shape and outward practice, though not upon the same principles'. As one government official observed, 'the people grow more fanatic; all the Presbyterians are growing to Independents and so must their teachers'. There were however many of the older and more conservative Presbyterian ministers who did not readily give in to this new trend. Foremost amongst these was Richard Baxter. Others were Thomas Manton, William Bates and John Humfrey. The list could be extended. Thus the major result of the Ejection for the Presbyterians was the creation of two parties amongst them.[1]

The Presbyterians were thus divided on the question of looking for an eventual return to the Church or looking to a future in separation from the Church; it was the conflict between Comprehension and Toleration. But there was a second cleavage over theology. Those who looked only for a toleration outside the Church tended to be traditional Calvinists like the generality of Independents; while those who looked for comprehension within the Church tended to moderate their Calvinism in the direction of Arminianism, a trend that was even more apparent among influential elements in the Church.

We consider first the cleavage between hopes of comprehension and hopes of a toleration. Clear evidence of the cleavage comes to light in 1668, the year that saw the failure of a very promising effort to bring about a measure of comprehension that would have brought back many Nonconformists into the Church. Baxter put the blame for the failure upon the 'Prelatists' malice', but Manton thought that the failure had come about because John Owen, accounted the leader of the Independents, had made a strong bid for a toleration

---

[1] Thomas in Nuttall and Chadwick, 205; *Rel. Baxt.* iii. 43; *CSPD*, 1671, 496 (September 21, 1671); Gordon, *Heads*, 83.

that had interfered with the proposals for comprehension.[1] Owen saw no future in comprehension and wanted only legal toleration so that Dissenters might continue to organize and build up gathered churches without fear of persecution. Owen heard of Manton's accusation. He could see that the Presbyterians were divided. He thought that it was high time that they realized that comprehension had no future and that the need was for Presbyterians and Independents to unite in a joint effort to seek a toleration in which both denominations could set up churches unmolested, outside the State system. He therefore called on Manton, taking with him Samuel Annesley, the most prominent amongst those Presbyterians who saw little future in comprehension. Owen's purpose was to persuade Manton that the Presbyterians should meet and come to a decision amongst themselves whether they should continue to work for comprehension or, what he regarded as inevitable, throw in their lot with the Independents in fighting for a toleration for gathered churches. Manton saw the insidious danger and, with Baxter's assistance, avoided a debate which all too easily might have meant the end of all hopes of a united English Church with its parish ministry. Baxter and his friends were not to be induced to walk into Owen's parlour.[2]

This was not the end of the matter, for as Baxter saw it there was some hope that Owen might be induced to walk into Baxter's parlour. In a recent publication Owen had used expressions that seemed to indicate that he was not wholly lost from the Presbyterian point of view. In Baxter's view he had conceded '1. That the people have not the power of the keys. 2. That they give not the power of the keys or their office-power to the pastors.'[3] At all events it can have been little more than a month after Owen's visit to Manton that Baxter approached Owen to see whether means could be found for reaching an accommodation between Presbyterians and Independents. Owen expressed himself very willing to enter into discussions. He refused to be the draftsman of a scheme for accommodation and put the work on to Baxter. Baxter was never backward in such matters and, as he himself records, drew up an 'abundance

[1] Cf. Hunter, 200–1. Henry Ashurst to Newcome, February 1, 1668, 'There will certainly now be room if the Independents do not frustrate our hopes, by rejecting that which the old Puritans would have leaped at; they say they desire more liberty.'

[2] Thomas in Nuttall and Chadwick, 203–5.

[3] John Owen, *A Brief Instruction*, 1667; *Rel. Baxt.* iii. 62. Cf. Watts, *Post. Works*, 160.

of theses' which Owen found too numerous.[1] Baxter produced a second draft.[2] Owen, after keeping this some time, wrote Baxter a hurried letter on January 25, 1669, containing a few cursory comments. Baxter replied at considerable length on February 16. In the middle of this letter, as if realizing that the argument was getting nowhere and that Owen was being elusive, he blurted out,

> The great things which hinder the Presbyterians and Moderate Episcopal Men from closing with you [Independents] are principally these. 1. Because they think that your way tends to destroy the Kingdom of Christ, by dividing it. . . . 2. They think, while you seem to be for a stricter discipline than others, that your way (or usual practice) tendeth to extirpate godliness out of the Land; by taking a very few that can talk more than the rest, and making them the Church, and shutting out more that are worthy, and by neglecting the souls of all the parish else, except as to some public preaching; against which you also prejudice them by your unjust rejections; and then think that you may warrantably account them unworthy. . . . [3]

With that outburst and the coupling of 'Presbyterians and Moderate Episcopal men' the cat is right out of the bag; Baxter's evident purpose had been to draw Owen into accepting such a compromise between the two denominations as might have paved the way for union with the National Church, which was the very reverse of the Congregational separatist system. In other words Baxter did not want a toleration opening the way to a multiplicity of sects, but comprehension within one broad based national church and the Independents committed in advance to accept it.

Owen's interest visibly cooled—to his credit he took no offence at accusations that the Independents talked more than the rest—he declared that he was still 'hearty for the work', but, though Baxter pressed him month after month, he got nothing from him until well on in 1670, and then obtained only the return of his papers and a cheerful expression of goodwill from Owen that he was 'still a

---

[1] *Rel. Baxt.* iii. 62.

[2] This document was printed as pp. 62–76 in Baxter's *Church Concord*, 1691. It is there misdated 'Acton, Nov. 21. 1688'. The reference to Acton is proof that 1688 cannot be right. The obvious date is 1668. The main title page of *Church Concord* gives the date for this work as 1667, which is doubtless also wrong. The same document exists in manuscript amongst the Baxter Treatises in D.W.L. as Treatises item No. 329; the MS., however, ends with a form of subscription—indicating its original purpose as an agreement to be signed by adherents from either side. [3] *Rel. Baxt.* iii. 67.

well-wisher to those mathematics'. Baxter and his party were not
to be induced to enter Owen's parlour; neither was Owen to be
induced to enter theirs.[1]

## The Indulgence of 1672

Time was moving on and for one reason or another the tide was
flowing strongly in favour of Owen's aspirations. Late in 1671,
when the mind of the King's advisers was moving in the direction of
a toleration, Lord Arlington's secretary, Sir Joseph Williamson,
was to learn a good deal about the party structure of Nonconformity;
he christened the Presbyterians who sided with Baxter, 'Dons',
and those associated with Samuel Annesley, 'Ducklings'. Whatever
the reason for this choice of terms, it is convenient and may be
adopted here. The Dons were a constant source of anxiety to
Williamson and the Court because they did not want a toleration
so much as a re-union with the Church, which it was not in the
King's power to give. He might arrogate to himself a power to
dispense with penal laws, but he could not dragoon an unwilling
Church into receiving unwanted dissident ministers. When Charles
issued his Indulgence of 1672, it satisfied Owen, who had no difficulty in wording an address of thanks to the King, but to the Presbyterians toleration was only a second-best and they shared with the
Anglicans their dislike of the King's exercise of the dispensing power.
So they were found wrangling over terms of their address of thanks
up to the very last minute. It was an ominous discord. When the
Commons, in the following year, forced the King to recall his
Indulgence, there were Presbyterians who gave their full support;
doubtless they expected Parliament to give them in return terms as
acceptable as they had received from the King.[2] In the event the
Bill that was to have done so failed, so that the net result of the
divisions amongst the Nonconformists was that they were left to
the full rigours of the repressive legislation against them which had
not been repealed.[3]

The same disunity did the Nonconformists disservice two years
later in 1674, when a new effort was planned from the Court for a
new Indulgence backed by the support of the wealthy and powerful

[1] Rel. Baxt. iii. 69 (145).
[2] Baxter hints at a political bargain, which there doubtless was. Rel. Baxt. iii. 103
(230).     [3] For a fuller account see Thomas in Nuttall and Chadwick, 206–13.

London Nonconformists. It failed, partly because Danby, now the King's adviser, was able to persuade the King to reverse the policy of the first half of his reign and attach himself to the Church instead of looking to the Dissenters, but partly also because of the manifest disunity among the Dissenters, with the Independents and Ducklings supporting the Duke of York's initiative for an indulgence while the Dons were entering into negotiations with the Bishops for a comprehension.[1]

The pro-Church or comprehension policy of Baxter and his friends had long been objectionable to the Independents and he had frequently been under fire from that quarter, but in these years estrangement was increased. Under the 1672 Indulgence London Dissenters had set up a Merchants' Lecture on a Tuesday each week at Pinners' Hall, and amongst those chosen as lecturers was Baxter. According to his own account;

> When I had preached there but four sermons, I found the Independents so quarrelsome with what I said that all the City did ring of their back-bitings and false accusations. So that had I but preached for unity and against division, or unnecessary withdrawing from each other, or against unwarrantable narrowing of Christ's Church, it was cried abroad that I preached against the Independents. . . .[2]

It is without surprise that we learn that in the following years the fortunes of the Dons reached their lowest ebb. When next the opportunity came for some redress of their grievances in the Commons during Shaftesbury's second Whig Parliament in 1680, it was Churchmen alone in the Commons who took any interest in comprehension; the Nonconformists in the Commons worked solely for an Act of Toleration.[3]

*New Efforts for Unity*

By that time also there had been another very significant change. Where Owen and Baxter had failed in arriving at an accommodation, the London merchants had very nearly succeeded. They had drawn up proposals for agreement between the two denominations. The

[1] Thomas in Nuttall and Chadwick, 216–21.
[2] *Rel. Baxt.* iii. 103 (§227). The sermons in question probably belong to the end of 1673 or the beginning of 1674.
[3] Thomas in Nuttall and Chadwick, 229–31.

proposals had been considered by ministers in the Bristol area and
revised by the London ministers.[1] Apart from copies of the proposals at various stages of revision we have little or no information as
to the progress of the negotiations; it would seem therefore that
they were kept very secret for fear of causing resentment in Government circles. The same fear may have been the reason why the
agreement was not implemented. In the first instance there may
have been delay because it was thought wise to wait until the Toleration Bill of 1680 was on the Statute Book. When it failed and persecution was not only renewed but redoubled, the old fear would
make it imprudent. One thing that would seem clear from an examination of the proposals is that they were not drawn up by anyone
whose object was to draw the two main parties into an agreement
that would prepare the way for both eventually to be re-united
with the Church, such as had been Baxter's ambition in his negotiations with Owen. Their purpose was not Baxter's purpose, but the
quite different one of making Nonconformity strong and united,
so that it did not suffer the reverses that had too often been its lot
in the past. The proposals, once laid on one side, were not seriously
taken up again until two years after the Revolution of 1688.[2]

In the intervening ten years Baxter again came under attack
from the Independents, this time for defending the use of a liturgy
in the interests of 'catholic communion'.[3] But when the persecution
of the last years of Charles II gave place to the renewed Indulgence
policy of James II in 1686 and 1687, the Dons began to enjoy something of an Indian Summer. From the side of Dissent Baxter and
his colleagues were able to persuade the Dissenters to support the
Church in its hour of danger from a Roman Catholic king, while,
from the side of the Church, John Tillotson, the future archbishop
(at this time Dean of Canterbury), and other moderate churchmen
were able to win over Archbishop Sancroft and others and bring
about a large measure of agreement between churchmen and

[1] The earliest known proposals in the series are reproduced in D.W.L. *Occasional
Paper*, No. 9, 1960. The West Country revision is contained in a copy in the Forbes
Library in Gloucester Public Library, which has the original proposals on one page
with comments on the opposite page. The London revision which embodies most of
the West Country comments is reproduced in D.W.L. *Occasional Paper*, No. 6, 1957.
[2] They may have been ventilated during the period of James II's Indulgence policy
if a report to that effect in *The History of the Union*, 1698, 1 is to be believed.
[3] D.W.L. *Occasional Paper*, No. 8, p. 19; A. G. Matthews, *The Works of Richard
Baxter: an annotated list* [1932], 8, 42–4.

Dissenters.[1] Hopes of comprehension within the Church once more rose above the horizon. Had James remained longer on the throne, ironical as it may seem, comprehension might well have been achieved. As it was, the advent of William III, while it dispelled the fears of Roman Catholicism, replaced it by suspicions of a Dutch king and his Presbyterian sympathies. Parties resumed their former shapes; comprehension was doomed and the most that the Dissenters obtained was a toleration by Act of Parliament grudgingly granted.[2]

## Unity Achieved

With hopes of comprehension now out of the way, the road was clear for the resumption of an effort to unite the two main Nonconformist bodies, the Presbyterians and Independents. Although it must have been plain by the beginning of 1690 that all hope of comprehension had vanished, nothing was done immediately. The first definite move came at the beginning of July and was the foundation of a Common Fund managed by representatives of both denominations, to aid ministers, churches and students for the ministry and to co-ordinate charity hitherto undertaken sporadically and by individuals.[3] One of the earliest undertakings of the Common Fund was to set on foot a correspondence throughout the country to learn the nature and the extent of the need for assistance. From the document compiled as a result of this correspondence we learn incidentally that the ministers of Somerset, Wiltshire and Gloucestershire had set up an association and had 'already agreed upon an accommodation between Presbyterian and Congregational Ministers'.[4] From elsewhere we know that the agreement was signed on June 11, 1690 after being under consideration for six months before, and that the document in which it was contained was the revised agreement towards the revision of which West Country ministers had contributed ten years before. The fact that agreement had

[1] R. Thomas, 'The Seven Bishops and their Petition', in *JEH*, xii. 56–70.

[2] Thomas in Nuttall and Chadwick, 229–34, 246, 251. John Locke criticized the inadequacies of the toleration granted, but the Act was largely a revival of the Bill of 1680 which had to a great extent been framed by Dissenters themselves.

[3] I. G. Philip, 'Needy Congregational ministers in the West, *c.* 1676–8' in *CHST*. xix. 68–71.

[4] The document based on this correspondence was fully edited by Alexander Gordon in *Freedom after Ejection*, 1917; ibid. 47.

been reached in the area around Bristol may have stimulated the London Ministers to a renewed effort to do likewise. Between the end of October and the middle of December 1690 a committee was set up to prepare an agreement. At the outset they had before them the agreement of ten years before, which as we have just seen had been adopted in the West earlier in the year. There were a good many objections from the Independents. So a new paper of agreement was drawn up. Although there were still some Independents who would not accept it, it won wide approval and was assented to by the vast majority of ministers at a general meeting on March 6, 1691. It was subscribed by between 80 and 100 ministers, read to congregations on March 15th and published (with some modifications) as the *Heads of Agreement* the following month.[1]

This achievement—the Happy Union it was called—was greeted with great rejoicings. The Congregational, Matthew Mead, preached a sermon to celebrate the occasion on the text, *Two sticks made one*. Later in the year, in an address presented to William III, Mead again made this success the subject of congratulation. Even the aged Baxter, though the success meant the sunset of his hopes for comprehension, greeted it with a generosity worthy of emulation.[2]

Despite the celebrations and the rejoicings there were some rumblings of discontent. Nathaniel Mather complained in a letter to Thomas Jollie in Lancashire that Mead was 'marvellously taken with the specious nature of agreement and ... so dazzled that he doth not exercise his wonted discerningness'. Mather and two other Congregationals, Thomas Cole and Richard Taylor, refused to subscribe to the agreement. Nevertheless the agreement was a real achievement, even if it did no more than enshrine a *modus vivendi* already arrived at in practice in many parts of the country. In London the Happy Union, based on the agreement, had a short and unhappy life and came to an end within a few years, but elsewhere it formed the ground plan of Protestant Dissent and lasted for the best part of a century.[3]

---

[1] D.W.L. *Occasional Paper*, No. 6, pp. 2 and 12; Daniel Williams, *Answer to the Report*, 1698, 2, for the names of the members of the Committee; Giles Firmin, *Brief Review*, 1693, 28. Cf. *An Apology for the English Presbyterians*, 1699. 62 ff.

[2] Thomas in *Beginnings*, 1964, 36.

[3] D.W.L. MS. 12.78(43); letter dated April 3, 1691; Gordon, *Freedom*, 155–6. Alexander Gordon summed it up. 'From Northumberland to Cornwall, from Cheshire to Norfolk, we find these Unions. At least two of them have maintained a continuous

## ii. CALVIN NEAT OR CALVIN MILD

As we have noted, the consummation of the agreement was to Baxter, and doubtless to the party associated with him, a second best; it marked the failure of their hope of comprehension. But this hope of comprehension, as against a toleration, was not the only difference that distinguished the Dons from the Ducklings. There was also a theological difference, and here the influence of Baxter and his party was more enduring.

### Towards Arminianism

Samuel Annesley's associates, the Ducklings, were apt to be traditional Calvinists like the generality of Independents. But Baxter, from his first book until the end of his days, was an opponent of certain extreme positions often derived from, if not indeed implicit in, Calvinism.[1] The stand taken by Baxter aligned him theologically with influential circles in the Church of England, notably the Cambridge Platonists and other Anglican Rationalists, such as John Hales of Eton and William Chillingworth, and Latitudinarians such as Simon Patrick and John Tillotson.[2] The main lines of this common divergence from what we may call the more rigid Calvinism were five-fold. In the first place, absolute reprobation or predestination to damnation was stopped and access to universal grace on Arminian lines was put alongside the Calvinist election to salvation. As Simon Patrick put it, writing of his college days, 'the doctrine of predestination . . . had always seemed to me very hard and I could never answer the objections against it, but was advised by divines to silence carnal reason.' But he acknowledges gratefully that John Smith, the Cambridge Platonist, was not one of these divines, for he laughed him out of silencing 'carnal reason'. Patrick also acknowledged gratefully help from Baxter's

---

existence to this day, the Exeter Assembly (still purely clerical) and the amalgamated (1764) Assembly of Lancashire and Cheshire (which admitted laymen in 1826, and lay delegates in 1856)', Gordon, *Heads*, 97. For details of known Unions, see D.W.L. *Occasional Paper*, No. 6, pp. 15–16. In all probability the Oldbury and Dudley 'Double Lectures' originated as such a union for the Midlands (*Unitarian Herald*, 1862, 299).

[1] In its most extreme form, spoken of as Antinomianism, any participation of a man in his own salvation was denied. R. Thomas, *Daniel Williams 'Presbyterian Bishop'*, 1964, 12–13; Thomas in *Beginnings*, 1964, 48–50.

[2] Norman Sykes, *From Sheldon to Secker*, 1959, 145–52; *A Brief Account of the New Sect of Latitude Men* [by Simon Patrick], 1662; Philip Harth, *Swift and Anglican Rationalism*, 1961.

earliest book, *Aphorismes of Justification*, 'in which the doctrine of justification is cleared of many errors'.[1] This clearing of predestination meant, secondly, that moral conduct had a larger part to play in salvation than many Calvinists were ready to admit, who condemned this deviation as legalism.[2] In the third place, as with the Arminians of his day, Baxter sought to put a term to the endless division that had plagued Protestants since the Reformation by reducing to a minimum the number of fundamentals to be treated as obligatory. Like Chillingworth he sought to do this by basing his appeal on the Bible alone and repudiating all human additions and gratuitous interpretations that led to conflict; this was the doctrine of Scripture-sufficiency which was to play a dominating part in eighteenth century controversy. In the fourth place, and again in line with contemporary Arminianism, reason was not dismissed as 'carnal' or 'corrupt', but was given a position of first importance. Reason was the inalienable badge of humanity which no man could surrender and remain human.[3] It was the sole means by which it could be established whether the Bible was or was not revealed truth, as all Christians at that time and for long after claimed it to be. It was the sole means by which canonical could be distinguished from uncanonical scriptures.[4] Any belief, however august its authority, if it flouted reason, was thereby to be repudiated. We may add that these four positions allowed those who held them to be tolerant of large divergencies in doctrine; indeed mutual tolerance may be regarded as a fifth Arminian characteristic.

## Baxter against Antinomianism

We first come upon clear signs of this theological divergence as a party matter amongst Nonconformists soon after the Indulgence of 1672, when the Merchants' Lecture was set up at Pinners' Hall as a common platform for Presbyterians and Independents. We have already seen that Baxter's contributions to the Lecture came under attack from the Independents when he argued against

[1] Simon Patrick, *Works*, 1858, ix. 419, 438.
[2] E.g. Ebenezer Turell, *The life and character of . . . Benjamin Colman*, 1749, 26–7. Cf. G. J. Hoenderdaal, 'The Life and Struggles of Arminius' in G. O. McCulloh, *Man's Faith and Freedom*, 1962, 15.
[3] Richard Baxter, *The Scripture Gospel Defended*, 1690, pt. ii (*A defence of Christ*) 26: 'As reason is a witness that we are men'; Simon Patrick, *Works*, ix. 419.
[4] Richard Baxter, *The Saints Everlasting Rest*, 1651, Preface to pt. ii.

Christian disunity and enmity to the Established Church. But he was as fiercely attacked for his stand against what he regarded as false doctrine. As Baxter himself put it,

It was cried abroad that I preached against the Independents; especially if I did but say that man's will had a natural liberty, though a moral thraldom to vice, and that men might have Christ and Life if they were truly willing, though Grace must make them willing; and that men have power to do better than they do. It was cried abroad among all the party that I preached Arminianism and free will and man's power, and O! what an odious crime was this.[1]

Snippets from sermons of Baxter in 1674 were quoted in support of these criticisms. We may quote them too, although with the warning that they may be garbled reports torn from their context. In one sermon he is said to have asserted 'that they [the saints] have the assistance of the Spirit of God, but with this caution; a man's first believing is by extrinsical arguments, not by the operation of the Spirit, but his after-believing is by the Spirit'. The report of another sermon runs, 'Far be it from thinking Christ's righteousness is our formal righteousness. And 'tis an error (saith he) to say Christ's righteousness is so perfectly ours as there is no need of any of our righteousness, in order to our actual or final justification.'[2]

Criticism of Baxter went on until well into 1676. The attacks came from the Independents, but those Presbyterians who associated with Samuel Annesley held more orthodox Calvinistic views than Baxter, and so were closer in sympathy to the Independents with some of whom they associated. We should know little of this aspect of the matter were it not for the fact that at about this time Baxter drew up a paper setting out his position and sent it to Annesley, 'desiring him but to get it read to' those who sometimes met at his house 'of different judgments in such things' 'and to procure me their animadversions on what they did any of them dislike; instead of their unprofitable obloquy when I cannot hear them'.[3]

[1] *Rel.* iii. 103 (§227). Cf. *Rel.* iii. 154 (§279).

[2] Tobias Crisp, *Christ alone exalted*, from the address 'To the Christian Reader' by his son, Samuel Crisp—Sermons of January 27, 1673 [/4] and August 11, 1674.

[3] From 'The Preface long ago written' before *A breviate of the doctrine of Justification*, 1690, which forms the first part of *The Scripture Gospel defended*, 1690, where he tells us that the *Breviate* was 'written about thirteen years past' and the paper sent to Annesley (*The Breviate*) was sent about a year before that, taking us back to about 1676, the time with which we are concerned. Baxter has a similar account in D.W.S.L. MS. 59.11, fo. 24 ('Baxter Treatises', vol. 5, item 143).

This Annesley did not do; we may guess that, understandably, he had no wish to foment dissension with the other wing of the Presbyterians.

## The Unfriendly Debate

It was at about the same time that Baxter entered upon a project which had all the aspects of a party affair. In 1676 he drew up a series of manifestos which had a twofold object. One was to make it plain that there was nothing in the theological outlook of Nonconformists to hinder reunion with the Church of England, that Nonconformists as such were not 'fanatics'. The second object was to quell those forces of unreason and fanaticism which were prevalent amongst some Independents and which gave critics a handle against Nonconformity. A damaging example of such criticism had occurred when Simon Patrick in an unfriendly mood published in 1669 and 1670 his *Friendly debate between a conformist and a nonconformist*. As Baxter said of him,

> This learned man having met with the weak passages of some ministers (especially Mr. Bridge, and some of the then Independent Party, who in an excessive opposition to the Arminians spake something unwarily, if not unsoundly, under the pretence of extolling free Grace) he scrapes these together for matter of reproach.[1]

Baxter was too generous to his opponents; Patrick did not want for material to fill the four successive parts of his *Friendly debate*. As Patrick had expressly exempted him from his aspersions Baxter was unwilling to reply to the attack, though urged to do so by Owen.[2] His reply rather took the form of the pleas that he made for sanity at the Merchants' Lectures and later in the manifestos that he drew up in 1676. He drew up five such manifestos, but only one was published in 1676. 'Some of our political friends in Parliament and elsewhere', as Baxter explained, 'were against the publishing of them, saying they would increase our sufferings as exasperating, or offend some sectaries that dislike some words'.[3] The one manifesto that was published in 1676, *The judgment of Nonconformists of the interest of reason in matters of religion*, bore the signatures of fifteen supporters. All, with one doubtful exception, were Presbyterians and the

[1] *Rel. Baxt.* iii. 39 (§88).     [2] *Rel. Baxt.* iii. 42 (§93).     [3] *Rel. Baxt.* iii. 185 (§42)

first three signatories were Manton, Baxter and Bates, three of the Merchants' lecturers at Pinners' Hall.[1]

## Enter Tobias Crisp's Ghost

Efforts to allay the dispute had some success and for a dozen years it was allowed to rest. Then in 1687 Thomas Cole, an Independent who had been amongst those who had attacked Baxter's theology in 1674, was appointed one of the stated Merchants' lecturers in succession to John Collins. The following year he made the Lecture a platform for preaching High Calvinism in a manner that exasperated Baxter.[2] Baxter gave himself credit for showing considerable restraint and not making any sort of retort.[3] But at the end of 1689 a publication appeared which exhausted his patience. It was the reprint, after the lapse of half a century, of the sermons of Tobias Crisp, who had been in his own day a notorious Antinomian and who had died in 1643. But it was not so much the reprint itself that exasperated Baxter as the fact that it bore a certificate at the beginning signed by a number of ministers including some of his own Presbyterian friends, such as John Howe, who, as Baxter well knew, had little sympathy with Crisp's teaching. It seemed to Baxter a poor subterfuge that their certificate, while it expressed no approval of Crisp, merely certified the genuineness of certain added sermons, a fact which no one was likely to dispute. What made matters worse was that Crisp's son, Samuel Crisp, who was responsible for the publication, had added a preface in which he took the opportunity to attack Baxter and rake over the coals of the old controversy that had raged soon after the Lecture was founded. The result was an outburst from Baxter when it was next his turn to preach the Merchants' Lecture, on January 28, 1690. He accused the subscribers to the certificate of hanging out 'a sign to show where Jezebel dwelt'. Not very surprisingly the epithet gave offence. Baxter followed up his outburst with the publication of a book with the title, *The Scripture Gospel defended ... against the libertines.*

---

[1] The signatories were as follows: Thomas Manton, Wm. Bates, Richard Baxter, Thomas Case, Mat. Silvester, Edward Laurence, Samuel Fairclough, Joseph Read, John Turner, Benjamin Agas, James Bedford, Mat. Pemberton, Gabriel Sangar, Henry Hurst, Roger Morice. The other manifestos were not published until 1680 and were without signatures, being published as part of *The second part of the Nonconformists plea for peace*.        [2] Thomas Cole, *A Discourse of Regeneration*, 1689.
[3] D.W.L. MS. 59.11, fos. 24–6 ('Baxter Treatises', vol. 5, item 143).

For the rest of the year the Merchants' Lecture rang with the noise of attack and counter-attack as lecture succeeded lecture, Baxter's chief opponent being Thomas Cole. John Howe, one of the offending signatories to Crisp's book, had read neither the sermons themselves nor Samuel Crisp's preface. To pacify Baxter's fury and to exculpate himself he printed a paper in which he gently reproved the younger Crisp for his preface, saying, 'the part of a friend had certainly been done as well in advising against such a preface as in subscribing the certificate'. He disavowed any share in the elder Crisp's distinctive notions in the most handsome and forthright terms, but added that it might be right to suppose that the elder Crisp, good saintly man, could not really have meant anything so wicked as his words could be taken to mean. This did not satisfy Baxter, who was quickly at work on yet another paper with a postscript in answer to Howe's paper. Hearing of this, Howe visited Baxter and 'prevailed with him to stop it, before it was published and dispersed'; Howe also promised 'to prefix a declaration with reference to the names before Dr Crisp's sermons . . . before a book . . . then going to press'. This was accordingly done.[1]

## Exalting Reason and Goodness

John Howe was not alone in trying to dissuade Baxter from what seemed ill-advised controversy. So also did Francis Tallents. Writing to him from Shrewsbury Tallents admitted that he was 'troubled . . . at the new impression of Dr Crisp's books with the pompous show of names before it and the ill consequences that are like to follow'. But he pleaded with Baxter to 'lessen differences all that may be' and added, significantly for an understanding of what lay behind the dispute, that 'a great fault has been for about twenty years, to incline to neglect Christ under the pretence of exalting reason and goodness'—two words that sufficiently indicate the contemporary Arminian advance and the tendency of Baxter's own teaching.[2] It is probable that in this Tallents would have had

[1] The book was Πλανηλογία. *A succinct and seasonable discourse . . . with an epistle . . . relative to Dr. Crisp's works*, 1691. Cf. Thomas in *Beginnings*, 1964, 40–2. That the Antinomians should have been libertines if they had followed out the logic of their own doctrines was a belief to which John Locke also subscribed. Cf. R. Thomas *Daniel Williams 'Presbyterian Bishop'*, 1964, 12–14.

[2] Powicke, ii. 174–5; D.W.L. MS. 59.5, fos. 125, 124 (letter of Tallents dated February 12, 1689/90).

a good many of the older or more old fashioned Presbyterians with him. Amongst them would have been the renowned Yorkshire Presbyterian, Oliver Heywood, who likewise saw fit to lament the rise of rationalism, especially as it affected the manner of preaching, in those twenty years. Writing in 1695, Heywood observed that no minister need be 'ashamed of the Gospel of Christ' and continued:

> Though this may seem to be out of fashion amongst some that would be esteemed rational preachers and think treating of Christ is but conceited canting (though the great Apostle of the Gentiles mentions the name of Christ nine several times in his ten first verses of I Cor. I. and his Epistles some hundreds of times; yea, and glories in it, and professeth, I. Cor. 2. 2. I determined not to know any thing amongst you save Jesus Christ and him crucified).[1]

It is a sharp reminder that the old order was passing slowly away and there can be little doubt that Francis Tallents was right if he suspected that Baxter's influence was being thrown on the side of the newer ways of 'exalting goodness and reason'. Baxter of course 'treated of Christ' and doubtless did so in a manner that would have satisfied even Oliver Heywood, but what counted for much more in the contemporary scene was Baxter's insistence upon the place of reason as an enemy of false doctrine and of the type of 'treating of Christ' that was associated with such doctrine. It was Baxter's influence in this direction that meant much in subsequent Dissenting history.[2]

Baxter was by no means alone in the making of these newer trends. Powerful influences in the Church of England, commanding wide-spread respect, were perhaps chiefly in the minds of Francis Tallents and Oliver Heywood. Among Anglicans the most noted exponent of the new rational preaching was John Tillotson, who became Archbishop of Canterbury in 1691.[3] When we recall the long friendship that existed between Baxter and Tillotson, the mutual respect of these two men for each other, the one from the

---

[1] O[liver] H[eywood], *A New Creature*, 1695, pp. i–ii.

[2] When I claimed Baxter's influence on the side of the rise of rationalism at this period Dr Geoffrey F. Nuttall reminded me that Baxter's support should not be claimed wholly on one side or the other and pointedly referred me to Baxter's own assertion (*Rel. Baxt.* i. 118) that 'if you discover an error to an injudicious man, he reeleth into the contrary error and it is hard to stop him in the middle verity'. I hope the paragraph as now worded fairly represents the truth of the situation without reeling to much into the contrary error.        [3] Norman Sykes, *From Sheldon to Secker*, 1959, 149–53.

ranks of Nonconformity, the other from the ranks of the Church, and the similarity of their outlook in many important respects, it is not hard to see how the two strands of Presbyterian party differences, a desire for reunion with the Church and a desire for a rationally controlled theology, drew them together into a single policy of a sane central churchmanship.[1] Both had sought to achieve reunion of Nonconformity with the Church and had pursued that end until hopes of its success were finally laid low with the embittered Convocation of 1689.[2] Both had boldly asserted the claims of reason in religion, which, if accepted, would have made reconciliation of the warring factions easier. Thus Tillotson had protested:

> I cannot imagine how men can do greater disservice to religion than by taking it off from the rational and solid basis upon which it stands and bearing the world in hand [i.e. maintaining] that men ought to believe without reason; for this is to turn faith into credulity. . . .[3]

In the same spirit Baxter had exclaimed:

> What more can be done to the disgrace and ruin of Christianity than to make the world believe we have no reason for it?[4]

Both men realized to the full that such assertions courted the abuse of extremists, who were all too ready to fall into the fallacy of the undistributed middle and equate acceptance of reason with the dread heresy of Socinianism. Both took pains to dissociate themselves from the Socinian heresy and to point out the fallacy. Thus Tillotson could observe:

> I know not how it comes to pass, but so it is, that everyone that offers a reasonable account of his faith . . . is presently branded a Socinian; of which we have a sad instance in that incomparable person Mr. Chillingworth. . . . [5]

Baxter was as explicit:

> We deny not but some non-conformists and conformists did cast out their suspicion of two very learned rational men, Mr. Hales and Mr. Chillingworth, as if they favoured Socinianism, because they so much used and ascribed to reason in judging of matters of religion.[6]

---

[1] *MR*, xviii. 203–5, from D.W.L. MS. 59.2, fo. 76.

[2] Thomas in Nuttall and Chadwick, 237–53.

[3] John Tillotson, *Works*, 1820, x. 271. 'Bear in hand' = maintain, *O.E.D.* i. 731.

[4] R. Baxter, *Saints Everlasting Rest*, pt ii, 5. Cf. Henry Grove, *Letter to the Reverend John Ball*, 1737, 28.       [5] Tillotson, *Works*, ix. 271.

[6] R. Baxter, *The Judgment of Non-conformists, of the Interest of Religion*, 1676, 6.

Baxter rightly realized that the important lines of party demarcation were not those of Conformist *versus* Nonconformist but those
of reasonable religion *versus* fanaticism in all its forms. Thus he
could write:

> Among the other Church-troubling controversies of these times we
> find it is one and not the least, *How far man's reason hath to do in
> matters of religion*. And deep accusations we find brought against each
> other on this account, some suspecting others of Socinianism, as over-
> magnifying reason, and others insimulating such as they seem to differ
> from, as guilty of making religion seem unreasonable, and some (who
> go over the hedge where it is low) do lay this charge of unreasonableness
> in special on the Nonconformists.[1]

To his dying day Baxter never forgot the wound to good relations
inflicted by Patrick's *Friendly Debate*.[2] Patrick had gone 'over the
hedge where it was low' and laid the charge of unreasonableness 'in
special' on the Nonconformists. But Baxter was uncomfortably
aware that the hedge was indeed low; when Antinomianism raised
its head in the reprinting of Tobias Crisp's sermons, Baxter put
the affront to reason in the forefront of his counter-attack. 'Is it no
wonder', he asked, 'that such men would cast out reason from religion for their religion seemeth to be by mere instinct. But if it
must be *without* reason it is hard that they will make it all *against*
reason.'[3]

That the point of difference was well understood on both sides
can be seen from what Tobias Crisp's son put early in his attack
on Baxter in the nefarious preface to the reprint of his father's
sermons. Thus he could write:

> If learning must take the upper-hand of divinity then *Antichristian,
> Socinian, Pelagian, Arminian* doctrines would have jostled out Christ-
> ianity long since; for who more scholastically learned than Antichrist's
> doctors, and yet who greater dunces, like *Nicodemus*, in Christ's school,
> where we are to account all our own righteousness, much more our
> learning, dung. . . . God will ever make it good, that the poor of the
> world, for parts and self-excellency, are chosen by him to be rich in

---

[1] R. Baxter, *The Judgment of Non-conformists, of the Interest of Religion*, 1676, 1.

[2] E.g. Baxter in his *Scripture-Gospel Defended*, 1690, alludes to this twenty year old
wound, in pt. II (*A defence of Christ*) sig. A2, where he speaks of 'those conformists
that will write the next friendly debate'.

[3] Ibid. pt. II, 'To the Teachers of Dr Crispe's Doctrine', sig. 3.

faith; while the rich, with their gifts and parts, are most of them sent empty away. . . . A blind man may as well dispute of the colours in the rainbow . . . as the graceless scholar of the wisdom of God in a mystery which none of the princes of this world knew.[1]

The blind man knows that he is blind and the colour-blind man can have his defect demonstrated to him, but if alleged spiritual blindness cannot be demonstrated, if it remains on the level of mere assertion, if moreover one suspects, as Baxter suspected, that its assertion was a covert means of harbouring evil and licentious doctrines, what more can be said than Baxter's 'if it must be without reason, it is hard that they will make it all against reason', and continue to use such learning as one has to demonstrate wrong-headedness? For after all, 'What more can be done to the disgrace and ruin of Christianity than to make the world believe we have no reason for it?'

[1] Tobias Crisp, *Christ alone exalted, being the complete works*, 1690, 'To the Christian Reader' [p. 4].

# CHAPTER IV

# PRESBYTERIANS IN TRANSITION

*by* ROGER THOMAS

## A DECADE OF DISCORD

The Happy Union of Presbyterians and Independents came into being in April 1691 with the adoption of the *Heads of Agreement*, but three Congregational ministers repudiated it from the outset. One of them was Thomas Cole, whom we have met among Baxter's theological opponents. Another was Richard Taylor. A third was Nathaniel Mather, who repudiated the agreement firstly because its temper was not missionary, secondly because the cardinal principles of the Congregationals were passed over almost in silence or ignored, and thirdly because Congregational principles on ordination had been compromised by the Presbyterian insistence on ministerial control of admissions to the ministry and on the exclusion of irregular preachers.[1]

### Qualification for Ordination

The last point well illustrates at once how hard it had been for the two bodies to reach agreement, and, at the same time, how necessary it had been on the question of ordination to do so. There were some unintended results of the famous Toleration Act of 1689. One was that, as the Presbyterians saw it, the Act opened the door wide for any 'illiterate, conceited person' with a ready tongue to register as a minister and gather a Dissenting congregation if he could find a group of people sufficiently like-minded to accept him, which was not hard to do.[2] There were friends of the Dissenters amongst the magistrates who were 'ashamed . . . to see what fellows came in and demanded licences' under the Act as soon as it was

---

[1] Daniel Williams, *Answer to the Report*, in *Works*, 1750, iv. 323; Gordon, *Freedom*, 156; D.W.L. MS. 12.78, pp. 243–4 (letter of N. Mather to Thomas Jollie, April 3, 1691).

[2] *Exeter Assembly: Minutes*, 31. Another unintended consequence, despite an express provision of the Act, which was a sore point with Anglicans, was that it became impracticable to enforce church attendance by the imposition of the customary penalties for non-attendance (N. Sykes, *From Sheldon to Secker*, 1959, 91).

passed.[1] Not surprisingly Dissenters, both Presbyterian and Congregational, saw this as a danger likely to bring Nonconformity not only into disrepute but into a rapid degeneration. The Congregational system was held to be peculiarly vulnerable to this danger because it gave complete authority under God (whose guidance in the matter it assumed) into the hands of each particular congregation (or church) not only to choose its own ministers, but to determine his fitness and to ordain him.[2] One of the most notable things gained by the Presbyterians in the agreement of 1691 was that something approximating to the Presbyterian theory of ordination should obtain. It was laid down that ministers 'ought to be endued with competent learning and ministerial gifts, as also with the Grace of God', that congregations should consult with pastors of neighbouring churches before choosing a minister and that candidates for the ministry should 'give proof of their gifts and fitness . . . unto pastors of known abilities to discern and judge of their qualifications'.[3] In some districts (e.g. in Devonshire) this was interpreted to mean that ordinations should be kept firmly in the hands of the local association of ministers.[4] Some other differences of principle between the two bodies either were not mentioned or were only lightly touched upon. Nothing was said of church covenants, a feature of the Congregational system.[5] No steps were taken to decide whether admission to the church should be in the hands of the minister, as with the Presbyterians, or an act of the church itself, as with the Congregationals; nor was there any clear guidance whether a credible profession of faith should be sufficient for admission, as with the Presbyterians, or whether evidence should be submitted of an experience of the sanctifying work of the Holy Spirit on the individual soul, as with the Congregationals.[6] There was substance in Nathaniel Mather's assertion that the way was 'either to suppress our principles in silence or to speak of them so

[1] Giles Firmin, *Brief Review*, 1693, 30–1, where also Firmin refers to what the Congregationals called 'gifted brethren' as 'lay preachers'—an early but not the earliest use of this more derogatory term in the mouths of Presbyterians. Cf. D.W.L. MS. 12.78 (letter of Isaac Noble, July 14, 1690).          [2] Nuttall, *Visible Saints*, 85–6.

[3] *Heads of Agreement*, 1691, 6 (sect. II. 2) and 7–8 (sect. II. 7).

[4] *Exeter Assembly : Minutes*, 18, (May 8–9, 1694); p. 31 (§5).

[5] Nuttall, *Visible Saints*, 77 ff.

[6] A reference to this question of admission is barely hinted at in *Heads*, I. 3. A reference to church covenants is just discoverable in *Heads*, I. 4. Similarly a reference to gathered churches on the Congregational pattern may be discovered in I. 5.

darkly and by halves as that none can know what we hold or of what persuasion we are in these matters.'[1] Whether this was a matter of justifiable complaint was another question. The purpose was to achieve an agreed basis of co-operation between the two bodies and not to assert the idiosyncrasies of either of them; it was felt that on many matters the differences between them could be left unresolved, since they affected only the internal organization of congregations and not their mutual relations.[2] It was quite otherwise with the question of ordination and admission to the ministry; the success of the Union depended upon a reasonable agreement here.

## The Case of Richard Davis

The importance of this was that it was precisely here that trouble first arose. If the framers of the agreement had wished to put their finger on the spot that would cause most friction they could not have done so more adroitly. For the agreement was given no time to settle down before the United Ministers were called upon to deal with the consequences of a full-scale revival which had broken out in Northamptonshire and which was spreading through neighbouring counties under the leadership of Richard Davis, formerly a member of Thomas Cole's Congregational church in London. Davis had been ordained at Rothwell on March 22, 1690, and one of his earliest indiscretions in their view had been to refuse to allow neighbouring ministers to participate in his ordination, a custom that had grown up during the years and one that would be enshrined in the *Heads of Agreement* when it came into being a year later. Tales were long treasured in the district of devout followers travelling unheard-of distances to attend his church at Rothwell on a Sunday. Other less savoury tales were also told (amongst detractors) of strange psychic phenomena associated with the revival. Leaving such tales on one side the revival was characterized by two things of subsequent importance.[3]

[1] D.W.L. MS. 12.78 (34); letter of Nathaniel Mather to Thomas Jollie, December 17. 1690.                    [2] [William Lorimer], *An Apology for the Ministers*, 1694, 15.
[3] Norman Glass, *The Early History of the Independent Church at Rothwell*, Northampton, 1871; Gordon, *Freedom*, 184–7; Olive M. Griffiths, *Religion and Learning*, 1935, 96–9; G. F. Nuttall in *Journal of Theol. Studies*, n.s. xvi (1965) 104–8; Peter Toon, in *Evangelical Magazine*, December 1966, 34–9. [John King], *A plain and just account of a most horrid . . . plague*, 1692; Richard Davis, *Truth and Innocency Vindicated*, [1692]; Giles Firmin, *Brief Review of Mr. Davis's Vindication*, 1693; D.W.L. MS. 12.78, p. 285 (letter of Isaac Noble to Thomas Jollie, June 11, 1692).

One count against Davis was that he fell foul of the *Heads of Agreement* at the vital point mentioned above; he sent out missionary preachers and put them in charge of mushroom congregations, which drew members away from long established churches, and the men he chose were certainly never examined by approved neighbouring ministers for their suitability; in the eyes of Presbyterians they were just 'ignorant and rash intruders' unfitted to enter a pulpit.[1] But with the Congregationals, however much some of them may have disapproved of Davis, it was a very tender point to interfere with the sacred rights of the particular church in appointing a minister or with the guidance of the Holy Spirit which they believed to operate in such matters.

The second count against Davis and his missionary preachers was that they preached a heady and popular form of extreme Calvinism commonly spoken of as Antinomianism to which, as we have already seen, Richard Baxter was utterly opposed. True to its etymology it opposed what was called 'legalism' or the belief that obedience to law, divine or human, had a bearing upon a man's salvation. Stillingfleet briefly summed up the Antinomian principles 'as that God seeth no sin in his people, that no conditions are required on our parts, to make us partakers of the benefits of Christ's sufferings, that Justification is before Faith, &c.' Divine grace was all, the human contribution nought—a doctrine that logically (though doubtless not in practice) implied that if a man was saved through divine grace, he might be an arrant sinner and a scoundrel, and it could make no difference to his salvation. This closely touched the susceptibilities of the Presbyterians, who shared Baxter's antipathy to Antinomianism and were more likely to agree with Stillingfleet and the Church of England in opposing fanatical excess than with the Congregationals in harbouring it. The London Presbyterians determined that Davis must be firmly dealt with.[2]

As an extreme Congregational, Davis felt no obligation to accept the agreement between the two denominations. He might well repudiate any attempts to discipline him, as evidence of synodical pretensions on the part of the Presbyterians. But he received

[1] *Heads of Agreement*, ii. 7. Cf. *Exeter Assembly: Minutes*, 31.

[2] Edward Stillingfleet, *Works*, 1710, iii. 368, 370. Cf. R. Thomas, *Daniel Williams 'Presbyterian Bishop'*, 1964, 12–14. One of Baxter's objections to the Savoy Declaration of the Independents was its Antinomian tendency—*Rel. Baxt.* i. 104 (§149).

financial aid from London and attempts had been made to stop this. So he was induced to appear before the United Ministers in May 1692 to give some explanation of his activities.[1] As Stillingfleet summed it up without specifically alluding to his case: 'Suppose some set up Antinomianism. . . . It may be, some would have them come up to their brethren and answer to the accusations brought against them. But suppose they will not and others of the brethren say they ought not, and so fall into heats and disputes among themselves about it and make new parties and divisions.'[2] This is almost to a nicety what happened amongst the London ministers in the case of Richard Davis. The Congregationals were suspicious of anything that looked like synodical jurisdiction and, in any case, they might complain that if any were to deal with Davis it ought to be neighbouring ministers in the Midlands. The upshot was that it was decided to hold an enquiry at Kettering. When the enquiry was held Davis referred to it scathingly as the 'Kettering Inquisition' and refused to attend, asserting that the ministers had no synodical jurisdiction over him; in his absence it became a field day for all the disgruntled ministers of the neighbourhood, Presbyterian and Independent alike, who had suffered from Davisite activities, to air their grievances— which they did plentifully.[3] It had no other result and it was left to the London ministers to decide whether to take action or not.

## Daniel Williams and the Theological Issues

It may well have been that amongst the Presbyterians there were many who, for peace and quiet, would have been prepared to let matters slide, but there was at least one man amongst them who was not prepared to let the Davis case go by default. This was Daniel Williams, a Welshman as was Davis, but, unlike him, a devout disciple of Baxter.[4] He had taken up Baxter's cause when he had deputized for Baxter at the Merchants' Lecture at Pinner's Hall. He had succeeded to Baxter's place amongst the Merchants'

[1] Presbyterian Fund Minutes, July 1690, June 8, 1691, January 10, 1692; [John King], *Plain and Just Account*, 1692, 18. Davis had met the London ministers on an earlier occasion also, in 1691.

[2] Edward Stillingfleet, *Ecclesiastical Cases*, 1698, 142, from a charge delivered October 26, 1696. (Also in *Works*, 1710, iii. 653.)

[3] The long tale of their grievances may be read in [John King], *A Plain and Just Account*, 1692. Cf. Richard Davis, *Truth and Innocency Vindicated* [1692], 42–6.

[4] R. Thomas, *Daniel Williams 'Presbyterian Bishop'*, 1964; S. K. Jones, *Dr. Williams and his Library*, 1948.

Lecturers. It was he who at the meeting with Davis in May 1692 brought up the accusation of Antinomianism; and it was he who went down to Kettering to represent the London ministers at the enquiry that Davis refused to attend.[1] He did more; in the interim between the meeting in May and the enquiry at Kettering he published a book with the title, *Gospel-truth stated*, upon which he must have been engaged ever since Baxter's outburst against Antinomianism on the republication of Tobias Crisp's teaching. But Davis could refer to it not unreasonably as 'this plausible book, lashing . . . at us . . over the shoulders of Dr. Crisp'. It bore a testimonial signed by a goodly number of London ministers, all Presbyterian.[2] Coming out when it did and prefaced by such a testimonial, it looked like a Presbyterian manifesto and the Congregationals treated it as such. Williams himself admitted that 'considering the delay of any testimony against Mr. Davies' (*sic*) he had hoped that 'this might be some antidote, till we arrived at more'.[3] But more was not to be had while the Congregationals remained in the Union. They had been infuriated by Williams and his determination that Davis should not escape his toils. The Arminianism towards which Baxter and his followers leaned was as repugnant to them as Antinomianism was to Baxter. And now their arch-foe had given hostages to fortune by the publication of *Gospel-truth stated*. They eagerly grasped their opportunity. Attacks upon Williams's book were quickly under way. At a meeting of the United Ministers on October 17th Isaac Chauncy handed in a paper of objections signed by himself and five other Congregationals and at the end of the meeting seceded from the Union. His reason was, as he himself put it later,

> to clear myself of the imputation of concurring with certain ministers in exerting a synodical jurisdiction . . . I have never been accessory to any such proceedings, they being utterly contrary to my judgment; what they have done since October 17 I am a stranger to and know not but by hear-say.[4]

[1] Richard Davis, *Truth and Innocency*, 38–9.

[2] Published May 18, 1692 (with 16 signatures to the testimonial); 2nd ed. September 27, 1692 (with 48 signatures).

[3] Daniel Williams, *Defence of Gospel Truth*, 1693, 'To the Reader'. The unfortunate misprint, 'my testimony' is corrected to 'any Testimony' when reprinted in *The Works* of 1750.

[4] Isaac Chauncy, *Neonomianism Unmask'd*, pt. iii, 1693, 96–7, 98; *Answer to the Report.* 1698, 3.

He was alluding to the testimony against Davis, which, once the Congregationals began to fall away from the Union, was rapidly agreed upon and published by the 'United Ministers' on the last day of the year 1692.[1]

Perhaps it was the publication of this testimony that made abortive an agreement in doctrine negotiated earlier in the same month of December to meet objections in Chauncy's paper handed in in October 1692.[2] It was hoped by this agreement on doctrine that the Union would be restored, but though it was published in the following March relations did not improve.[3] In the following year, 1694, they took a decided turn for the worse. In the early part of the year Nathaniel Mather took the opportunity offered by two sermons at the Merchants' Lecture to attack Williams's alleged Arminianism (Semi-Socinianism, he called it). Williams replied when it came his turn to preach the Lecture. Both contributions to the Lecture were published.[4] The chief consequence of these exchanges was a determination on the part of his bitterest opponents, to have Williams voted out of the Lectureship. This they achieved at a packed meeting in August.[5]

## Disunity becomes Complete

It was a Pyrrhic victory, however. If the purpose was to cast the odium on Williams and isolate him from his friends it lamentably failed, for the three remaining Presbyterian Lecturers, William Bates, John Howe and Vincent Alsop left in a body and joined Williams in a new Presbyterian Merchants' Lecture set up at Salters' hall on the same day and at the same hour as the old Lecture.

[1] *The sense of the United Ministers, in and about London, concerning some of the erroneous doctrines, and irregular practices, of Mr. Richard Davis, of Rothwell in Northamptonshire*, was the full title of this seven page statement, dated 1693. A copy of this publication is printed in Calamy, *Abridgement*, 512–14.

[2] The agreement was reached on December 16, 1692. (Daniel Williams, *Answer to the Report*, 1698, 5.)

[3] It was published by March 4th under the title of *The agreement in doctrine among the Dissenting Ministers in London*, 1693.

[4] Nathaniel Mather, *The righteousness of God through faith upon all without difference who believe*, 1694; ('To the Reader' dated 14 '2d month' [April] 1694). Daniel Williams, *Man made righteous by Christ's obedience. Being two sermons at Pinners-Hall. With enlargements, &c. Also some remarks on Mr. Mather's postscript, &c.*, 1694. (Published June 11, 1694.)

[5] Letter from John Howe to William Taylor dated August 18, 1694 (Bodleian MS. Carte 80, fos. 820–1).

To complete the panel of six lecturers two new lecturers were appointed in the persons of Samuel Annesley and Richard Mayo.[1] The inclusion of Samuel Annesley is of some importance since it marks the end of the old division amongst the Presbyterians of Dons and Ducklings. Their difference over concord with the Church of England had ceased to have much importance when Convocation had made it plain in 1689 that there was no hope of comprehension within the Church of England and when the union between Congregationals and Presbyterians had come into being in 1691.[2] But there was still the other difference. Annesley and his friends had more sympathy than Baxter with traditional Calvinism and so were closer to the Congregationals. It is significant that Annesley was not amongst those who signed the testimonial to *Gospel-Truth*. But now, two years later, the Congregationals had succeeded in alienating those that were closest to them amongst the Presbyterians, as became abundantly clear when Annesley joined the break-away Merchants' Lecture at Salters' Hall.[3]

At the end of 1694, following the sorry dissensions over the Lecture, a new effort was made to find a basis of agreement. The Congregationals drew up five Arminian propositions which they stipulated the Presbyterians should disown. Did they perhaps hope that Williams would refuse to disown them while the rest of the Presbyterians would do so? If so, they were again disappointed, for Williams and the other Presbyterians agreed to the proposal but added seven Antinomian propositions, which they required the other side to disown, drawn 'generally in the words of the Assembly, to which we hoped they would be more easily induced to assent'. To these disclaimers of Antinomian tenets they could not obtain Congregational agreement. By their refusal the Congregationals did

---

[1] The secession took place on November 7, 1694. *Answer to the Report*, 1698, 9.

[2] There were however renewed efforts to revive the 1689 proposals for comprehension in 1696. H. G. Horwitz, 'Comprehension in the later seventeenth century: a postscript' in *Church History*, xxiv (1965), 342–8. Cf. John Newton, *Methodism and the Puritans*, 1964, 4.

[3] The Pinners' Hall Lecture continued for the time-being with the two remaining lecturers, Thomas Cole and Matthew Mead. *The History of the Union*, 1698, claims that the managers delayed filling the vacancies in the hope that Bates, Howe and Alsop would return. Only in February 1695 did they fill the vacancies, the new lecturers being the Congregationals, Stephen Lobb, Thomas Gouge and Nathaniel Mather, and the Presbyterian, Timothy Cruso. Cruso was amongst the few Presbyterians who did not sign the testimonial to *Gospel-Truth*, and he played no part in the controversy.

their cause harm, for at a later date Bishop Stillingfleet could quote their failure on this occasion to denounce Antinomian errors as leaving them open to serious suspicion of still entertaining them.[1]

Instead of coming into the new proposals and paving the way to a restoration of the Union, the Congregationals began an attack on Williams for immorality. His friends rallied to his support, however. His character was cleared and the attack proved a complete fiasco. As Edmund Calamy described it:

> The angry party came upon him with open mouths, summoned witnesses from Dan to Beersheba, made the strictest search and inquiry that was possible into his words, actions and behaviour in all the places where he had lived and from all the servants that were within reach and ever lived with him. . . . But it so fell out that this zeal of theirs was so far from doing Mr. Williams any real damage that, contrary to the design of his enemies, it made his innocence the more conspicuous.[2]

During these years of dissension, from September 1692 to April 1695, the Congregationals not only deserted the Union but also dropped out of the management of the Common Fund. The disruption of the Union thus became complete and final with the foundation of the Congregational Fund in the Autumn of 1695.[3] It was only in London that it was the end, however, for the Union continued in other parts of the country, but even in the country it was the beginning of the end, though the end there came much more slowly. Attempts seem to have been made by the new Congregational Fund in its early days to disrupt the Union in the country but on the whole they met with very little success.[4] The country could ill afford dissensions on the scale they had reached in the metropolis. Moreover relations eventually improved in the metropolis itself, though the Union was never restored. With the improvement the two Funds were less willing to act as cut-throat rivals and the older fund at least long retained something of its character as a common fund.[5] Nevertheless, when a quarter of a

---

[1] Edward Stillingfleet, *Works*, 1710, 377–8. Daniel Williams, *Answer to the Report*, 1698, 6–10.

[2] Calamy, *Hist. Account*, i. 357. Williams appealed to the Ministers to adjudicate and his character was cleared on April 8, 1695 (*Gospel-Truth*, 3rd ed., 1698, 301–5).

[3] Established December 17, 1695. *CHST*, v. 134–48; Gordon, *Freedom*, 157, 183; *CR*, 1852, 20.

[4] *Exeter Assembly: Minutes*, 29–36.                    [5] Gordon, *Freedom*, 183–4.

century later fresh theological differences again separated the two denominations, the Fund from which a church was aided tended to determine its denominational allegiance no matter what its denominational origin had been, and throughout the country Dissenters tended to line up under one or other denominational name.

Once the London Union had been irrevocably broken in 1695, less interest attaches to the subsequent stages of the dispute which became more and more acrimonious. Stephen Lobb in a desire to restore the fortunes of his Congregational colleagues, which had by this time sunk to a low ebb, made a new attempt to isolate Williams from his friends by producing evidence that he had denied what some of his Presbyterian friends had asserted and that, further, in doing so he had fallen into the dread heresy of Socinianism. This heresy was made all the more notorious by reason of a noisy controversy going on at the time in the Church of England which had made Socinianism one of the bogy words of the day, not least amongst Dissenters; and we find William Bates heading a deputation to appeal to the king to take action against Socinian and other errors, so adding to the agitation that issued in the Blasphemy Act of 1698.[1]

Lobb's contention against Williams was specious rather than well-founded and would probably have ended in nothing had it not been for John Howe's hope that, by conceding that Williams had blundered, the Congregationals might be won over to repairing the breach in the Union. Williams, however, refused to be made a scape-goat for a blunder he had not made, nor was he prepared to see Antinomianism gain ground on the strength of admissions that would allow the case against it to go by default. The authority of Bishop Stillingfleet's writings on the subject had been used as evidence against him. So Williams appealed to the bishop for his considered judgment on the point at issue. Stillingfleet replied very fully in a letter dated November 10, 1697 and came down firmly on the side of Williams, affirming that Howe's proposed admission 'hath no foundation in Scripture ... is contrary to the tenor of it ... is attended with very bad consequences which naturally follow from it'. Lobb made a desperate effort to make the Bishop

---

[1] H. J. McLachlan, *Socinianism in seventeenth-century England*, 1951, 318; R. Thomas, *Daniel Williams 'Presbyterian Bishop'*, 1964, 17; John Howe, *Sermon preach'd on the late day of thanksgiving*, 1698 (William Bates's address); Bennett, 188.

see that Socinianism was involved in what Williams taught, but
the Bishop would have none of it, strongly opposed to Socinianism
though he was.[1]

## Soberer Counsels Prevail

Soon after this foray, which lasted on into 1698, tempers cooled
considerably and to that extent relations between the two bodies
improved. Stillingfleet's letter to Williams and his subsequent
correspondence with Lobb may have contributed to this end.[2]
But two other factors had perhaps a greater influence. One was that
the two bitterest opponents of Baxterianism and of the Union,
Mather and Cole, both died in 1697 within a few months of each
other. They had been the main instigators of Congregational
opposition and with them died the main stimulus to controversy.
The other factor was that at about the same date Tory and High
Church fortunes had begun to revive. The Tories had only reluctantly acquiesced in the Act of Toleration and even at the time that
it was passed (when their fortunes were low) they had been strong
enough to prevent the repeal of parts of the Test and Corporation
Acts, by which Dissenters could only hold office on condition that
they took the sacrament in the Church of England; they had also
succeeded in weakening the Act of Toleration itself by removing
from it the clause giving exemption to Dissenting schoolmasters.[3]
Three incidents in 1697 bore witness to a reviving Tory agitation
against the Dissenters. The Lord Mayor of London elected that
year, Sir Humphrey Edwin, a Presbyterian, saw fit to attend a Dissenters' Meeting in state with the mayoral sword of office. This
taking the sword to a 'nasty conventicle' produced a Tory howl of
dismay. 'Many heartily wished', as a sober commentator put it,
'that this action had been waived, as tending to enrage; yet were
utterly to seek for the horridness of the crime'. But the mischief was
done. Tories saw cause to be infuriated against the practice of
occasional conformity, as it was called, whereby Dissenters qualified

[1] R. Thomas, *Daniel Williams 'Presbyterian Bishop'*, 18-21; Edward Stillingfleet,
*Works*, 1710, iii. 369-411. Stillingfleet thought it might be easier to detect Socinian
leanings in Baxter than in Williams, but does not fail to absolve Baxter also.

[2] Lobb died June 3, 1699. Stillingfleet predeceased him on March 27, 1699.

[3] R. Thomas, *Daniel Williams 'Presbyterian Bishop'*, 22; Thomas in Nuttall and Chadwick, 251.

for office, and the agitation against it did not cease until it culminated in the Occasional Conformity Act of 1712.[1]

The second incident was the falling of a letter into wrong hands, thus advertising to the world a strengthening of Dissenting organization which struck horror into the hearts of such High Churchmen as the notorious Francis Atterbury. Since 1694 West Country Dissenters had been pressing for a more effective national organization. Now that at last something was being done its discovery at an untoward moment led to a clamour which put a damp upon the undertaking and made the London Dissenters, who had perhaps never been very eager for the scheme, think that it would be advisable that it should be dropped.[2]

The third incident constituted a more serious menace. Joshua Oldfield was cited to appear before an Ecclesiastical Court for keeping school without a bishop's licence and without having subscribed to the Book of Common Prayer and the whole of the Thirty Nine Articles as required under the Act of Uniformity. After considerable litigation the case was eventually dropped when William III intimated that 'he was not pleased with such prosecutions'. The royal intervention secured the immediate object but left open the opportunity for fresh attacks whenever the Tories should feel that the time was opportune.[3]

From now onwards the Dissenters would find themselves engaged in efforts to defend themselves against inroads upon their liberties and it was doubtless borne in upon them that their internal feuds could only do them harm when threatened from without.

Whatever the reasons for stifling their quarrels, Stephen Lobb took the initiative, shortly before his death, in offering an olive

---

[1] *DNB* under Edwin (H.); *CSPD*, 1697, 408, 451, 467, 484. For Sir Humphrey Edwin as a Presbyterian, D.W.L. MS. Morrice 'Entry Books', ii. 189. Cf. R. Thomas 'Presbyterians, Congregationals and the Test and Corporation Acts', in *UHST*, xi. 118. Perhaps the earliest shot in the agitation was Daniel Defoe's *An enquiry into the occasional conformity of Dissenters*, 1697, which may well have been the 'foolish pasquil, reflecting on the Lord Mayor' which was 'fixed upon the door of St. Pauls' before Sir Humphrey attended a thanksgiving day service at the cathedral on Thursday, December 2nd (*Postman*, November 30th–December 2nd). Cf. Barlow, 71–3.

[2] *Some reflections on a model now in projection by the Presbyterian Dissenters*, 1689; Francis Atterbury, *Rights, Powers and Privileges*, 1700, Appendix ii; *Exeter Assembly: Minutes*, 19–21; D.W.L. MS. 12.78, 271; Chetham Soc, n.s. 24, 352; Calamy, *Abridgement*, 498; Calamy, *Hist. Account*, i. 408.

[3] Calamy, *Abridgement*, 551–4; J. E. G. de Montmorency, *State Intervention in English Education*, 1902, 170–4; Barlow, 59–60.

branch. As Daniel Williams put it, 'when Mr. Lob and his brethren found they could not gain their point, but that his party became suspected of all Crisp's errors, by that time much exploded through the prevalency of the opposite party, they thought fit to draw a sort of confession, wherein they cleared themselves of the most dangerous of Crisp's opinions. And Mr. Lob desired me to put the best sense on that confession, that a period might be set to those debates.' The Congregational declaration was published over five signatures and Williams responded with a pamphlet entitled *An end of discord*.[1]

It was an end of discord but not a restoration of the broken Union. Probably the chief outcome of the conflict was that Presbyterianism had become predominantly and consciously Baxterian. It was a loosening of the rigours of Calvinism that would have considerable future consequences.

QUEEN ANNE TIME

## A New London Union

The end of discord did not mean the restoration of the Union. But with the Tories once more powerful and with the accession of a Stuart to the throne in the person of Queen Anne, in itself a reminder of unhappier times, the Dissenters had reason to look to their liberties. Though the Union was not restored the Presbyterians and Independents so far joined forces as to organize the protection of their civil liberties. In this they welcomed the co-operation of the Baptists and formed the General Body of Protestant Dissenting Ministers in and about London, which on occasion presented addresses to the throne and, what was more important, set up a permanent Committee of Three Denominations to keep watch over their common interests. Thus London had an organization at once looser and wider than that operating in many parts of the country. At the same time, apart from the two Funds, though it had no

---

[1] D.W.L. MS. 12.56(6) a letter of Daniel Williams to Robert Nelson, October 28, 1712. The 'confession' was published under the title of *A declaration of the Congregational ministers in and about London against Antinomian errours and ignorant . . . persons intruding themselves into the ministry*, 1699.

national representation, it was the only organization operating nationally on behalf of Dissenters.[1]

The creation of this Committee was opportune, for three times in the Queen's first Parliament the Tories were strong enough to carry a Bill in the Commons against the practice of Occasional Conformity. Each time, however, it was defeated in the Lords where the prevailing Whig interest prevented it. During the middle years of the reign the Tories were out of power, but, when they returned following the Sacheverell affair in 1710, they quickly succeeded, first in passing an Act against Occasional Conformity (1712), and then, in the very last year of the reign (1714), the Schism Act suppressing Dissenters' Schools and Academies. But it was not only in Parliament that the Dissenters had to face antagonism, nor were Occasional Conformity and Dissenters' education the only subjects of attack in the abundant ill-tempered pamphletage of the time. The consequence was that the controversial energies of Dissenters were more and more directed into parrying attacks from without, and they had less time for disputes amongst themselves. For this reason it is not easy to trace out developments in Presbyterian thought during this period and yet there can be no doubt there were very important developments in outlook. As so often happens, men emerge from a conflict with their outlook changed in many respects from that with which they entered it. The best that we can do is to examine the differences which we have already noted as coming to the front and trace out such indications as there are of developments taking place.[2]

[1] Norman Sykes, *From Sheldon to Secker*, 94–101. The Committee was composed of representatives from each of the three denominations appointed by the denominations acting separately, possibly by Denominational Boards set up for the purpose; at least this was the method employed at a later date. The Committee at first consisted of four Presbyterians, three Independents and three Baptists. In 1716 it was increased to six Presbyterians, five Independents and five Baptists. At the end of the same year or the beginning of 1717, the Committee was further increased by the addition of laymen, three appointed by the Presbyterians and two each by the Independents and Baptists. The Salters' Hall meetings in 1719, when controversy broke out over advice to the Exeter congregations, were in fact meetings of the General Body called together by their Committee. The Body split into two parties and the Committee's activities dwindled, although it seems to have held together sufficiently to present addresses to the throne in 1722 and 1727. With the accession of George II in 1727 the Body once more became active and the practice began of making appointments to the Committee annually.

[2] T. Bennett, *Laws against Nonconformity*, 1913, 192–8; P. M. Scholes, 'Parliament and the Protestant Dissenters, 1702–1717', London M.A. Thesis, 1961; Norman

We have thus to consider differences over ecclesiastical polity, over tolerance, over the Arminian alternative to Calvinism, over the place of reason in religion and over Scripture sufficiency.

In assessing these changes we are aided by the fact that Edmund Calamy, who was destined to take the place of Daniel Williams as the unofficial head of the English Presbyterians, left very informative records of his activities and of events and developments that affected him. He was in many ways a typical Baxterian but, though he stuck to the theological pattern inherited from Baxter more rigidly than some of his younger contemporaries, he did so with a magnanimity that was perhaps more faithful to Baxter's genius than Baxter might have been himself.[1]

## Presbyterianism—a New Image?

Under the new conditions of Tory ascendancy he was soon drawn into the work of presenting the Dissenting case. In 1696 had appeared a life of Baxter clumsily edited from Baxter's own writings by one of the most unskilled of editors, Matthew Sylvester. Calamy had tried to assist Sylvester but with very little effect on the final product. To the historian it is a mine of information that might have been lost in a better managed book, but at the time a briefer less cumbrous volume would have done better service to the Dissenting cause. Calamy doubtless appreciated this and when such service was sorely needed he decided to publish an abridgement. It appeared in 1702, forty years after the Ejection, and acted as something of a counterblast to Clarendon's celebrated *History of the Rebellion* (then beginning to appear) which was well calculated to revive, and was perhaps intended to revive, ancient antipathies against the Nonconformists. To us Calamy's *Abridgement of Mr. Baxter's History* may be less redolent of Baxter's vehement character and racy English but it was none the less effective in its day. Its effectiveness can be measured by the controversy it evoked. Anglicans evidently felt that some reply was called for; there were several, of which the most impressive was *The reasonableness of conformity* by

---

Sykes, *From Sheldon to Secker*, 1959, 89 ff. For attacks on Nonconformist orders and on the validity of Nonconformist baptisms see George Every, *The High Church Party*, 1956, 128–30.

[1] Baxter's adherence to 'discipline' naturally conflicted with his catholicity (Richard Schlatter, *Richard Baxter and Puritan politics*, 1957, 33–7).

Benjamin Hoadly. This led to a series of rejoinders in the course of which Calamy printed a long 'Introduction'.[1]

Calamy himself said of his 'Introduction' that he 'never published anything so maturely weighed as this Introduction'. In truth it marked an epoch in the evolution of Dissent and gives us a fair measure of the position which English Presbyterianism had now reached. In the main it is an attack upon impositions in religious observance, but in the course of it Calamy admits that what he had been outlining might be represented as a 'mere independent scheme' and he continues:

> Whatever name it is given, that which confirms me in my adherence to this principle, is this; that it secures to all their undoubted rights. . . . Each worshipping society must determine for itself all necessary circumstances and each private Christian has his judgment and discretion left untouched. . . . The pastoral office also remains uninvaded. Each pastor is still free to pursue his commission, to teach whatever Christ commanded. . . . Synods still have their use, in a way of consultation, admonition and advice to repress disorders, determine differences and regulate by consent such things as are of common concernment.[2]

The position now reached was not Calamy's unsupported opinion. In his memoirs he says of this 'Introduction' that he 'freely communicated it to several of' his 'brethren, who signified their concurrence'. Only Daniel Williams (as Calamy put it) 'apprehended', 'when the proper season came', that 'he could overthrow the whole fabric with ease'. Calamy urged him to do it quickly, for, as he said, 'the principles there advanced were spreading so wide and prevailing so generally . . . that if he neglected the present opportunity' it might be too late.[3] But Williams never did.

Wisely, Williams never did. The episode brings into high relief the part that he had played in the long drawn out conflict with the Congregationals. It was clear what construction he had put upon the *Heads of Agreement* concerning synods. It was doubtless he above others who had determined that Richard Davis should not

---

[1] Calamy, *Hist. Account*, i. 376–80. One section of Calamy's *Abridgement* (1702) grew into his great series of biographies of the Ejected Ministers (*Cal. Rev.* 1934, pp. xx ff.). The 'Introduction' appeared in the second part of his *A defence of moderate Nonconformity*, 1704. Part I was 1703; part III, 1705.

[2] Edmund Calamy, *A defence of moderate Non-conformity*, part II, 1704, 87–9.

[3] Calamy, *Hist. Account*, 29–30.

escape the clutches of the London ministers. And he was still unrepentant at heart when Calamy sought his opinion upon an 'Introduction' that laid all his synodical ideals in the dust. But Williams had had his bellyful of conflict. Moreover the times were menacing, it was not a 'proper season' and if he had renewed the fight for the right of presbytery he would have fought almost alone. But it is not difficult to see what his case would have been. Following Baxter in his desire to have firm discipline as well as catholicity, he could have argued that Calamy's scheme provided no protection against the intrusion of illiterate upstart preachers, nor any protection against ministers and churches wallowing in what Tillotson had described as the 'luscious doctrine of the Antinomians'. But then no matter what self-imposed discipline the Presbyterians might have agreed upon for themselves, there was little likelihood of the Congregationals falling in with them and, even if they had, the Toleration Act left the door open to all and sundry (except Socinians and Roman Catholics) to form Dissenting congregations beyond the reach of any discipline. There was common sense in Calamy's ready acceptance of the situation, hopeful that persuasion and common sense might prevail where discipline was dead.[1]

This 'independency' of the Presbyterians as expounded by Calamy is an instructive product; the outcome of a generation of hard experience, it shows how far they had travelled. Hoadly, in answer to Calamy's 'Introduction', betrays no little surprise at the transformation and notes

> the peculiar abilities of this writer [Calamy] at once to defend the cause of the Ejected Ministers and to propose a scheme as is as little agreeable to their main cause as to that of the Established Church. Nay, I think there is reason to judge that the best of them would sooner have chosen the continuance of the present Establishment than the alteration of it into such an one as is here contrived.[2]

---

[1] John Tillotson, *Works*, ed. Thos. Birch, 1820, ix. 11; L. G. Locke, *Tillotson*, 1954, 96. In spite of Calamy's large inclusiveness there were Congregationals who quarrelled with Calamy's scheme (*A letter from a Congregational minister in the country*, 1704; Calamy's *Defence*, part II, 1704, 391–414). Church of England men also lamented the breaches made in discipline by the Toleration Act (Norman Sykes, *From Sheldon to Secker*, 91). Cf. Alex. Gordon in *CL*, 1885, 523, for Socinianizing Huguenots availing themselves of the shelter of the Toleration Act.

[2] Benjamin Hoadly, *The Reasonableness of Conformity*, 4th ed., 1720, 528.

I

Doubtless Williams would have said Amen; so too might Baxter. Calamy's own grandfather, too, might have been called in evidence against his grandson. But many of the ejected ministers were still living when Calamy published his 'Introduction' and they had recently issued a manifesto, just forty years after Black Bartholomew Day, in which they certainly expressed no such sentiments as Hoadly would have expected of them.[1]

Calamy did not stand alone. When his 'Introduction' was published in 1704 his colleagues stood him a supper, a good eighteenth century token of approbation. John Howe, himself an ejected minister, commended the work. Even more impressive support came from the aged John Locke, the doyen of the new age, then in the last year of his life, who sent Calamy a message that he 'thought it such a defence of Nonconformity as could not be answered and that standing to the principles there laid down' Calamy 'had no occasion to be afraid of any antagonist'.[2]

## A New Spirit of Tolerance

No wonder that Locke praised it. Calamy had been deeply influenced by Locke's *Letter concerning toleration*. In the light of it he had re-modelled the teaching of Baxter. In one respect he had gone even further than Locke himself. Locke (here no doubt showing traces of early Congregational influence) had envisaged freedom for each worhipping society to make and enforce its own rules, it being understood that those who did not accept the rules should be excluded from that society but not persecuted.[3] Calamy, however, clearly envisages a measure of toleration within the worshipping community itself. He defines no limits, and doubtless there would have had to be limits, but Calamy seems to be prepared to leave the matter to the good sense of those who were loath to be exacting in their requirements. It is something of a revivification of the old spirit of comprehension in a new setting. It could be argued that as Calamy is far from explicit he never intended any such extension of Locke's argument. But what is conclusive is that he acted on the principle of a good deal of internal latitude and toleration within the Church. Moreover, if he was to take Locke

---

[1] *A letter from some aged nonconforming ministers to their Christian friends touching the reasons of their practice* (August 24, 1701), 1st ed. 1702.

[2] Calamy, *Hist. Account*, ii. 30–1.          [3] Nuttall, *Visible Saints*, 76–7, 117.

seriously, he was almost bound, as a Presbyterian, to make this extension, for Locke speaks like a Congregational in outlook and, in this respect, like a good disciple of John Owen by whom he had been taught in his student days. Locke speaks of individual worshipping societies governing their own affairs, but to Calamy, as a Presbyterian, the Church was not the particular worshipping society, but the whole Church, the Church Universal, however much split by dissensions. In this setting, if there was to be genuine toleration, it had to be toleration within the Church as a whole. Hence Calamy's extension of Locke.

The point is vital, for Presbyterian development was to be precisely along these lines of a reluctance to discipline the heretic within the gates, whereas the Independents, some of whom welcomed Locke's teaching on toleration as much as Calamy had done, continued to think of each particular church exercising discipline within its own society and they assumed that an accepted standard of orthodoxy might be exacted of members.[1]

It is instructive to find Calamy as an exponent of toleration in both aspects. In the more generally accepted sense a striking example occurred in 1703. The Quakers in New England complained of severe laws made against them and appealed to the London ministers to show their dislike of these laws and to use their influence with their co-religionists in New England to get them modified. This the ministers of the Three Denominations very willingly did. The letter that they sent bases itself firmly on the arguments made familiar by Locke. With evident satisfaction Calamy reproduces the letter entire in the second edition of his *Abridgement*. From the tone of the letter it is by no means impossible that he penned it.[2]

The example of toleration in its other aspect takes us into a somewhat wider field, for it illustrates not only a growing tolerance amongst English Presbyterians, but also a growing divergence between them and their Scottish Presbyterian brethren.[3] The year

[1] E.g. Isaac Watts and Philip Doddridge. Isaac Watts, *Works*, 1810, 500 f.; R. Thomas, 'Doddridge and liberalism in religion' in G. F. Nuttall, *Philip Doddridge*, 1951, 126-7, 148-9.

[2] Calamy, *Abridgement*, 670-2; Carl Bridenbaugh, *Mitre and sceptre*, 1962, 62-5; Susan Martha Reed, 'Church and State in Massachusetts, 1691-1740' in Univ. of Illinois *Studies in the Social Sciences*, iii (1914), 99 ff.

[3] Cf. John Locke in his letter to Limborch (February 29, 1693) in *MR*, xiii, 355; John Toland in his life of Milton (p. 25) preceding his edition of Milton's *Complete collection of . . . works*, Amsterdam, 1698.

1707 had seen the successful achievement of the Union with Scotland. But long before this there had been close contact between English and Scottish Presbyterians; they shared the same name, and Scottish Universities were among the centres where English Dissenters, especially the Presbyterians, received University education when Oxford and Cambridge were closed to them.[1]

These and other reasons may have led to an invitation to Calamy to visit Scotland and the Presbyterian General Assembly at Edinburgh in 1709. While he was there he sat in as an honoured guest at the meetings of the Assembly. Among other business that came up was the case of a certain minister who was accused by the Synod of Aberdeen of being 'deficient in knowledge and unsound in principles'. He had been subjected to a gruelling examination and a report of the questions ('above one hundred in number') together with his answers was read to the Assembly. On this Calamy says:

> Some of these answers, it must be confessed, were but weak. Others were as proper, as would, I believe, have been returned, off hand, by many whose sufficiency was no way called in question.
>
> The Assembly seemed to be at a loss what to do with this man. The moderator stepping down and whispering in the ear, as the questions were read over, asked me what my apprehensions were. I frankly answered that we in England should reckon this way of proceeding, the Inquisition revived; at which he could not help smiling. Lord Forbes, who sat on the bench above me, asked what passed between the Moderator and me. . . . I freely told him and he immediately fell to laughing. The Lord President, who sat on the seat above him, inquiring what he laughed at and he giving his account, joined also in the laugh. At last the Commissioner, who could not well help observing this, stepped down and whispered the Lord President of the Session and asked what was the occasion of this laughing? Being told, he could not forebear joining. In short it was whispered from one to another, till it went the round of the Assembly. I heard of it afterwards at Aberdeen.[2]

Indeed he did. It was Aberdeen that had made the complaint and when Calamy visited that town he was told that 'it was not well taken' that he should represent the conduct of their synod of Aberdeen 'as a revival of the Inquisition'. So far from palliating the offence, Calamy said that, being asked the question, he thought it

---

[1] O. M. Griffiths, *Religion and Learning*, 178–82.
[2] Calamy, *Hist. Account*, ii. 155–6.

became him to signify his 'real apprehensions of the matter without any collusions' and went on to defend his point of view.[1]

When Calamy disparaged the inquisitorial procedure of the Scottish Assembly it will be noted that he was passing on from the Lockean toleration outside a given worshipping society to the more exciting toleration of differences within the same society. He was not just criticizing the Scottish Assembly, he was criticizing the traditional Presbyterian discipline of recalcitrant individuals.

Calamy's practice was in accord with his belief. As we shall see later, in 1716 he was one of a number of London ministers to ordain an assistant who had only a few months before been dismissed by his senior minister for Arminianism. Again in 1723 Calamy took part in the ordination of George Benson at Abingdon although he knew quite well of his leanings towards Arminianism. We have too the case of John Fox, in 1713, who had doubts about the doctrine of the Trinity and was in difficulties about subscribing such of the Thirty Nine Articles as was required under the Toleration Act; Calamy's recommendation to him was to do as he himself had done, to refrain from subscribing, keep himself to himself and trust that the omission would go unnoticed. More striking still was the report of Robert Wodrow, in a letter to Lord Grange of 1728, that North-ern Ireland Nonsubscribers 'are sending over some of their young preachers to London, where Dr Calamy and the Non-subscribers ordain them indefinitely and they return ordained ministers'.[2]

## Contrasts with a Generation Earlier

We have some measure of the progress towards a wider tolerance if we recall that in 1697 William Bates, one of the heroes of the Ejection and one of the leading Presbyterian ministers of the time, led a deputation of Dissenting ministers in an address to William III appealing for measures against Socinians and Deists, thus adding to the agitation that issued in the Blasphemy Act of the following year. We may contrast too the treatment meted out to Thomas Emlyn for heresy in Dublin in 1702 at the instance of the Pres-byterian congregation there. As Hoadly summed it up, 'the

[1] Calamy, *Hist. Account*, ii. 199. Cf. Stirling corresp. at the University of Glasgow, BE. III. 81.

[2] Benson MSS. (Calamy to Benson January 31, 1723); *MR*, xvi (1821), 134–5; R. Wodrow, *Correspondence*, 1842–3, iii. 169. Cf. Edmund Calamy, *Divine Mercy Exalted*, 1703, p. v. For non-subscribers, see below p. 162.

Nonconformists accused him, the Conformists condemned him, the secular power was called in and the cause ended in an imprisonment and a very great fine: two methods of conviction about which the Gospel is silent'.[1]

In his attitude to tolerance Calamy was perhaps more typical of contemporary Arminian trends than Baxter had been. In other respects he remained more loyal to his Baxterian original than did some of his younger contemporaries who were moving on and following Baxter's lead with greater consistency but less fidelity.

## Calamy's Baxterianism

Like Baxter, Calamy believed that the old traditional orthodoxy in all its essentials stood in no danger from Reason or from Scripture. It is interesting to note his reactions at critical junctures when orthodox doctrines came under debate. On one occasion in 1704, it was the question of the verbal inspiration of the Bible which had become (and long remained) a subject of heart-searching because of the trenchant enquiry into the subject published long before by the eminent Dutch Arminian publicist Le Clerc and translated into English as *Five letters concerning the inspiration of the Holy Scriptures*. Calamy preached a series of Merchants' Lectures attacking Le Clerc's criticisms.[2] On another occasion, in 1719, it was the doctrine of the Trinity. Again Calamy preached a series of Lectures to uphold the traditional doctrine in opposition to those who argued that it was not to be found in Scripture. But when it came to dealing with men whose minds were open to the newer criticisms where Calamy's was closed, he gave them, as we have seen, every assistance, ordaining as ministers men who had departed widely from the orthodoxy which Calamy so firmly defended. This gave an air of inconsistency to his activities which puzzled more traditional souls. One such summed him up as 'a zealous man for the Kirk and would

[1] The address of William Bates is printed in John Howe's *Sermon preech'd on the Day of Thanksgiving*, 1698. Cf. Bennett, 188. The Emlyn case is quoted from Hoadly's Introduction in Urbano Cerri, *An account of the state of the Roman Catholic religion*, [published] by Richard Steele, 1715, pp. xi–xii.

[2] The *Five letters*, published in 1690, were translations of certain letters (attributed to Aubert de Versé) in *Sentimens de quelque theologiens de Hollande*, 1685, and *Defense de Sentimens de quelque theologiens*, 1686. Thomas Secker (the future Archbishop) amongst others was studying these Letters in his student days, *circa*. 1714; E. Calamy, *The inspiration of the Holy writings*, 1710, which were the Merchants' Lectures, August 22, 1704 to June 11, 1706, at about monthly intervals.

be more useful if more consistent. . . . Wherever his diocese reaches he encourages persons of latitude enough.'[1] In fact he was only a consistent Baxterian who believed that the truth could stand on its own feet and that men must exercise charity to differences of opinion.

Not only did Calamy defend the heretic while attacking the heresy. He was also a Baxterian in theology firmly adhering to the Middle Way (or Baxterianism) throughout his life. Thus we are told, 'Dr. Calamy was bred in the Middle Way and his whole preaching was in that strain. He never troubled them [his congregation] with predestination.'[2] In other words Calamy retained the Calvinist doctrine of election but dropped that of absolute reprobation, substituting for it the Arminian doctrine of sufficient grace for all. Calamy himself reports an argument he had with Bishop Burnet in which the Bishop endeavoured to convince Calamy 'that such as declared for the middle way must at last, when pressed, fall into the Arminian scheme'. But Calamy was not to be convinced.[3]

## A Growing Arminianism

There were, however, younger ministers who would have agreed with Burnet and who found themselves unable to stop short at the middle position sanctified by Baxter's name. Perhaps the best documented case is that of Joseph Standen in the West Country, who in the years following 1706 was under attack from the orthodox John England. But Standen stood firmly by his Arminianism.[4] Another was Samuel Bourn who, when elected as minister at Crook near Kendal in 1711, refused to subscribe the Westminster Assembly Catechism.[5] There was John Rastrick of King's Lynn, of an older

[1] 1732 MS. Report, p. 47.

[2] *CHST*, xix. 87 (letter from T. Steward to Samuel Say, April 1734) from D.W.L. MS. 'Say Papers', p. 64 (No. 108)

[3] Calamy, *Hist. Account*, ii. 471. Cf. *MR*, xvi (1821), 259-60; Thomas in *Beginnings of Nonconformity*, 48-50.

[4] D.W.L. MS. 38.90—replies to John England, prepared for publication, but not published. John England's side of the controversy was *A View of Arminianism compared with Moderate Calvinism*, 1707.

[5] Samuel Bourn, 1689-1754, *DNB*. There was also an unidentified Mr H., probably in the Eastern counties, about whom Isaac Watts wrote to Samuel Say in 1708. He had been falsely accused of Socinianism; the comments of Watts makes it clear that his sin was Arminianism. (D.W.L. MS. 'Say Papers'). See below, p. 187.

generation, whose version of the Middle Way savours more of
Arminius than of Baxter.[1] There were doubtless others of whom
little or nothing is known and there were some whose formative
years were in the time of Queen Anne, but whose attacks on Calvinism are only known to us from publications of a later date. One
of these was Joseph Dodson who in a sermon in April 1719 could
use these expressions about Calvin and his followers:

> Let not any of us who admire the learning and judgment of Mr. Calvin
> join with him in reproaching those who are of a different persuasion
> from him in matters of religion. . . . Whereas Melancthon's disciples
> are generally very mild and gentle, those of Calvin, on the contrary, are
> men of a rough and unfriendly behaviour toward those who differ
> from them in matters of religion.[2]

Another was Nicholas Billingsley of Ashwick in Somerset, who was
even more outspoken:

> Many, or most of them [our predecessors], were brought up, and lived
> and died in what we call Calvinism. But for my part I cannot persuade
> myself that this did in its nature contribute to the piety or usefulness
> of those reverend fathers. But I ascribe it to something else, in which
> they were worthy the imitation of us all. Had they preached nothing
> but the Calvinistical doctrine of the Decrees, with all the natural
> consequences of it, had they never delivered anything inconsistent with
> it, it is my opinion that in that case, instead of bringing people to
> repentance and the love of God, they would have hardened them
> against it and driven them to presumption or to despair.[3]

Enough has been said to show that despite the paucity of evidence
in this formative period of thought there were Dissenters (all those
mentioned above may properly be counted as Presbyterians) who
were finding it impossible to rest in Baxter's Middle Way and who
were finding themselves obliged to pass on to a full Arminianism, as
Burnet had argued they must.[4]

[1] John Rastrick, *A sermon . . . at the ordination of Samuel Savage*, 1714.
[2] Joseph Dodson, *Moderation and Charity*, 1720. See below, p. 165.
[3] Nicholas Billingsley, *Rational and Christian Principles the Best Rules of Conduct*,
1721, p. xviii.
[4] It may be noted, for the somewhat fluid denominational associations at this time,
that Dodson was receiving grants from both Presbyterian and Congregational Funds.
Joseph Standen was educated at the expense of the Common Fund (before the split),
1691–3, by John Tomlyns, a Congregational (Presb. Fund minutes, i. 24, 30, 44, 76,
99, 116).

Closely akin to the more specifically Arminian teachings were an emphasis upon the use of reason and upon the sufficiency of Scripture, both characteristic of Arminianism. The emphasis on reason cannot but have been helped forward by current scientific developments, by the promotion of the scientific spirit fostered by the Royal Society, and by Locke's philosophy. Thus Baxter's emphasis upon reason was reinforced.[1]

## Calamy and the Place of Reason

Calamy is as typical in this respect as in others. He tells us himself how this aspect of Baxterianism lost him the appointment as minister at Salters' Hall when Nathaniel Taylor died. He happened to place on record about Taylor that 'he was for such a religion as might be a reasonable service, and not for living upon, or being governed by mere spiritual sensations, sudden transports and the variable workings of the affections'. This opinion of his fell into the hands of a prominent member of the Salters' Hall congregation, Sir David Hamilton, who had very different and less rational ideas, and Calamy was not appointed. As they stand Calamy's words could well be a good summary of what Baxter asserted in relation to fanatical sects on more occasions than one, but in Calamy's day there was a more sceptical spirit abroad than seems to have affected Baxter. It is not hard to find examples of this more sceptical spirit in Calamy and amongst other Presbyterians.[2]

Soon after 1707 the delusions of certain French prophets from the Continent were having a remarkable vogue in London and even in Calamy's own congregation. Calamy was not impressed and went so far as to challenge one of them with the promise that he would 'fall in with their dispensation' if a certain prophesied resurrection of a dead man did actually take place as foretold, if the other would 'entirely quit the said dispensation' if the resurrection did not take place.[3] We have too the account of how James Peirce, a Presbyterian

[1] Gordon *Heads*, 98–100.

[2] Calamy, *Hist. Account*, i. 476–7. Sir David had published a book (anonymous), *The private Christian's witness for Christianity: in opposition to the notional and erroneous apprehensions of Arminian, Socinian and Deist of the age . . .* , 1697.

[3] Calamy, *Hist. Account*, ii. 94–9, 104–5, 108–9. The French Prophets carry us back to the persecution of the Huguenots and to the conflict in Holland between Pierre Bayle and Pierre Jurieu (whom Calamy dubbed 'the Apocalyptical Monsieur Jurieu'—*Hist. Account*, i. 182). Cf. Calamy, *Hist. Account*, i. 182; i. 36. Cf. James Sutherland, *Background for Queen Anne*, 1939.

minister at Exeter, refused to be duped by a vision of a headless horse on a dark night in the graveyard outside his study window, to find to his satisfaction on the morrow that the said horse had a white body and a black head, making the head invisible in the darkness.[1] Doubtless the list of salutary instances of common sense scepticism could be lengthened, but perhaps we nowhere get a better indication of the feeling of the time than in a jocular remark of a Presbyterian student, Thomas Secker, who later conformed and became Archbishop of Canterbury. He had been retailing some of the marvel-mongering explanations of the Aurora Borealis that was particularly brilliant in 1716. He followed these with an account of an attempted scientific explanation of the phenomenon, adding that those who offered it 'were doubtless either Presbyterians or Atheists', a valuable chance testimony to the scientific spirit becoming prevalent amongst Presbyterians at the time.[2]

## A Contrast

This newer and persistent scepticism contrasts markedly with a certain credulity that was frequent enough only a generation earlier. We may instance Baxter's last book, *The certainty of the worlds of spirits*, 1691, with its incredible catalogue of credulities. Baxter's intention may have been scientific enough in one sense, that of demonstrating by means of evidence the existence of spiritual beings, but it evinces little appreciation of the worthlessness of much of the evidence adduced. How quickly such credulity was passing away we may see when we consider an account of exorcism that was originally intended to have formed part of Baxter's book. It was not until six years later, however, in 1697, that it was published.[3] When it did thus belatedly find its way into print, it was promptly greeted by an Anglican minister with the exclamation, 'I beseech you, Gentlemen, consider the evil you have done in publishing a wild story, for religious truth, in this sceptical and irreligious age'.[4] It was one of the blessings of the newer outlook that

---

[1] *MR*, xvi, 330.

[2] *MR*, xv. 67 (Thomas Secker to his sister [March 1716]). Cf. R. Thomas in *Inquirer*, September 27, 1958, 311.                [3] Published in *The Surey Demoniack*, 1697.

[4] Zachary Taylor, *The Surey Impostor*, 1697, 1. On the delayed publication of *The Surey Demoniack*, see *The Lancashire Levite Rebuk'd*, 1698, 2 and *The Surey Demoniack*, Preface, p. [1]. Cf. F. Nicholson and E. Axon, *The Older Nonconformity in Kendal*, 1915, 175-9.

Queen Anne's age saw the passing away of witch hunts. Soon after the last trial in England for witchcraft in 1712 (in which the judge nullified the jury's verdict of guilty by passing a derisorily inadequate sentence) a Deist claimed that the disappearance of witch-hunts was due to free-thinking imported from Holland; the great Richard Bentley took him severely to task for this claim and asserted that it was not atheistical free thinking that had done away with witchcraft, but the influence of the Royal Society and the College of Physicians.[1] Either way it was the rise of reason that had put an end to witch beliefs.

## John Locke's Rationalism

As with toleration a notable contributor, whether as inspirer or as exponent, to the more radical rationalism had been John Locke. The noticeable difference of tone between, shall we say?, the Cambridge Platonists and Tillotson or Hoadly, between Baxter and Edmund Calamy, may well be traced back to the criticism that we associate with the name of John Locke.[2]

To both Baxter and Locke reason was the ultimate guardian of truth in religion and in other matters, but though they both appealed to reason they had rather different conceptions of reason in mind. Prior to Locke it was generally characteristic of English philosophers to regard innate knowledge as rational, including our knowledge of God, the obligation of duty, the immortality of the soul and so on. Baxter certainly held this belief in innate knowledge, as did many with whom he was in essential agreement. But it was against the validity of such innate knowledge that Locke's life work had been directed. His aim was to replace it by reason in the sense of what we should call empirical knowledge and to discourage excursions into realms with which our minds were not capable of dealing.[3]

[1] R. Trevor Davies, *Four Centuries of Witch-Beliefs*, 1947, 5, 181; *A Discourse of Free-Thinking* [by Anthony Collins], 1713, 30; *An Answer to the Discourse on Free-Thinking* [by Richard Bentley], 1713, 33–4. Collins is doubtless referring to Balthasar Bekker's famous work, *De Betoverde Wereld*, 1691. Bekker tried to get rid of the awkward fact that witchcraft was countenanced in the Bible by means of highly forced and allegorical interpretations. For this his Calvinist colleagues excommunicated him. In England sceptics found a more successful compromise, viz. witchcraft in the Bible was all right; contemporary witchcraft was all wrong, lacking sufficient evidence (Francis Hutchinson, *Historical Essay concerning Witchcraft*, 1720).

[2] Norman Sykes, *From Sheldon to Secker*, 1959, 145/6, 149/50.

[3] J. W. Yolton, *John Locke and the Way of Ideas*, 1956; A.-L. Leroy, *Locke, sa vie, son oeuvre*, 1964, 24.

Great as this difference was, it made little immediate difference in religion since Locke believed that he could derive all the essentials of accepted religious belief as readily by means of his conception of reason as Baxter had done by means of his. Nevertheless a consistent Baxterian, putting his ultimate reliance in reason, when confronted with Locke's argument and accepting it, was bound to put his reliance in empirical rather than in implicit knowledge for the defence of religion. To have done otherwise would have been to abandon that very confidence in reason that was essential to his Baxterianism. The outcome was a more exacting and scientific and, to some extent, a more sceptical use of reason.

Whatever the precise influence of Locke's philosophy may have been there is no doubt that his *Essay concerning human understanding* was becoming the text-book of the age. Characteristic was its entry into Dissenting academies. Joshua Oldfield, who conducted an academy first in Coventry and, from 1699, in London, embodied Locke in his teaching. So too did Thomas Dixon at Whitehaven by at least as early as 1710. Samuel Jones at Tewkesbury (amongst whose students may be counted Joseph Butler of the *Analogy* and Thomas Secker, the future archbishop) was teaching from Locke at about the same time. At Taunton, where Henry Grove was tutor, Locke, if not actually taught, was being read by students. These were all Presbyterian centres of learning and they do not exhaust the list of academies where Locke's influence was at work in these years.[1]

Nothing perhaps illustrates the enquiring spirit of the age so well as the activities of some of the more intelligent students in the academies. With the little information that we have it is surprising that we know so much. At Tewkesbury Butler was carrying on a clandestine correspondence on philosophy with Samuel Clarke, who was perhaps England's most eminent philosopher after Locke died in 1704. At Exeter, where the tutor was Joseph Hallett, the tutor's own son, another Joseph Hallett, was carrying on a similar correspondence in 1710 with William Whiston, Sir Isaac Newton's successor at Cambridge. Later we hear of another student at the same

---

[1] Joshua Oldfield, *An essay towards the improvement of reason*, 1707, 5 etc., McLachlan, *EETA*, 128, 126, 293. We may add the use of Locke by John Jennings at Kibworth, and by Doddridge at Northampton, both Congregational academies. There is evidence of Dissenting laity in London reading Locke. Cf. below, p. 191.

academy corresponding with Samuel Clarke. There was no dearth of enquiry into new developments of thought.[1]

## The Theory of Ordination

This newer mood of scepticism and enquiry did not touch the ecclesiastical practice or teaching of Dissenters immediately or directly except in one respect, that of the theory of ordination and what was conveyed, with or without the laying on of hands, when a minister was ordained. According to Presbyterians only ministers could ordain a man to the ministry and hand on the succession. Was this a piece of superstitious priestcraft conveying some hidden power? Whatever it had been or might have been, ordination for Presbyterians was cleared of any superstitious attachments at about this time.

Perhaps the event that brought the question into the immediate foreground was the publication, in 1706, of the anonymous *Rights of the Christian Church*. By Matthew Tindal, the book was a withering attack on High Church pretensions in this respect and on any similar pretensions that there might be in other bodies. Of it Calamy wrote that there had not 'been a book published in many years that made more noise'. His estimate of its importance may be gauged from the fact that he printed a full summary of it. His estimate of the insignificance of the numerous published answers to it is obliquely hinted at in the bland observation with which he concludes his summary, that he would have been 'glad to see a good answer to the book, upon the *jure divino* bottom, of any particular form of church government'.[2] These last words point the moral for the Presbyterian form of church government. Amongst other matters *The Rights* had attacked the High Church theory of the apostolic succession and of claims for the validity of episcopal ordination and it did not forget a side glance at any similar claims by Dissenters. There can be no doubt that *The Rights* caused English Presbyterians seriously to reconsider their own position; and they were ready enough to repudiate any superstitious or sacerdotal claims of which they might be suspected. One instance amongst

[1] McLachlan, *EETA*, 129–30; W. Whiston, *Memoirs*, 2nd ed., 1753, 128–30 (May 1, 1710). (Characteristically Whiston believed himself to be corresponding with Hallett the father when he was really corresponding with the son); Letter of Hubert Stogdon to Clarke in the British Museum. [2] Calamy, *Abridgement*, 701, 709.

several gives an outspoken expression of this. When Thomas Morgan was ordained at Frome in 1716 the proceedings were published with a preface by Henry Chandler of Bath. Chandler's preface was neatly summed up by a Presbyterian student at the time in London in these words:

> He makes no scruple of telling the world that the essence of a minister consists in his fitness and the people's choice, and that all his brethren do is declaring him to be such antecedently to their declaration and then giving good advice and praying for him. And upon his proposing the question, What then is the use of ordination? he answers, If you mean by ordination imposition of hands, ask them that know, for I do not. In the Apostles' time it was a method of conveying miraculous gifts, etc.[1]

It might be thought that Chandler was doing no more than assimilating the Presbyterian to the Congregational theory, under which the essence of ordination, according to the Savoy Declaration, consisted in election by the church and the separation of ordinands by fasting and prayer. But in fact he was concerned with the very similar declaration in *The Rights* that ordination consisted soley in 'the suffrages of the people'. And he was careful to include against both *The Rights* and the Congregationals the Presbyterian claim that ministers had a special part to play; they were there not merely to advise and pray but also to give their decision that the person to be ordained was a fit person to be so set apart for the ministry. Other Presbyterians who responded to the challenge in *The Rights* were even more explicit; it was quite in character that Daniel Williams asserted that 'unless self-conceitedness be allowed as the fittest standard' some must judge of a candidate's fitness and that they who were best fitted to judge were other ministers.[2] All taint of superstition and irrationalism was thus repudiated without conceding the central Presbyterian contention that ministers should hand on the succession.

---

[1] *MR*, xvi (1821), 573 (letter of Thomas Secker to John Fox, dated February 13, 1717); Nicholas Billingsley, *A sermon preach'd at the ordination of Mr. Thomas Morgan*, 1717, Preface. Cf. D.W.L. MS. 'Say Papers' (Isaac Watts to S. Say, November 1, 1709) p. 4. (Printed *MR*, iv. 10.)

[2] [M. Tindal] *Rights of the Christian Church*, 3rd ed., 1707, 358, ch. ix. 52, referring to Acts xix. (Cf. *MR*, xvi (1821), 134); Daniel Williams, *The Ministerial Office*, 1709, 55. Cf. James Peirce, *Presbyterian Ordination prov'd valid*, 23, 24; Edmund Calamy, *The Inspiration of the Holy Writings*, 1710, 385, 393.

It is not without significance, for the scientific and rational interests of the time, that Thomas Morgan, who was ordained on the occasion just mentioned, in his confession of faith gives a good example of the influence of contemporary science upon an impressionable student. The opening passage of his confession is a slice out of Sir Isaac Newton. On it the London student, already quoted, commented:

> How it must edify the hearers to understand that the mutual attractions of bodies was as their quantities of matter directly and as the square of their distances reciprocally! And without doubt a man that was acquainted with the sublimation of the vapours in the natural alembics of the hills must be able to raise the affections of his auditory to heaven without difficulty.[1]

Morgan's excursions into the uplifting possibilities of 'modern' science were a little jéjune no doubt, but they were quite in the spirit of the age and are to be found exemplified also in Addison's famous hymn which had appeared a few years earlier in 1712, and which is still vociferously sung:

> The spacious firmament on high
> With all the blue ethereal sky
> And spangled heavens, a shining frame
> Their great original proclaim.

Perhaps this picture was more successful in raising the affections of an auditory to heaven!

### Too Fast and Too Far?

These glimpses into the scientific mood of the time give us some slight feeling of the exhilaration felt at the sense of new worlds of thought and knowledge opening up a way to the better understanding of God and his world. It was not everyone however who felt any such exhilaration and the sense of emancipation that attended it. There were those who noted the change with grave misgivings and resentment and who did not let it go by unchallenged. The examples we have taken from Thomas Morgan's ordination lie a little beyond the confines of Queen Anne's reign, but they are

[1] *MR*, xvi (1821), 573. Morgan's confession of faith is printed with N. Billingsley, *Sermon preach'd at the ordination of Mr. Thomas Morgan*, 1717.

evidence of a mood that had clearly been gathering force for some time. The very last months of the Queen's reign saw an orthodox Presbyterian, a Scotsman, John Cumming, minister at Cambridge, bewailing *The general corruptions and defection of the present time, as to matters of religion*. He complains of those who make their own reasonings 'the rule of truth, and by vain reasoning exalt themselves against the knowledge of God. . . . '

> Their proud maxim is that they are bound to believe nothing of which they have not a distinct idea. Socinianism and Arianism threaten to lay the axe to the root of Christianity: not only the Arminian errors, but even the vile texts of Pelagius are the only notions now in vogue. The doctrines of Election and Predestination [and he goes through the catalogue of Calvinist tenets] are not only generally exploded as irrational, but profanely bantered and laughed at as ridiculous.[1]

And later he has a special word for the Dissenters on the dangers of Arminianism.[2] All in all he provides us with an eloquent testimony to the developments taking place during the previous years with which we have been dealing—of which he disapproved. And his wrathful dismay gives us fair warning that old ways of thought would not give way to new without a struggle.

One phrase that Cumming used is particularly noteworthy; it is his reference to those who refuse to believe anything 'of which they have not a distinct idea'. One could hardly desire a clearer indictment of the influence in some quarters of the philosophy of John Locke. He may have had the Deist John Toland's *Christianity not mysterious* in mind, for Toland deliberately built his Deism on Locke's Theory, but, as we have already seen, Locke's thought was beginning to have considerable influence in Dissenting circles.[3] We have noted Calamy's respect for Locke and his welcome for his lead in the movement for toleration. We have noted that Locke's philosophy was being taught or read in Dissenting academies. And we have noted too the effect of his contribution to scientific thought in modifying an older conception of reason. There was yet another field in which Locke gave a lead with considerable influence later on Presbyterian thought; this was in Biblical criticism. Cumming

---

[1] John Cumming, *The General Corruptions*, 1714, 8–9.     [2] Ibid. 30.
[3] Locke had had to defend himself against Stillingfleet on account of Toland's extension of his doctrine of ideas. See the published exchanges between Locke and the bishop in 1697.

does not allude to it unless perhaps in his omnibus reference to Socinianism and Arianism, the Arminian errors and 'even the vile texts of Pelagius'. Possibly the effect of a more radical Biblical criticism was not apparent in Dissenting circles by 1714. But the Queen's reign saw notable advances in Biblical scholarship. Overtly advances in this field were the monopoly of Anglicans of whom the most important were John Mill, Samuel Clarke and Locke himself. As usual at this period it was the Anglicans who provided men in the van of theological advance. Nevertheless the influence of Locke, Mill and Clarke in Biblical studies upon Presbyterians at a later time was so considerable that some account of it must be given here.

*Scripture Sufficiency*

Baxter had been utterly confident that everything that mattered in Christianity was made safe and secure by a simple adherence to Scripture. Thus, speaking of Socinianism he could declare that 'if there is nothing against Socinianism in Scripture, it is no heresy: if there be (as sure there is enough and plain enough) judge them by that rule and make not new ones'. Calamy would have said Amen, though whether, living when he did, he could have felt the same robust confidence is another matter. When the Presbyterians and Congregationals were drafting their *Heads of Agreement* in 1691 they had before them an earlier draft in which conformity to one or other of several acceptable confessions of faith was made obligatory, but in the final version they prefaced this reference to the confessions with the requirement that 'a Church acknowledge the Scriptures to be the Word of God, the perfect and only rule of faith and practice'. They evidently felt the same unquestioning confidence as Baxter that there could be no material conflict between Scripture and traditional belief. But since 1691 much water had gone under the bridge; writings had appeared that made a vital impact upon Biblical thought and their influence would be felt for long years to come.[1]

Two of these writings came from the pen of John Locke. The first was *The reasonableness of Christianity as delivered in the Scriptures*, in 1695, four years after the *Heads of Agreement*. Ostensibly

---

[1] R. Baxter, *The Judgment of Nonconformists of the interest of reason*, 1676, 2; Thomas in *Beginnings*, 1964, 53; *Heads of Agreement*, 14 (sect. viii). D.W.L. *Occasional Paper*, No. 6, p.11.

K

the theme was the same as that of Baxter's *The reasons of the Christian religion* of 1667, but the emphasis in Locke's title that the Christianity was that 'delivered in the Scriptures' deftly advertised the fact all too apparent from its pages that, whatever else it was, the Christianity delivered in the Scriptures was very different from the Christianity delivered in the creeds. The essentials of Christianity were reduced to the Apostolic confession that Jesus was the Christ. Not very surprisingly the book, as Locke himself reported, displeased 'our divines both conformist and nonconformist'. Calamy's voluminous silence on the book, of which he cannot have been ignorant, is almost vocal: Isaac Watts delivered himself of the mildly worded protest that Locke had 'sunk some of the divine themes and glories of that dispensation too much below the original design'. The Scriptures in Locke's hands were not doing what was expected of them—or of him.[1]

From examining the Gospels as he had done in the *Reasonableness* Locke went on to draw up paraphrases of the Pauline Epistles. Before he died in 1704 he had worked through five of the Epistles—Galatians, Romans, I and II Corinthians, and Ephesians. These paraphrases appeared posthumously one by one with a collected edition in the year 1707. This collected edition was prefaced by an 'Essay for the understanding of St. Paul's Epistles, by consulting St. Paul himself'. The sting was clearly in the tail and the appeal was once again away from the commentators and creeds to the fountain head, in this case St Paul 'himself'. It was also a protest against the customary way of reading the Bible 'crumbled' into verses as set out in the Authorized Version or by daily chapters. The mistake, as he said, was 'to snatch out a few words, as if they were separate from the rest, to serve a purpose, to which they do not at all belong and with which they have nothing to do'. Instead of this his attempt had been to read one of the Epistles 'all through at one sitting and to observe as well as I could the drift and design of his writing it. If the first reading gave me some light, the second gave me more.'[2]

---

[1] *MR*, xiii (1818), 612—'theologis nostris tam conformistis quam non-conformistis displicere audio' (*Works*, 1812, x. 51); Isaac Watts, *Works*, 1810, iv. 469; R. Thomas 'Philip Doddridge and liberalism in religion' in G. F. Nuttall, *Philip Doddridge*, 1951, 127.
[2] J. Locke, *Paraphrases and notes on the Epistles of St. Paul*, 1707, pp. viii, xv; Thomas in *JEH*, iv. 186.

Locke had worked through only five of the Epistles in this way before his death. It says something for the novelty of the idea and the impact that it made upon those searching for light in obscurity that two leading minds among the Presbyterians later took up the work where Locke left off and attempted the same method with the remaining Epistles. James Peirce was at that time at Newbury in Berkshire; later he went to Exeter where, as we shall see, he was ejected for heresy in 1719, and there subsequently he published continuations of Locke's paraphrases between 1725 and 1727, completing Colossians, Philippians and Hebrews. George Benson who was a protégé of Edmund Calamy and whose first ministry was at Abingdon (1723–29) completed the work on the Pauline Epistles and added paraphrases of the Catholic Epistles, his volumes appearing between 1731 and 1749.[1]

## Mill's New Testament

The year 1707 which saw the appearance of the collected edition of Locke's paraphrases saw also the appearance of another Biblical work of major importance. This was John Mill's *Novum Testamentum*, on the preparation of which he had been engaged since 1678. During these thirty years Mill had collected an incredible number of variant readings, computed at something like 30,000. It was these variant readings that did the mischief and made the work controversial, for they seemed 'quite plainly to render the standard of faith insecure or at least to give others too good a handle for doubting'.[2] It was asked what became of the verbal inerrancy of the Scripture if the true text was submerged beneath such a welter of variant readings. Was not this a free gift to the Deist cause? It takes an effort to realize that the inerrancy of the divine text was then taken quite seriously and even so mild an inroad upon that theory as was made in Le Clerc's *Five letters concerning the inspiration of the Holy Scriptures* (published in this English translation in 1690) found Calamy, as we have seen, making a full-scale defence of the traditional belief fourteen years later. In such an atmosphere the very number of Mill's variants was disturbing, but even more disturbing was the nature of some of them. Thus we may note the

[1] A. Gordon, *Addresses Biographical and Historical*, 1922, 121–8; Brockett, 79.

[2] Daniel Whitby, *Examen variantium lectionum Joannis Millii*, 1710, quoted from Adam Fox, *John Mill and Richard Bentley*, 1954, 106.

somewhat suspicious comment of a review in the *Journal des Savans* soon after the work was published:

> We observe on the subject of the infinite number of variae lectiones which Mr. Mill has collected together that to read them with profit one must have great judgment and a great fund of theology. Those who will give attention to I Jn v. 7, 8, and the places where the doctrine of the Trinity is dealt with, will easily recognise the truth of this reflexion.[1]

For all his numerous variants Mill's principal text was still the old 'received text' of Stephanus, the *Textus Receptus* as it is called. Had he attempted a revision based on an assessment of the value of the variant readings the result might have been even more disturbing, but this Mill did not do. Any such task was left to others.[2]

It is to the honour of a Presbyterian, Daniel Mace, that he was amongst those who realized that the need was to abandon the *Textus Receptus* and draw up a revised text taking account of the newly collected manuscript evidence. What is more, he not only saw the need but actually gave it effect in an edition of the New Testament which was published in 1729 and which was so remarkably in advance of its time that it suffered severely from adverse critics on that account, so severely, we may suspect, that further efforts of a similar kind in England were discouraged and the initiative in this direction passed from England to the Continent.

Mace's New Testament was printed in a very beautiful, sensible and apparently unique Greek type, anticipating that of Porson by getting rid of the countless disfiguring ligatures that were then and long afterwards the delight of printers of Greek. Moreover it was set out intelligently in paragraphs, thus putting into effect one of Locke's desiderata and at the same time anticipating the practice of the English Revised Version. Parallel to the Greek Mace printed a new English translation which if not without merit is too much a product of its century to arouse much enthusiasm today. What is more to his credit is that in a remarkable number of places where he departed from the *Textus Receptus* his judgment has been upheld by modern critics. He evidently possessed a good measure of that 'great judgment' enjoined by the *Journal des Savans*. He had the

---

[1] Adam Fox, op. cit. 83.

[2] E.g. Edward Wells whose New Testament was appearing 1709-19; Adam Fox, op. cit. 95-7.

courage (or temerity) to omit the spurious reading of I John v. 7, 8, and adds a long note setting out convincingly the manuscript evidence against it.[1]

## Samuel Clarke

The work of Locke and Mill would take time to permeate the theological world of thought. As we have just seen, the results of intensive study by Peirce and Mace did not bear fruit until 1725 and 1729. But a work that appeared in 1712, a few years later than those of Locke and Mill, made an immediate impact. It was a serious attempt to come to grips with Scripture's real teaching and was made by Samuel Clarke in his *Scripture-doctrine of the Trinity*. It was a determined effort to discover what exactly Scripture did teach on a single doctrine, that of the Trinity. The outcome may have been *a* doctrine of the Trinity, but it was certainly not *the* doctrine of the Trinity as commonly entertained, and enshrined in the confessions of faith. Its enemies dubbed it Arianism, the same name as was given to a very similar doctrine being taught by Isaac Newton's successor as Lucasian professor at Cambridge, the eccentric William Whiston, in his *Primitive Christianity reviv'd* which appeared at about the same time. The importance of Clarke's book, as time went on, was not so much that it was about the Trinity (though it was this that made it controversial at the time), but that it set a new standard of exact investigation into what Scripture did in fact teach and that it demonstrated that it could not be assumed that the teaching of Scripture was necessarily in accord with received Christian belief. The 'Gospel' could no longer be regarded as something known and certain beforehand, but had become, like truth itself, something only to be elicited at the end of a close and scientific investigation. Clarke thus reinforced the lesson of Locke and to a lesser degree that of Mill. At the time, however, what caused alarm was that the sacred doctrine of the Trinity was once more being challenged and that it was being challenged more

[1] Daniel Mace's edition appeared without his name as *The New Testament in Greek and English, Containing the original text corrected from the authority of the most authentic manuscripts: and a new version* . . . , 2 vols. 1729. Cf. Adam Fox, op. cit. 97–102; McLachlan, *Essays*, 230–47. Mace was appointed minister at Beckington in Somerset in 1717 (Presb. Fund Mins. ii. 320, etc.). Did Lord Chancellor King, to whom Mace's New Testament was dedicated, pay for the remarkable and apparently unique Greek type and the production of the book? Cf. McLachlan, *Essays*, 237.

effectively on Scriptural grounds alone than ever it had been by the Unitarian Anglicans of twenty years before. Controversy broke out immediately, but it was mainly Anglicans who were concerned in it; as with the earlier, Socinian or Unitarian controversy, the few Dissenters who took part did so in defence of the received doctrine.[1] It was not long, however, before there were Dissenters who began to feel the weight of Clarke's argument and were impressed by his case.

The hitherto easy belief in the sufficiency of Scripture might become a cause of serious heart searchings. If a man was inclined towards Arminianism, if he was for tolerance in religious matters, if he looked to Scripture to end old theological feuds and put a reasonable in place of a dogmatic or imposed faith, if, in a word, he was a consistent Baxterian, prepared to abide by his principles (even if it meant departing from the doctrine that, he believed, followed from these principles), Clarke's book might disturb him but it could not daunt him. But if he was an old-school divine to whom the sufficiency of Scripture was a mighty sword when it supported his cause against Popish innovations, he would begin to realize that it was double-edged and that his old-school divinity was beginning to come under the other cutting edge. Moreover, whatever the official teaching in the Dissenting academies, students were alive to what was passing in the world of thought. Locke and Mill and Clarke and Whiston were being read for the new light that they threw on old problems and the consequence was that the stabilities of the old orthodoxies could no longer be preserved immune.

## Matthew Henry's Commentary

When Queen Anne died whatever subterranean influence the newer Biblical criticism may have had on Dissenters it had not emerged above ground. The most notable contribution of Dissenters to Biblical studies bore quite a different character. It was Matthew Henry's famous commentary whose first volume appeared in 1707, the year that saw the publication of Mill's New Testament and the collected edition of Locke's paraphrases. Unlike them, however, it broke no new ground and its great merit lay in the fact that it was so able an exposition of old-school divinity that down to very recent

[1] E.g. John Hughes *of Ware*. See above, p. 122.

times it remained in high favour with evangelically minded theologians. Ironically it thus outlived Locke and Clarke, being still reprinted when they were almost forgotten, for as they had superseded older work so they themselves would be superseded by newer advances in scholarship, while Matthew Henry would go on as the grand repository of unchanging orthodoxy and the great bastion against novelty. At the end of the Queen's reign, to the general eye, Matthew Henry would be evidence enough that at least the Dissenters were unaffected by the fresher winds of theological change.

### THE SALTERS' HALL WATERSHED, 1719

When George I ascended the throne, the developments which had been quietly taking place amongst Dissenters were hardly apparent to the outside world, and low-churchmen or Latitudinarians, amongst whom advanced beliefs had long been making progress, were apt to regard the Dissenters as backwoodsmen sticking to an outworn creed. Thus Benjamin Hoadly, Calamy's adversary of an earlier day, now the rising star of Whig Anglicanism and soon to be created a bishop, could say without serious risk of contradiction:

> Amongst our Nonconformists the same logics and the same bodies of theology (as they are called) descend from generation to generation. The same systems and syllogisms, definitions and distinctions pass on current for Divinity; and Calvin and the Gospel go hand in hand, as if there were not a hair's breadth to choose between them.[1]

And elsewhere he adds:

> It is all with them right and good, just as Christ left it at first and Calvin found it above fifteen hundred years afterwards.[2]

Events of the next few years would undeceive him and necessitate a very different estimate.

---

[1] U. Cerri, *An account of the Roman Catholic religion ... with a large dedication* [by Benjamin Hoadly] ... [Published] by Richard Steele, 1715, p. xlviii.

[2] Cerri, *Account*, p. x.

*Scripture or Interpretation*

The earliest of these events was one much talked of amongst London Presbyterians at the time, though probably soon forgotten. It is none the less significant of the changing climate of opinion. In 1716 Daniel Wilcox, Presbyterian minister at Monkwell Street, London, dismissed his assistant, Henry Read, for Arminianism. Read may have been no more than a faithful Baxterian, but Wilcox demanded his subscription to doctrinal articles designed to entangle him in contradictions with what he was known to have preached. Read refused; the London ministers took up his case; they advised Wilcox against dismissing him, but Wilcox flouted their advice. Later in the year Read was one of several to be ordained by leading Presbyterian ministers, one of whom was Edmund Calamy. Wilcox defended his action in an anonymous pamphlet with the title *The duty of holding fast the form of sound words* (1717). For him the form of sound words was the Westminster Confession, one of whose purposes, he asserted, was 'to be a test of truth and error'. To the question 'Is not the Bible . . . test sufficient?' his reply was that 'a man may be Protestant or Papist, Calvinist or Arminian, and no discovery made of him'. 'The calling any to the Assembly's Confession of Faith', he added, 'we by no means take to be calling of them *from* the *Scripture* but a putting them to the trial in what sense they understood Scripture'. This was quite in accord with the *Heads of Agreement*, where Scripture, though the 'only rule', is given a determinate sense by reference to one or other of the Confessions of faith there named. But the writings of Locke and Mill and Clarke had not gone for nothing and in 1716 the time had gone by for this sort of argument to go unchallenged. And challenged it certainly was, and that very promptly, in a monthly journal, the *Occasional Papers*, conducted by Dissenters, mostly Presbyterians. The author on this occasion was Moses Lowman, who wrote, 'It looks a little oddly . . . to assert the Scripture as the only rule and that men must judge for themselves and then, at the same time, to claim authority to the Church in matters of faith'.[1]

[1] Thomas in *JEH*, iv. 183–4; Calamy, *Hist. Account*, ii. 364; Edmund Calamy, *The principles and practice of moderate Nonconformists*, 1717; *Occasional Papers*, ii, no. 1, p. 15 (the author of this particular paper was Moses Lowman, an Independent); Dudley Ryder's diary—transcript in Harrowby MSS., July 3, 1716, November 20, 1716. Henry Read was not at the time an ordained minister; the usual practice for a

## The Bangorian Controversy

Before the next occasion on which developments in Dissenting thought would come into the public eye a controversy was to break out in the Church of England that would illustrate that similar, and indeed greater, advances had been taking place within the Establishment. It was the notorious Bangorian Controversy which broke out in 1717 and which was to affect Dissenters more than they probably realized at the time. It arose out of a sermon preached on March 31st by Benjamin Hoadly, now elevated to the see of Bangor. Nowhere perhaps do we find almost the whole range of interrelated beliefs that we have been considering better brought together than in this sermon. For its Arminianism what could be more downright than this?

> Religion in St. James's days was virtue and integrity as to ourselves, and charity and beneficence to others; before God, even the Father. James i. 27. By degrees it is come to signify, in most of the countries throughout the whole world, the performance of everything almost, except virtue and charity.

Or could the point of Scripture sufficiency be more explicitly stated than in this?

> I have mentioned these particulars not only to show the evil . . . but to give you occasion to observe that there can be no cure for it, in Christians, but to go back to the New Testament itself; because there alone we shall find the original intention of such words, or the nature of the things designed to be signified by them, declared and fixed by our Lord or his Apostles from him.

Even the use to which Locke had put Scripture in his *Reasonableness of Christianity* is exhibited:

> And the notion of the Church of Christ . . . at first was only the number, small or great, of those who believed him to be the Messiah, or of those who subjected themselves to him as their King in the affair of religion.

But above all it was a plea for tolerance:

> If he [Christ] had but at first enlightened the powers of this world, as he did St. Paul, and employed the sword which they bore and the

---

man intending to enter the ministry at this time was for him to be first licensed to preach; thereafter he was expected to proceed to ordination in due course or on taking up full responsibility for a pastorate.

favours they had in their hands to bring subjects into his kindgom, this had been an expeditious and an effectual way, according to the conduct of some of his professed followers, to have had a glorious and extensive Kingdom or Church. But this was not his design, unless it could be compassed in quite a different way.[1]

It was not, however, as a general exposition of what we might call the new theology (unpopular though that was in certain quarters) that made the sermon an immediate cause of controversy, but as a frontal attack on those High Church Tory elements in the community whose aim had long been to undermine the freedom enjoyed by the Dissenters under the Toleration Act. Indeed they had succeeded during the latter years of Queen Anne in passing the Occasional Conformity Act and the Schism Act and had, in a word, 'employed the sword which they bore and the favours they had in their hands' against the Dissenters to some purpose. The moment chosen by Hoadly for preaching the sermon made its significance inescapable. It was preached on March 31, 1717, only a few days after a great meeting of Members of Parliament had been held to agitate for the repeal of the penal Acts against Dissenters, and, when it was published in April, it appeared as the climax to a series of pamphlets written as part of the agitation against these Acts.[2] Its purpose in support of the repeals could not be missed. Contents and timing were more than Tory flesh and blood could bear and the outburst of acrimonious, unrestrained, sustained fury against the sermon and its author was immediate and scandalous even for those days and it has remained a remarkable exhibit ever since.

Whatever Dissenters may have thought of the doctrines taught in the sermon they could not but welcome Hoadly's forthright support of their cause against the penal laws.[3] But the sermon did something more; it gave active encouragement to all those amongst the Dis-

[1] Benjamin Hoadly, *The Nature of the Kingdom, or Church, of Christ*, 1717, 5, 9, 10, 21.
[2] Pamphlets for this purpose included *The repeal of the Act against Occasional Conformity considered* [by Edmund Calamy (Calamy, *Hist. Account*, ii. 369)]—March 22nd; *The Dissenters claim of right*—March 27th; *Two questions of present importance* [by William Harris (*Prot. Diss. Mag.* ii. 224)]—April 1st; *The case of the Acts against the Protestant Dissenters*—April 18th; *Of the removing the incapacities of Protestant Dissenters* (*Occasional Papers*, ii, No. 4)—April 10th; *Two and twenty queries*—March 22nd; *The second part of the State anatomy* [by John Toland]—April. For the meeting on March 26th, see *Political State of Great Britain* (ed. A. Boyer) xiii (for April 1717), 391. For the political situation see Barlow, 57 ff.
[3] Samuel Chandler, *The History of Persecution*, 1736, 391.

senters who had been slowly feeling their way towards the theology
there so boldly advocated. This was a disturbing by-product of the
sermon that many Dissenters were to find very distasteful. One
observer reported the situation in these words: 'I find by conversations I have had with some ministers and comrades that there is a
perfect Hoadly mania among our younger ministers in the north.'[1]
He was writing of Northern Ireland, but the same 'mania' was to be
discerned in England. In London the *Occasional Papers*, published
monthly from 1716 to 1719, not only welcomed Hoadly's writings
in the Bangorian Controversy; they also afford an excellent source
for the study of 'Hoadly mania', if that be the appropriate term, for
it was a very sober mania.[2] But there were certainly manifestations
of an ebullient hopefulness abroad that the bad old times were about
to succumb to the new spirit. It only wanted time before there must
be a serious conflict among Dissenters between the old immovables
and the new invincibles. When the conflict came, it was a conflagra-
tion.

## Exeter Heresy

The spark that set the flame alight came from students at the
Exeter Academy, an academy maintained by Joseph Hallett, one of
the Exeter Presbyterian Ministers and a colleague of James Peirce.
We have a valuable account of the beginnings of the trouble from
one of the students, John Fox, who entered the Academy in 1708.
His account is,

> while I lived here some of us fell into the Unitarian scheme about the
> Trinity. The first in it was Mr. Joseph Hallett, our tutor's eldest son,
> who held a secret correspondence with Mr. Whiston, then publishing
> his 'Primitive Christianity '. . . . I was more intimate with him than
> with any of the rest of the young men, but I knew nothing of his
> notions till our class was lectured on Pictet's chapter concerning the
> Trinity. He then laid several books on that subject in my way, which
> extremely surprised me. . . . I remember that what startled me most
> was the famous Mr. Boyse's answer to Emlyn. . . . But the bare

[1] Thomas in *JEH*, iv. 180.
[2] The authors of the *Occasional Papers* were Simon Browne, Benjamin Avery,
Benjamin Grosvenor, Samuel Wright, John Evans, Jabez Earle, Moses Lowman and
Nathaniel Lardner. All but Earle were Nonsubscribers in 1719 and he disowned his
subscription later. All but Lowman and Lardner were Presbyterians, and Lardner
later became a Presbyterian.

quotations which Boyse made from Emlyn, in order to answer him, seemed to strike so strongly that I began to doubt from that moment, notwithstanding my own natural prejudices and all the art and learning of Mr. Boyse. We were about five or six of us who understood one another in this affair, but we conversed with great caution and secrecy. And from this small beginning sprang the grand quarrel and dispute at Exeter; for the notion by degrees got abroad among some conceited citizens, who perhaps at first talked of more than they understood; then the ministers began to be alarmed, and the danger of heresy was uppermost with them. . . . At length they began to dispute and consequently to be angry, all which laid the foundation for that war which broke out soon afterwards.[1]

Secrecy seems to have been successfully maintained for a number of years and when something did leak out it was owing to the indiscretions of a later student, Hubert Stogdon. He had been so impressed by his reading of Samuel Clarke's *Scripture-doctrine* that in the exuberance of youth he gloried in his new found faith.[2] Towards the end of 1716 he admitted as much to a very orthodox minister who was horrified at what he heard. Older men than Stogdon had been impressed by Clarke's arguments; they were more discreet, but their very reticences aroused disquiet. James Peirce, one of the four Exeter Presbyterian Ministers, was one of these. He had deplored the heterodoxy of his friend, the eccentric William Whiston, when he first heard of it in 1708, but since then he had given concentrated attention not only to what Whiston had written but also to what had been written by Clarke and by Locke. As a result he had found that he could not deny that these men had had the better of the Scriptural argument. Whether for this reason or because tolerance was one of his principles, he was unwilling to see young Stogdon suffer

[1] John Fox, 'Memoir of himself' in *MR*, xvi (1821), 131. Cf. Brockett, 78–80. Fox was mistaken over one matter. The events that he records took place in 1710 and the work of Whiston could not have been *Primitive Christianity*, 1711–12. The work which was the subject of the correspondence was in fact 'Directions for the study of divinity' in Whiston's *Sermons and Essays*, 1709 (W. Whiston, *Memoirs*, 1749, i. 146–50). Fox's use of Unitarian for this period is unusual. For Thomas Emlyn see H. J. McLachlan in *UHST*, xiii (1963), 19–21.

[2] Stogdon wrote to Clarke, in a letter dated October 29, 1717 (preserved in the British Museum) 'Ten thousand thousand thanks to you for the benefit I have received from the incomparable work, your *Scripture-doctrine:* and it has in a great measure delivered me from the fetters which prejudice, education and tradition had thrown on my reason and understanding'.

for his independence of thought and he was not unmindful that Stogdon was a more than promising student who had already done useful service to the Dissenting cause in controversy with the Church of England.[1] The time was approaching when Stogdon should apply to the Exeter Assembly for ordination but 'there were apprehensions that it would raise a feud and contention'. Rather than risk a rebuff, three of the Exeter ministers, Peirce, Hallett and John Withers, gave Stogdon a letter of commendation which led to his appointment to a small but useful sphere of ministerial activity in the neighbouring county of Somerset, beyond the bounds, and out of the clutches, of the Exeter Assembly. It was a charitable action which nevertheless led to serious trouble.

The following year, in March 1718, the Managers of the Presbyterian Fund in London, took the same lenient view of Stogdon's deviations from orthodoxy as the three Exeter ministers had done and made him a grant from the Fund. The Managers knew of his unorthodoxy and some of them were made uneasy by the decision. We are told that in the meeting that took this decision, 'Mr. Tong was silent for some time, and then went out'. The orthodox stalwarts in Devon might have maintained a similar disapproving silence, had not the news burst upon them in August that Stogdon was about to be ordained at Shepton Mallet over the border in Somerset. Patience was exhausted and one of the Devonshire ministers wrote to Mr Tong in London giving a gloomy picture of the growth of Arianism in Devonshire. In London Tong gathered a number of ministers together to discuss the situation and a reply was returned deprecating the ordination of candidates unsound on the Trinity and recommending a warning to congregations if ministers were suspected of unorthodoxy. In September the Exeter Assembly met for what turned out to be extraordinarily stormy debates. An effort to stampede the ministers into a declaration against Arianism met with tough opposition especially from the ministers who had hustled Stogdon out of the county by their letter of commendation. This

[1] In 1714 Stogdon had written *A defence of the Caveat against the new sect of Anabaptists, &c. In answer to Mr. Reed's Reply.* The *Caveat*, of which this was a defence, had been written by John Withers, one of the ministers to sign the letter which led to Stogdon's appointment outside Devon. The new 'Anabaptists' were Anglican clergy who insisted upon 're-baptizing' converts from Dissent, because they refused to recognize Dissenters' baptisms. Cf. Alex. Gordon, *Addresses Biographical and Historical*, 1922, 126–8.

did nothing to allay apprehension about the growth of Arianism, and the Trustees of the Exeter ministers' fund, commonly known as the 'Thirteen', wrote to ministers in London for guidance as to the best action to take about those of their own ministers who had aroused suspicions. Edmund Calamy was one of the ministers applied to and his hand may be discerned in the cautious advice that came back to the Trustees that they should consult with respected ministers in their own neighbourhood, since they would have a better knowledge than London ministers could have about the situation with which they had to deal.[1]

## John Shute Barrington

The Exeter Trustees acted on the advice given, by choosing seven respected local ministers as advisers, often referred to as the 'Seven'. Whether by design or because respectability and conservatism coincided the men they chose were of the orthodox party.[2] In the meantime Peirce, who could see trouble brewing and who could have no confidence in the advisers chosen by the Trustees, was writing to London in order to try to save the situation. One at least to whom he wrote was John Shute Barrington (later to be Lord Barrington) who was at the time taking a prominent part in the attempt in Parliament to secure the repeal of the legislation which disabled Dissenters from holding office in central and local government. Since 1717 he had been one of the lay members of the Committee of the Three Denominations which had done much to promote the repeals. Barrington's had been a liberal influence on this Committee; early in 1718 he had initiated a paper of advice to ministers 'full of the most generous and free principles imaginable, particularly not only precepts of charity to all Christians, but one paragraph express to exhort them to carry it well to the Deists and maintain their liberties, because any hardship used to them would be contrary both to humanity and the Christian religion, and the rest . . . of the same strain'.[3]

When the Trinitarian controversy arose in Exeter one of its

---

[1] Thomas in *JEH*, iv. 163–70. Cf. Brockett, 82–8.

[2] Allan Brockett points out that the choice of the 'Seven' was probably determined by their proximity and accessibility, but the upshot was the same (Brockett, 90).

[3] It would be valuable if a copy of this paper in full could be located. Quoted here from *MR*, xvi. 633—a letter from Thomas Secker to John Fox, dated May 20, 1719.

unfortunate consequences was to impede the Bill for the repeals in
Parliament, for one of the Harley family, Sir Edward Harley, who
had once been a Dissenter and who was still the chief manager of
the Wharton bequest for Dissenting ministers, was trying to clog
the Bill with a provision requiring subscription to Trinitarian
orthodoxy. During the passage of the Bill in the winter of 1718–19
Harley's amendment nearly succeeded. For this, if for no other
reason, Barrington was anxious to quiet the dispute in Exeter, but
also he was himself a man of the newer more tolerant ideas. He had
been a friend of Locke during his life-time and was still a devoted
disciple. To him it seemed that the best way to deal with the
dangers in Exeter was to persuade the Committee of Three Denominations in London to take the matter in hand and prepare specific
advice to deal with the situation. For this purpose he drew up a
paper of 'Advices' and laid it before the Committee on February 5,
1719. The main substance of the 'Advices' was, first, to secure that
when accusations of heresy were made they should not be left to
the vagaries of rumour and gossip but should be substantiated by
adequate witnesses; and, second, to secure that, if it became necessary to apply a test of orthodoxy, that test should be adherence to
Scripture as the perfect and only rule of faith and not to any formula
of merely human composition. The Committee approved the
'Advices' after making sundry alterations, but not without a good
deal of argument. The Committee also took the further step,
against Barrington's advice, of deciding to lay the 'Advices' before
the full body of London ministers 'that so', as Calamy reports,
'what was done might have the more weight'. It was suspected that
this move was in reality a delaying tactic, for time was running
short. In view of the deliberations in London, the 'Seven' Devonshire advisers had been persuaded to defer a meeting on February
9th when they would have delivered their very different advice to
the Exeter Trustees, but they could not be expected to defer
presenting their advice indefinitely, especially when they had heard
of the much more liberal advice that was to be expected from
London.[1]

---

[1] Brockett, 89–90. Thomas in *JEH*, iv. 165–71. Barrington and six other laymen
were members of the Committee of Three Denominations at this time (since 1717—
T. Crosby, *History of the English Baptists*, 1738–40, iv. 172). Barrington brought his
proposal direct to the Committee of Three Denominations on February 5th.

*The General Body Meets*

The paper of 'Advices' initiated by Barrington was brought before the General Body of London Ministers, meeting at Salters' Hall, on February 19th. But preliminaries prevented it from being considered until a second meeting on February 24th, when the crucial debate took place. The 'Seven' in Exeter had consulted with friends in London and the nature of their proposed three-point advice was known. It may have been in the Committee that it was decided to tack on to Barrington's 'Advices' the first and part of the third clause from the proposed advice of the 'Seven', omitting the second. The first two clauses of this advice ran as follows,

> 1. That there are some errors in doctrine, that are a sufficient foundation for the people to withdraw from the communion of their ministers holding such errors. 2. That the denying the true and proper Divinity of the Son of God, viz. that he is one God with the Father, is an error of that nature, contrary to the Holy Scriptures and the common faith of the reformed Churches.[1]

It did not go unnoticed that the Committee had omitted the second clause and the debate in the General Body of Ministers took place on an attempt to have this second clause included in the London 'Advices' along with the first and part of the third which it had been agreed to insert. It was obvious that the inclusion of this second clause, asserting the central doctrine of the Trinity, would have prejudged the issue as to whether the disputed doctrine was or was not in accord with Scripture and it would have defeated Barrington's purpose, which was to allow a latitude of interpretation where Scripture was not self-evidently clear. Eventually a division was taken. Those who were against inserting a declaration concerning the Trinity in the 'Advices' were to go up into the gallery, while the others remained below. As the division proceeded slogans were bandied about. 'It was very indiscreetly called out by some persons,

---

[1] James Peirce, *Western Inquisition*, 171; *Account of the reasons* [by Josiah Eveleigh], 1719, 10; Brockett, 90. Alexander Gordon mysteriously attributed to the first clause an importance that it did not possess, seeing in it 'a charter of Independency in its most unrestricted form' (A. Gordon, *Addresses Biographical and Historical*, 151—cf. 137–8). That the clause had no such implication is proved by the fact that Robert Wodrow saw nothing extraordinary in similar action in Scottish Presbyterianism. His words to William Livingstone were 'Your people are better natured than many here, who leave ministers upon far less provocations' (*Correspondence*, 1843, iii. 162).

*You that are against persecution, come up stairs!* Which was pretty evenly balanced by one on the other side, calling out, *You that are for the doctrine of the Trinity, stay below!*' When order was restored after complaints about these misrepresentations and the division was allowed to proceed quietly, it was found that those against the inclusion of a declaration on the Trinity in the 'Advices' had carried it by 57 votes to 53. It had been a long debate and the meeting adjourned immediately to proceed with the consideration of the 'Advices' seriatim at a further meeting called for the following week on March 3rd.[1]

## The Bible Carried it by Four

It had been a momentous decision in favour of the Baxterian principle of Scripture sufficiency. Sir Joseph Jekyl, Master of the Rolls, as an interested onlooker, summed up the whole in one brief summary that 'The Bible carried it by four', which came about as near to the truth as six words could.[2] Report has it that Benjamin Hoadly, who, as we have seen, had already suffered for the same cause from Tory elements in his own church, 'was pleased to say on this occasion that it was the first convocation or assembly of divines since the time of the apostles that carried a question for liberty'.[3] Back in the West Country Hubert Stogdon applauded the 'noble spirit of Christian liberty in London', while Barrington published the decision to the world as a 'noble stand', a phrase which Daniel Wilcox (whom we have already met dismissing his assistant) adopted as a handy title for a bitterly satirical opposition pamphlet in the stormy pamphlet war that ensued. Thomas Morgan of the Newtonian confession of faith was amongst the many who joined in; he lectured Mr Tong and others on *The Nature and consequences of enthusiasm*.[4] Enthusiasm in its technical sense of laying claim to private revelation was becoming a recognized evil in the eighteenth century and the accusation of enthusiasm was not calculated to be a compliment to sober Presbyterians.

[1] Thomas in *JEH*, iv. 171–2.
[2] William Whiston, who reports this remark (*Memoir*, 1749, i. 220) that 'the Bible carried it by four', counted the list of names of those who signed the Nonsubscribers' 'Advices' and found the number to be 73. He then deducted 4 and found the Subscribers to number 69. This was excellent mathematics, but deplorable history, for the numbers signing the 'Advices' were quite different from the numbers on either side in the division on February 24th.          [3] Thomas in *JEH*, iv. 181.
[4] 1719. Other pamphlets from Morgan's pen followed in the next three years.

L

*Disruption*

The defeated minority at the meeting on February 24th spent the week before the next meeting on March 3rd in rounding up support for an effort to get the decision reversed or its effect nullified. According to one report,

> several of our brethren renewed a debate to the same purpose with that which before was agreed should be laid aside 'till we had gone through the advices', and would not acquiesce in the determination of the majority, even in the method of proceeding. Instead of this they withdrew from our Assembly and went by themselves to subscribe their names to a certain roll of paper wherein was contained (as we were told) the first Article of the Church of England and the 5th and 6th Answers of the Assembly's catechism.[1]

Thus the General Body split into two factions: the seceders, from their action in demanding a subscription to the Trinitarian Doctrine, earned for themselves the name of Subscribers, while those who remained with the Moderator and continued deliberations upon the Committee's 'Advices' came to be called Non-Subscribers. Eventually, after two more meetings attended only by the Nonsubscribers the 'Advices' were completed and despatched to Exeter accompanied by a letter in which the Moderator was careful to say that the 'Advices' came from men who were themselves orthodox on the doctrine of the Trinity. So ended the Salters' Hall debates.[2]

In Exeter the 'Advices' came too late. The 'Seven', after postponing their meeting on February 9th, met again on March 4th (doubtless after hearing the outcome of the London meeting on February 24th when their own crucial second clause had been voted down by a majority of four) and tendered their uncompromising advice to the Exeter Trustees without waiting to hear of any further developments from London. The Trustees lost no time in requiring the Exeter ministers to subscribe to the Trinitarian doctrine. Peirce and Hallett refused and were ejected. By the time the dreaded London advice came down to Exeter Peirce had already (on March 15th) preached to a hastily organized new meeting, where he and Hallett became colleagues.[3]

---

[1] *Authentick Account*, 1719, p. [19].     [2] Thomas in *JEH*, iv. 175.
[3] Brockett, 92–5.

We need not pursue the subsequent dispute into the multifarious ramifications of the controversy in the public press nor recount the steps taken by the Subscribers belatedly to nullify the effect of the official London 'Advices' by adopting and sending 'Advices' of their own of a very different character. These subsequent angry proceedings did nothing to heal the wounds caused by the split. We have rather to consider its long-term consequences.

Had the controversy been confined to Devonshire it might well have been remembered only as a rather disgraceful local affair to be consigned eventually to the limbo of forgotten things, but Barrington's intervention had brought it on to the national stage and diverted attention away from particular dogmas to the whole question of dogmatic authority. As a result the London ministers had divided over a matter of vital principle that would have far-reaching consequences all over the country and down the years. It had created a watershed between liberal and creed-bound Dissent, a watershed tending to carry Presbyterians one way and Independents the other.

### The Differences Denominational?

In the Salters' Hall split itself each of the three denominations had been to some extent divided internally. The Baptists were nearly equally divided between the General Baptists, who almost all sided with the Nonsubscribers, and the Particular Baptists, who were almost all Subscribers. Leaving the Baptist votes aside, the Nonsubscribing majority was made up largely of Presbyterians with a mere handful of Independents, while the minority was made up of most of the Independents together with an almost equal number of the older and more conservative Presbyterians.[1] The

[1] No analysis of the denominational allegiances of those participating in the crucial vote of February 19th is possible for no division list has survived, if ever one was made. But analyses of the list of signatories put out by either side, by the Non-subscribers in the *Authentick Account* and by the Subscribers in *True Relation*, notably by F. J. Powicke in *CHST*, vii. 165 ff. (cf. *Transactions of the Bapt. Hist Soc.* v. 172 ff. and Tudur Jones, 136). Subject to slight revision of Powicke's analysis the allegiance of the signatories by denominations is as follows:

|  | Scottish Presb. | English Presb. | Independents | General Bapts. | Partic. Bapts. | ? | Totals |
|---|---|---|---|---|---|---|---|
| *Authentick Account* (Non-subscribers) | 0 | 48 | 8 | 14 | 2 | 1 | 73 |
| *True Relation* (Subscribers) | 3 | 27 | 28 | 1 | 14 | 5 | 78 |

figures make it apparent that at the time of the split the division was far from being wholly along denominational lines; but a dozen years later it had virtually become so. During these years several of the Presbyterians who had been Subscribers in 1719 are known to have 'disowned their subscriptions', while at the end an observer could report that the Independents in London were solidly Calvinist, with one doubtful exception, and that heterodoxy was almost wholly confined to the Presbyterians.[1] The difference had thus begun to take firmly denominational lines, though employing denominational names that had originally had ecclesiastical rather than doctrinal meanings.

It is clear that from the time of the split a tendency developed for men to gravitate to the denomination that they found more congenial on grounds of doctrine or of freedom of inquiry. Thus Nathaniel Lardner, who was to become famous for Biblical enquiries directed against the Deists and who had considerable influence later in undermining traditional orthodoxy, elected to be counted with the Presbyterians; he has often been reckoned as an Independent, and doubtless he was so originally, and so he has been counted as one of the few Independents to vote with the Nonsubscribers at Salters' Hall, but in 1730 he had come to feel more at home with the Presbyterians.[2] An opposite instance was that of Thomas Reynolds, friend and fellow-student of Edmund Calamy. At Salters' Hall he voted with the Subscribers. Soon afterwards he had a violent dispute with his assistant, James Read, who had taken the other side. Interrogate Read as much as he liked, he could get from him no admission of unsoundness on the Trinity, but it was enough for Reynolds that, though Read 'confessed the truth of the

Tudur Jones names as Independents who were Nonsubscribers, Moses Lowman, Jeremiah Hunt, Nathaniel Lardner, John Conder, Thomas Simmons, David Jennings, Arthur Shallet, John Eaton, Robert Lamb and James Read. The inclusion of James Read is a mistake, owing to a misreading of the Evans List of Dissenting ministers and congregations (D.W.L. MS. 38.4). Lardner later became Presbyterian. Conder distinguished himself by 'voting on both sides', i.e. he signed the subscription to the doctrine of the Trinity with the Subscribers and the 'Advices' of the Nonsubscribers; he did not sign the Subscribers' Advices.

[1] 1732 MS. Report p. 89. According to a letter of Andrew Gray, dated February 16, 1724/5, the Presbyterians, Jabez Earle, Daniel Mayo and John Barker had by that date disowned their subscriptions (Stirling Correspondence, University of Glasgow MSS., BE. IV. 106).

[2] Nathaniel Lardner, on becoming Assistant to William Harris at Crutched Friars, attached himself to the Presbyterians (Three Denom. Minutes pp. 11, 24).

doctrine, he quitted the importance of it'; so Reynolds dismissed him. Calamy called this 'a piece of management I could no way approve of, though I heard what could be offered on both sides distinctly'. John Evans, with whom Reynolds had collaborated in joint church activities, took Read for his own assistant on his dismissal by Reynolds. Reynolds soon found his Presbyterian associations uncongenial and, although he did not sever his official connection with the Presbyterians, his sympathies lay elsewhere.[1]

## The Denominational Funds

A further reason for the progressive widening of the division between the two denominations was the contrasting policies of the two London Funds, which, as we have already seen, originated in the split of the Common Fund in 1695. In December 1719, Edmund Calamy, who prided himself on avoiding entanglements with either party, but who was to all intents and purposes a Nonsubscriber, carried a motion on the Presbyterian Fund that the side a minister took in the controversy should be disregarded in considering his case for a grant from the Fund.[2] This was in complete contrast with the policy of the Congregational Fund. Joseph Dodson in Cumberland, whom we have already met expressing his dislike of Calvinist intolerance, had been receiving grants from both Funds, and he now had a serious complaint that the sermon in which he had criticized Calvin had led to the withdrawal of his grant, but it was the Congregational, not the Presbyterian, Fund that took this action.[3] Nor was this an isolated instance of discrimination, for at a later date it became the established practice under the rules of the Congregational Fund to investigate a man's opinions before making a grant and to restrict grants to those who were orthodox.[4] The

[1] Thomas Reynolds, *Answer to the Revd. Mr. Simon Browne's Letter*, 1723, 14. See below, p. 204 ff.

[2] Presb. Fund Minutes, December 7, 1719 (ii. 357). This was amended at the following meeting (January 4, 1719, 20, ii. 358) to read 'any otherwise than the law directs', referring to the requirement under the Toleration Act for ministers to subscribe the Anglican Articles. But like the provision in the Toleration Act—Calamy for one never qualified under the Act by signing the Articles—the provision was something of a dead letter from the start. The Managers of the Fund continued to make grants without asking questions about doctrine.

[3] Presb. Fund Minutes, ii. 327, 346, 366, 390. Cf. above, p. 136.

[4] Cong. Fund Minutes. For this period they are not extant, but when resumed in 1738, it is with a careful revision of the rules and the inauguration of a book in which records of applicants' orthodoxy were entered.

Presbyterian Fund made no such restrictive rule and continued to make grants to orthodox and unorthodox alike. As much as anything this difference in the policies of the two Funds determined that Salters' Hall should be a watershed not only in London but all over the country and that the names Presbyterian and Independent should be attached to the two different outlooks. With the poorer churches in the country only orthodox ministers could gain admission to the Congregational Fund, so that the less orthodox naturally gravitated to the other Fund and made it, as time went on, progressively heterodox.

It would, however, be putting the cart before the horse to attribute the progressive liberalization of Presbyterian congregations to the policy of the Presbyterian Fund. The growth of liberalism was far from being a movement confined to the grant-aided, usually country, churches, but, as we shall see in a later section, the liberal lead came from the churches and their ministers in the great towns, churches that needed no grants and so were not affected by the contrasting policies of the two Funds. And in London it was not merely the great influence of Edmund Calamy and of one or two others that brought about a settled liberal policy; it was a greater sensitiveness amongst ministers and laymen alike to the implications of their Presbyterian heritage from Baxter, and a deeper realization that dissension was inevitable and concord impossible if reliance were placed elsewhere than on the accepted authority of the Bible and of Reason.[1]

Although the controversy at Salters' Hall was precipitated by Clarke's *Scripture-doctrine of the Trinity*, the underlying root difference went much further back to the semi-Arminian reaction against the more inhuman forms of Calvinism. The Antinomian Controversy in the Sixteen Nineties revealed a tendency of the two denominations to part company over matters of doctrine as well as over matters of church polity. The importance of Salters' Hall was that it brought back this double difference between Presbyterians and Independents at a time when it was hoped that it was passing away. Moreover it largely replaced the ecclesiastical by the theological differences. By 1718, before the conflict broke out, amity between the two denominations had progressed so far that there was

---

[1] Leading London laymen with advanced views are listed in *MR*, xiv (1819), 107. Cf. Dudley Ryder, *Diary*, 1939.

real hope that the union of 1691 might be restored and the dividing names dropped in favour of the more general term of Protestant Dissenter.[1] It may to some extent be indicative of the closer harmony that had been growing up that when the conflict did break out both denominations were split internally, although in significantly different proportions. Some of the most outspoken leaders of the Nonsubscribers were indeed drawn from the ranks of the Indepents. Moses Lowman, who was writing in what was to become the Nonsubscribing interest as early as 1716, affords a striking example. Barrington, too, whose 'Advices' were the immediate cause of the split was a member of an Independent church although he sat on the Three Denominations Committee as a lay representative appointed by the Presbyterians—another sign that the older denominational lines of demarcation were being softened.[2] Indeed it is not too much to say that, had there been no Presbyterians with their Baxterian or semi-Arminian tradition to siphon off the incipiently liberal elements in Dissent, the split would have been wholly internal to the Independent denomination, just as it was in New England at a later date. But, as things were, one of the chief effects of the Salters' Hall controversy was to act as a watershed carrying the Independents increasingly one way theologically and the Presbyterians another and to bring back into extended use the older denominational names to differentiate the two streams. As a consequence churches with mixed denominational origins and churches whose denominational origins were beginning to be lost in the mists of obscurity came to bear the familiar denominational labels quite regardless of their origins and solely because they were carried into this or that stream on either side of the watershed.[3]

---

[1] Calamy, *Hist. Account*, ii. 401, speaking of 'closer union' says, 'The thoughts of several were working that way, and somewhat of that nature had been actually under the consideration of some of them, and some previous steps had been taken in order to it'. (The quotation is from the original manuscript, which is fuller and more definite than the printed version—*UHST*, xiii (1966), 168–71.)

[2] Barrington was of Thomas Bradbury's congregation (Congregational). He left it for Jeremiah Hunt's congregation (also Congregational) after the split at Salters' Hall because Bradbury was an embittered Subscribing partisan. Cf. Alex Gordon, 'Our Presbyterian forefathers' in *CL*, xi (1885), 623–4.

[3] Amongst Unitarian congregations that were originally Congregational may be counted Duckinfield and Bridport.

*The Division not over Dogmas*

This rejuvenation of the older denominational labels for theological differences is an odd and remarkable feature of the situation. It looks like an unaccountable pouring of new wine into old bottles. Why were not the new parties called Arians and Trinitarians, or Arminians and Calvinists? The truth is that these opposing terms would have been inappropriate for, if one party could properly be called Trinitarian and Calvinist, the other could not be called Arian or Arminian, for their protest was not against certain doctrines but against being enslaved to doctrines unless they were convinced that they had scriptural warrant.[1]

There were plenty at the time to confuse the issue by maintaining that the controversy was merely for and against the Trinity. There were also those who could not believe that the Nonsubscribers really meant what they said when they claimed that their opposition was not to the doctrine of the Trinity or to any other doctrine as such. Robert Wodrow in Scotland persisted in believing that there could be no 'plausible reason for non-subscribing, but some real dislike of the doctrine declared in the confession or articles to be subscribed'.[2] But whatever may have been the case at Exeter and elsewhere, the controversy in London at Salters' Hall was not over the acceptance or rejection of the doctrine of the Trinity, but about the question how the truth of this and other doctrines should be decided; it had been over whether the decision should be referred to the confessions of faith or to the Bible and whether the Scriptural plank in the Arminian platform should be adhered to. There would have been small ground for quarrel if the Bible had been as explicit as the Athanasian Creed on the doctrine of the Trinity. But it was not, and with Clarke's *Scripture-doctrine of the Trinity* as an awful example of departure from the Trinity of the Creed on supposedly Scriptural grounds, it was not as clear to the Subscribers as it had been to Baxter that Scripture was a sufficient safeguard for orthodox doctrine. But the admission of the Subscribers that the Bible was no sure safeguard was tantamount to an admission that the doctrine in dispute was not to be certainly found there. If so, what right had they to insist upon it? Theirs was a more serious admission than any

---

[1] The difference does, indeed, go back as far as Cromwellian times, which makes the Presbyterian name more appropriate than might at first sight seem the case.
[2] Robert Wodrow, *Correspondence*, ed. T. M'Crie, 1843, iii. 57.

made by the Nonsubscribers. The Nonsubscribers for their part insisted that theirs was 'the more effectual course to prevent the growth of errors concerning the doctrine of the Trinity'. At this the Subscribers were incredulous and called the assertion 'very extraordinary' and pointedly added that 'it will be *difficult* to persuade *any* of the *same faith* with us of the justice of this *apprehension*'.[1]

It is not hard to see that the underlying difference lay between those who were willing to rely on the integrity of human reason and those who regarded it as corrupt. Some doggerel verses of the day gave popular form to the Nonsubscribers' faith:

> All who with judgment view'd the case
>   Said Liberty was good,
> And wisely saw no truth could fail
>   Which on that bottom stood.[2]

Free inquiry was the term that came into vogue. Nevertheless the Subscribers were right that the days of Calvinist orthodoxy were numbered if they conceded their adversaries' point.

Thus the clash was not between one dogma and another, but between dogma on one side and the refusal to impose (or submit to) dogma on the other. That is why, in what has gone before, we have spoken of the liberal movement in Dissent. The liberal movement was not so much that characterized by the various doctrines that have at one time or another been thought of as liberal, but the movement to leave the mind free and unfettered in its search for truth.

## Two Estimates of Freedom

Edmund Calamy was quite definite that, as he bluntly told George Chalmers, the doctrine of the Trinity was 'not the point in question' at Salters' Hall.[3] Similarly Isaac Watts, in ladylike prose, wrote to Cotton Mather in America, 'I confess, if the matter of debate at London were the glorious doctrine of the Trinity . . . there would be more just occasion for some fervour of spirit. . . . But while the subject of the contest in this city is reduced to this one point, viz. which is the best way to preserve truth and peace,

---

[1] Italics as in original. Thomas in *JEH*, iv. 185; *Authentick Account*, 30; *Vind. of the Subscribing ministers*, 1719, 47.

[2] *The Subscribers*, 1722.          [3] Calamy, *Hist. Account*, ii. 414.

whether by subscribing the words of Scripture or human forms, I think a happy medium might be found out to secure liberty and the gospel together . . .'.[1] At first sight it would appear that Watts and Calamy, one an Independent and the other a Presbyterian, were in complete agreement against subscription, and one begins to wonder why Watts did not carry as much weight with the Congregational, as Calamy did with the Presbyterian, Fund. But there was in fact a considerable and important difference. Calamy was prepared to be as bold as anyone in his defence of traditional doctrines by argument, but in his dealings with others and especially with younger ministers he made no attempt to put any restraint upon their intellectual freedom. In the cause of freedom he could quote, as Baxter might have done, Chillingworth's 'let all men believe the Scripture and that only, and endeavour to believe it in the true sense and require no more of others; and they shall find this not only a better but the only means to suppress heresy and restore unity'.[2] Though now a Nonconformist, Calamy in his thinking looked, as Baxter had done, to a church commensurate with the community and was unwilling to exclude from its service any man sincerely trying to follow Chillingworth's advice. Watts, with his different background, acted quite otherwise. Although at times his own orthodoxy was not above suspicion he wished nevertheless to maintain a standard of orthodoxy. If a student for the ministry presented himself, he would not indeed require from him a subscription to specific doctrines but he did require of him a statement of his faith in his own words, and if his statement was not considered adequate he was not accepted.[3] The student was thus left 'free'; if he did not satisfy, he could go elsewhere, but that was not a freedom that Watts was in a position to withhold, but it seems to be the sum total of what he meant by his 'medium . . . to secure liberty and the gospel together'. So far from Watts giving a liberal lead to the Congregational Fund, his was indeed the practice that the Fund actually adopted; it ascertained a man's opinions and rejected him if he did not come up to the required standard of orthodoxy. While

---

[1] Matthew Henry, *Disputes review'd . . . With a preface by I. Watts*, 1719, pp. v–vi. Cf. a letter of Isaac Watts to Cotton Mather, February 11, 1720 (Massachusetts Hist. Soc. MS.).       [2] Calamy, *Hist. Account*, ii. 417.

[3] Doddridge, *Corresp.* iii. 515 (September 18, 1740). He makes this requirement explicit in the letter to Cotton Mather, cited above.

the King's Head Society for the training of students, which was composed of the more persistent Subscribers, required its students to put their names to a confession of faith drawn up by their tutor, Abraham Taylor, the Congregational Fund attained the same ends by less ostentatious means.[1]

## Liberal Independents

Watts no doubt believed that he meant more by liberty than in fact he did, and there were certainly other established Independents who would not lightly let themselves be deprived of a liberty of thought that they had hitherto enjoyed. It is noteworthy that when the London Congregational Body which appointed representatives to the Three Denominations Committee was reorganized in 1727, there was a hot dispute as to the qualifications to be required of a minister before he could be accepted on the official list of the denomination. Some wished to have it laid down that 'those only should be accounted Congregational ministers who some way or other manifested their agreement to the Savoy confession of faith and order of Congregational churches'. Others argued in favour of admitting 'those who had been known and approved preachers and chose to be ranked among the Congregational ministers, and did not design to vote in the Body of Presbyterian or Baptist ministers'. It was significant of a lingering respect for a fuller freedom that the latter more liberal method was adopted.[2]

It is possible to exaggerate the extent to which the Independents closed their ranks. The extent to which they did in fact do so may also be misleading if it is read back into the time before 1719, and before the dogmatic reaction set in. We have already noted amongst leading Nonsubscribers the names of Independents such as Moses Lowman, Nathaniel Lardner and John Shute Barrington. Others could be added to the list.[3] And there would always be Independents exercising a large measure of freedom—as indeed there are in most denominations, whatever the restrictions imposed.

[1] King's Head Society Minutes (New College, London, MS.), vol. i, printed statement of faith with signatures attached.
[2] T. S. James, *History of the Congregational Board* (also printed in the *Congregational Year Book*, 1867, 409). It was also decided that the term 'Third Body' should be employed instead of Congregational to avoid the term Congregational being misapplied. Cf. Congregational Board Minutes, December 5, 1727.
[3] E.g. John Jennings of Kibworth and Thomas Rowe.

Nevertheless the distinction was established by these events that the Presbyterians exercised a genuine liberty within the communion of their church while the Independents came more and more to impose a standard of orthodoxy, and, though they might call it 'freedom within the Gospel',[1] or, with Watts, securing 'liberty and the Gospel together', it exhibited, if not a misunderstanding of what liberty of thought really entails and of the faith in human reason on which it rests, at least an unwillingness to trust to reason and to the integrity of the human mind. If they suspected that the Gospel as it had come down to them from Calvin and the Reformation was in peril, they were doubtless right, but the time might come when such an attitude would arouse more than the smile of a tolerant Bishop Hoadly at those who found it all 'right and good, just as Christ left it at first and Calvin found it above fifteen hundred years afterwards'.

## Presbyterian Arminian Trend

Liberty, which now became progressively the badge of the Presbyterians, was something to be used and not merely cherished. Wodrow was wrong in supposing that the 'reason for non-subscribing' was 'some real dislike of the doctrine . . . to be subscribed'. Had he said that the reason was a doubt whether the doctrine had more than mere human authority and a disinclination therefore to impose it he would have been nearer the mark. Freedom might well lead to certain doctrines being called in question. At the time of Salters' Hall the doctrine that chiefly aroused doubts was the doctrine of the Trinity; but this was only because of the recent controversy arising out of Samuel Clarke's *Scripture-doctrine of the Trinity*, which its enemies considered heretical, dubbing it Arianism. Arianism was a term of abuse which was doubly inappropriate. From the point of view of those who followed Clarke it was inappropriate because they claimed that their belief, whether heretical or not, was not the heresy of Arius. It was still more inappropriate when applied to the Presbyterians, because the trend amongst them was not so much towards Arianism as towards Arminianism. Amongst the Nonsubscribers the two or three ministers who might properly have been called Arian or Clarkean

*Inquirer*, January 27, 1962 (letter of March 29, 1957).

were not invited (or not allowed) to put their names to the Non-subscribers' manifesto.[1]

In the years following the split those younger ministers who favoured Clarke's scheme defected to the Church of England where the tolerance of Arianism was greater than amongst the Presbyterians.[2] These defections were a minor scandal. In the 1732 Report, when the author comes to assessing the unorthodoxy prevalent amongst the Presbyterians, he knows of Calvinists, he knows of Middle Way men and he knows of Arminians, but amongst Dissenters he has no word about Arians. And this is not because he does not know about Arianism; he knows a great deal about it and he knows that this was the reason why a large number of younger ministers had conformed to the Church of England and he evinced no little surprise that 'those persons that could not digest one article of faith, are on a sudden so enlightened as to be convinced it is their duty to subscribe to 39'.[3] There can be little doubt that the trend amongst Presbyterians was towards Arminianism and not towards Clarke's Arianism, though his insistence upon Scripture-doctrine chimed well with their Arminianism. Indeed the term 'Scripture-doctrine' would be a favourite term on the title pages of their publications as time went by, but more often than not the doctrine that came under Scripture scrutiny was some item of Calvinist doctrine that was being found to be at once objectionable and unscriptural.

*Biblical Doctrine*

Although the trend was towards Arminianism the accusation of Arianism tended to stick, but if we ask what meaning it conveyed we find that it applied not so much to those who propagated Clarkean teaching as to those who did not propagate Calvinism and who endeavoured to maintain a catholic unity by keeping close to the Bible and by refusing, so far as they could, to be drawn into discussions not germane to its religious and moral teaching. F. J. Powicke in his bicentenary study of Salters' Hall, though he employed the traditional term Arian for these men, summed up what

---

[1] E.g. Martin Tomkins and Luke Langdon. It is also noticeable that the two Read brothers were not included in the first printed list of Nonsubscribers; they were however in the list printed in the *Authentick Account*. There may have been some doubt about them initially.

[2] Calamy, *Hist. Account*. ii. 503–6.          [3] 1732 MS. Report, p. 85/6.

they stood for under four heads that savour more of Arminianism than of Arianism[1]: (1) they were for intellectual freedom; (2) they held that salvation did not depend upon doctrinal agreement; (3) they laid exceptional stress upon the practical aspect of Christianity—a stress much needed in their day; (4) they were often pioneers of the modern study of the Bible. It matters little whether we use the term Arian or Arminian to describe them, though Arminian is clearly more appropriate. The truth is that they simply wished to get on with their primary duty as ministers to serve their flocks. They wished to avoid contentious disputes on what they held to be irrelevant issues; they wished to foster sound morality; they wished to avoid fanaticism and excess and believed that a humble and patient study of the Bible would foster all the essentials of religion.

The day was yet far off when Biblical authority would give way to the over-riding authority of reason and it was evident that the great need was to understand exactly what the Bible did in fact inculcate. Hence the years that followed Salters' Hall are remarkable for the number of ventures to do just this. In the years 1725 to 1727 James Peirce ventured to do this by his attempts to follow John Locke in the production of paraphrases of Pauline Epistles and, later, work on the same lines was taken up where he left off by George Benson. The year 1729 saw Daniel Mace's remarkable achievement in publishing a new text and translation of the New Testament, while the following year, 1730, saw the first of Nathaniel Lardner's long series of volumes entitled *The credibility of the Gospel history*, a once famous, and still valuable, source of Biblical criticism, called forth by the new urge to discover what Scripture really taught and to undermine the more slip-shod criticism prevalent in the Deist controversy.[2]

[1] F. J. Powicke, 'An Apology for the Nonconformist Arians of the Eighteenth Century' in *UHST*, i. 111–23.          [2] See above p. 147 ff. and below, p. 190.

# CHAPTER V

# THE BREAK-UP OF THE OLD DISSENT

*by* JEREMY GORING

## Dissent, a Dying Cause?

By the end of the third decade of the eighteenth century both
Presbyterians and Independents were beginning to be concerned
about a reported decline in their numbers and influence. Matters
were brought to a head in 1730 by the publication of an anonymous
*Enquiry into the state of the Dissenting interest*. The author of this
pamphlet painted a very pessimistic picture of the situation, suggest-
ing that men were losing sight of the fundamental principles of
Protestant Dissent: many of the younger Dissenters, he suggested,
'know no other reason for their separation than because 'tis a sin
for the Minister to wear a surplice or bow towards the altar'.[1]

This pamphlet, which turned out to be the work of a young
Presbyterian minister called Strickland Gough, provoked a good
deal of discussion. Gough's old tutor at Taunton academy, Henry
Grove, said that the laity were as much to blame as the ministers;
they had 'grown cold and indifferent to Nonconformity and in some
company been ashamed to be known for Dissenters, only because
the favours and preferments of the world and public fashion are
not on their side'.[2] But most other commentators disagreed with
Gough. Philip Doddridge, Independent minister at Northampton,
did not see any great cause for alarm; he said that the numbers of
Dissenters in his part of the country had increased in recent years.[3]
Another Independent, in a private report which was prepared at
Doddridge's instigation, gave the reassuring information that the
number of Dissenters attending public worship in London had
hardly altered since 1695, but he did point out that the population
of the city had risen in that time.[4] What he said was confirmed by
another anonymous writer with an intimate knowledge of the

[1] *Enquiry*, 26.
[2] H. Grove, *A sermon preached at the ordination of Thomas Amory*, 1731, 32.
[3] Doddridge, *Free thoughts*, 1730, 31.        [4] 1732 MS. report, 81–3.

London scene, who observed that, although the interest had been weakened by ministers conforming to the Establishment, several city congregations had recently been 'raised almost from nothing'. But he had to confess that in 'the two Southern counties' (presumably Hampshire and Wiltshire) economic factors had produced a decline: 'The strength of our interest lies amongst the middling and trading people; and therefore where trade and populousness decrease in a place, our meetings must be expected to grow emptier there.'[1]

The causes of this decline, if decline there was, were not only social and economic; they were also to a certain extent political. By 1730 the political situation, paradoxically, was not favourable to English Dissent, which, like many religious minorities, tended to flourish most when governments were unfriendly. The Whigs, who had been in power since 1714, were the Dissenters' allies; Walpole based his policy upon an expansion of trade and could not afford to lose the support of the powerful London merchants, the majority of whom were Dissenters. Admittedly he did not permit the repeal of the Test and Corporation Acts but he did allow an Annual Indemnity Act, which, although not in fact annual and not completely indemnifying, probably gave most Dissenters as much relief as they could hope for.[2]

## Politics and Dissent

In any event attempts to obtain the repeal of the Test and Corporation Acts in the 1730s did not arouse universal enthusiasm amongst Dissenters. Some provincial Dissenters, notably those in Bristol and Liverpool, pressed hard for repeal, but the majority of Londoners were content to leave matters to the committee of rather dilatory Deputies who from 1732 onwards were engaged in negotiations on the matter with Walpole. The first chairman of this committee was a leading London banker, Samuel Holden, who may or may not have been a creature of the Prime Minister. Holden himself was a Presbyterian but his principal supporters seem to have been Independents. Indeed many London Presbyterians were impatient at the slowness of his methods and agitated for a more active policy of lobbying M.P.s. Foremost among these advocates of activity was Benjamin Avery, who had left the Presbyterian

[1] *Some observations upon the present state of the Dissenting interest*, 1731, 9, 20, 30–1.
[2] N. C. Hunt, *Two early political associations*, 1961, 122 ff.

ministry after Salters' Hall and had gone into practice as a physician. In 1736 he succeeded Holden as chairman of the Deputies and thereafter there was a marked intensification in the efforts to obtain repeal. Walpole, however, remained adamant that the time for repeal was inopportune.[1]

Avery was the leading figure behind *The Old Whig*, a weekly newspaper which first appeared in March 1735, at a time when many London Presbyterians were feeling the need to re-affirm the principles of civil and religious liberty for which, they believed, the old Whigs of the seventeenth century had stood. The early issues of the journal championed the Englishman's right to freedom of worship, always provided of course that this right was not extended to Roman Catholics. Closely associated with Avery in this project were several London ministers, Benjamin Grosvenor, Samuel Chandler, George Benson and James Foster. All except one were Presbyterians: the exception was Foster who had begun life as a Presbyterian but had later become a General Baptist. All without exception belonged to the party that had opposed subscription at Salters' Hall. All would have joined wholeheartedly with Grosvenor in looking forward to a time when 'a man might travel with his own religion and conscience about him as safely through the whole world as every traveller wishes to do with his money'.[2]

## Presbyterians and Independents

The difference in outlook between Presbyterians and Independents which revealed itself in the campaign for the repeal of the Test and Corporation Acts was but one of a number of factors which were tending to separate the two denominations.[3] The old ecclesiastical differences, though less important than formerly, were still significant. The author of the 1732 report on the state of Dissent in London listed a number of these. While Presbyterian ministers were generally chosen by a mixed body of people including subscribers and church members, the Independents gave the right to vote only to fully accredited members.[4] While Presbyterians often

[1] N. C. Hunt, *Two early political associations*, 1961, 130 ff.; R. Thomas, 'Presbyterians, Congregationals and the Test and Corporation Acts' in *UHST*, xi. 124 ff.
[2] Colligan, *Eighteenth cent. Nonconf.*, 40.
[3] Cf. above, p. 163 ff.          [4] 1732 MS. report, 93–4.

M

admitted people to communion on the sole authority of the minister, the Independents invariably required prospective members to give an account of their experience that satisfied the whole church.[1] Again, Presbyterians, when they assembled for days of prayer, 'never do it as a church, but their doors are open to all comers'.[2]

This policy of opening their doors to all 'sincere' comers had the disastrous consequence, so this critic maintained, of destroying the purity of the church; they 'admit all sorts of persons that will but say they are Christians into their communion, be they Arminians, Calvinists, Free Thinkers, Arians or Socinians; it is all one to them'.[3] Unlike the Independents the Presbyterians were unwilling that the use of their meeting-houses should be restricted to special gatherings of people set apart from the rest of society by a peculiar experience of God's saving grace and by a distinctive ecclesiastical organization; in their trust deeds they often made it clear that their buildings were for the use of Protestant Dissenters in general, not of Presbyterians in particular.

Further points of difference in ecclesiastical theory and practice were mentioned by Isaac Watts in an undated letter to his brother. He was writing of a rather earlier period, but what he wrote was probably as true of 1730 as it was of 1700. He placed particular emphasis on differences in ordination. Presbyterians were ordained to the ministry at large, Independents to that of a particular church. While Presbyterians were ordained by the laying on of hands of their ministerial colleagues, Independents preferred to restrict the role of ministers present to that of witnesses. In general the Independents tried in every way to minimize the importance of the minister: they tended to reverse the Presbyterian view that it was the minister's task to rule in the church and 'the people's duty to consent'.[4]

## Arian or Arminian

The greater freedom accorded to Presbyterian ministers may help to explain why they were on the whole more heterodox in their theology than their Independent brethren. In the 1730s the form that this heterodoxy took was not, as has sometimes been suggested,

[1] 1732 MS. report, 94–5.                    [2] Ibid. 96. Cf. Studies, 1964, 33–6.
[3] 1732 MS. report, 87.
[4] Watts, Posth. works, ii. 159–60; Studies, 1964, 31–3. Cf. above, p. 142.

Arianism.[1] Many Presbyterians may in fact have been Arians, but, as has been pointed out above, their Arianism was not a dominant factor in their thinking and preaching.[2] While it is true that from time to time and from place to place subscription to the doctrine of the Trinity did become an issue, it was more a symptom than a cause of friction. This was true even of the Exeter Assembly where subscription to the doctrine was compulsory for all ordination candidates from 1719 until 1753: as at Salters' Hall the fundamental issue was that of the sufficiency or insufficiency of Scripture. Outside the Exeter Assembly the Trinitarian question seems to have been the concern of only a small minority of Dissenters. Foremost among these was Isaac Watts, who attached unusual importance to the doctrine. In at least one case where the Trinity became a local issue at this period it transpired that Watts was behind it: at Kidderminster in 1743 those who were concerned with upholding orthodoxy were found to be using a set of questions supplied by the Doctor, the first of which read: 'Do you believe that Jesus Christ was God equal with the Father from all eternity?'[3] Another who was remarkable for the great store that he set by Trinitarian orthodoxy was James Sloss, minister of Castle Gate Independent chapel, Nottingham, who in 1736 preached eighteen sermons on 1 John v. 7 (a text which scholars had long ago shown to be of dubious validity) and thereby sparked off a long a bitter controversy.[4]

The continuous and universal cause of controversy in the fourth and fifth decades of the century was not Arianism but Arminianism. The Lime Street lectures organized by strictly orthodox London Independents in 1730-1 for the express purpose of countering 'the errors of the day' were all on such subjects as Particular Election, Particular Redemption, the Imputation of Adam's Sin and the Insufficiency of Natural Religion.[5] Moreover, Strickland Gough's

[1] The emphasis upon Arianism as the major heresy of the age is found, e.g. in Colligan's *Arian movement*, where it is stated that 'an analysis of the pastorates at the Presbyterian and Independent meeting-houses in England proves that between the years 1730 and 1750 very few of them were untouched by Arianism' (p. 93). If 'Arminianism' be substituted for 'Arianism' the truth of this statement is indisputable.

[2] See above, p. 172 f.

[3] Benson MSS. (Bourn to Benson, October 7, 1743, and Bourn to Watts, December 2, 1743).

[4] A. R. Henderson, *Castle Gate, Nottingham*, 1905, 140 f.; Sloss, *Doctrine of the Trinity*, 1736.

[5] *A defense of some important doctrines of the gospel*, 1732, pp. iv-vi.

delightful tale of 'the lady who would not suffer her daughter to marry an Arminian merely because he was so' seems to confirm that it was Calvin's scheme rather than that of Athanasius which was popularly believed to be in danger of demolition.[1]

The London survey of 1732 mentioned Arianism along with Socinianism and Deism but made it clear that it was 'the spreading of Arminianism which generally leads the van'.[2] It found that only nineteen out of forty-four Presbyterian ministers were entirely free from the taint of this form of heterodoxy, while all but one of the Independents were classified as orthodox Calvinists.[3] These figures are probably not strictly accurate: for example, among the Independents, Watts, whose Baxterian principles were soon to cause him to lose favour with the leading Independent lay patron William Coward,[4] is listed as a Calvinist. More correctly he should have been set down not with strict Calvinists like Bradbury and Guyse but with Jeremiah Hunt, the one Independent who was regarded as of doubtful orthodoxy and against whose name was the bewildered comment: 'It is difficult to say what he is.'[5] This is another way of saying that Hunt was a 'Middle Way Man'.

Of the twelve London Presbyterians categorized as Middle Way men in 1732 two, Nathaniel Lardner and Edward Sandercock, had until recently been Independent ministers.[6] Their change of allegiance probably meant that the only Middle Way men left among the London Independents beside Watts were Hunt and Moses Lowman, both of them strong individualists presiding over small but select congregations of liberal-minded Dissenters and looking for intellectual companionship not to their own denominational brethren but to those more radical Presbyterians who were coming to be known as 'new scheme preachers'.

## New Scheme Preachers

By 1730 something resembling a liberal 'party' within Dissent was coming into being. Those who may be regarded as members

---

[1] *Enquiry*, 28.          [2] 1732 MS. report, 82–3.

[3] Ibid. 87–9, 91. The Presbyterian figures were: Calvinists 19, Arminians 13, Middle Way men 12.          [4] Doddridge, *Corresp.* iii. 251 (Farmer to Doddridge July 14, 1737).

[5] 1732 MS. report, 92.

[6] For Lardner, see above, p. 164. Sandercock is first listed as a Presbyterian in 1732. (Three Denoms. mins. i. 32). Consequently his name was struck off the list of London Congregational ministers and the words 'joined with the Presbyterians' added in the margin (*CHST*, ii, 51–2).

would have repudiated any partisan label; they thought of themselves as 'mere' Christians whose grand design was to make an end of all parties and factions in the Church. Nevertheless, though their meetings were informal, their programme ill-defined and their organization practically non-existent, this group of ministers did possess certain of the characteristics of a party. They had a common identity and a common purpose. They were for the most part younger men who had been educated at one or other of the more radical Dissenting academies and who had entered the ministry after Salters' Hall. In theology they were Arminian, in philosophy Lockean, in churchmanship Baxterian. Their over-riding purpose was the restoration of Christianity to its 'original purity'. But to their opponents who did not share their conception of the character of primitive Christianity, they were simply heretics, innovators, 'new scheme preachers'.

Foremost among these heterodox divines was Samuel Chandler, who ministered to the important Old Jewry congregation in the city of London from 1726 to 1766. The 1732 report lists him as an Arminian and describes him as a popular preacher whose sermons are 'more suited to bring people to church than to make serious Christians'.[1] Chandler, like Lardner, Lowman and Hunt, had completed his education at Leyden: it was here that he probably first met the works of Limborch, Locke's Dutch Remonstrant friend, whose History of the Inquisition he translated into English.[2] In 1729 he became involved in a long and bitter dispute with the strictly orthodox Independent John Guyse, who described one of Chandler's sermons as 'the boldest attack on the doctrines of the Reformation that ever was made by a Dissenter'.[3] But his sermons were not so much 'attacks' on Calvinist doctrines as affirmations of things which many Calvinists tended to overlook. The difference between his outlook and that of his more orthodox contemporaries is vividly illustrated by the titles of two sermons preached in London in 1746: *Christ the great propitiation* by Samuel Wilson, and *Christ the pattern* by Samuel Chandler.[4] By this date Chandler had become

[1] 1732 MS. report, 53, 89.

[2] Leyden was a stronghold of Arminian teaching, while Utrecht was more sternly Calvinistic. Chandler's translation of Limborch's work appeared in 1732.

[3] *A letter to a friend . . . a reverend bookseller*, 1729, 38.

[4] These two sermon titles are consecutive in the D.W.L. calendar of pamphlets. Samuel Wilson, a strict orthodox Independent, had been one of the Lime Street lecturers in 1731.

rather more orthodox in his theology than heretofore, calling himself a 'moderate Calvinist', but his emphasis on the significance of the life as distinct from the death of Christ was thoroughly Arminian.

Also on the Arminian list in 1732 was another of the *Old Whig* group, George Benson.[1] In 1729 he had been forced to vacate his Abingdon pulpit 'because his people would not swallow down Arminianism'[2]; he had then come to London and had succeeded in getting himself accepted by the congregation at King John's Court, Southwark, where the previous minister had been an orthodox Calvinist and a 1719 Subscriber. Unlike Chandler, Benson seems to have become progressively more heterodox in his views, and in later life seems to have embraced Socinianism. In so far as there was an Arminian 'party' among the English Presbyterians in the middle years of the century Benson (though he himself would have repudiated the idea most strongly) was its leader.

Part of Benson's importance lay in the fact that he kept up a regular correspondence with a large number of provincial ministers who shared his theological opinions. Among these was his fellow-Cumbrian, Henry Winder, minister at Castle Hey (later Benn's Garden) Chapel, Liverpool from 1718 to his death in 1752.[3] In his memorial tribute to his old friend Benson described how Winder had laboured to enlarge the minds of the Liverpool people: 'He showed them the injustice of all impositions on the consciences of men and that human authority in matters of religion is ridiculous and absurd.'[4] It was partly to illustrate this 'absurdity' that Winder wrote *A critical and chronological history of the rise, progress, declension and revival of knowledge*, the first instalment of which appeared in 1745 and for which subscriptions were paid by most of the leading theologians in Britain.

Another Liverpool Presbyterian in the circle was John Brekell, who had an influential ministry at Kaye Street from 1729 to 1769. Benson corresponded with him regularly and wrote a commendatory preface to his sermon on *The Christian warfare*, a work which contained a trenchant criticism of the Calvinistic doctrine of Election.[5] Here were struck the first notes of the theme later developed in Brekell's *Grounds and principles of the Christian revelation*:—

[1] See above, p. 133, 147.                    [2] 1732 MS. report, 8.
[3] For Winder see Anne Holt, *Walking together*, 1938, 100 ff.          [4] Ibid. 104.
[5] H. D. Roberts, *Hope Street Church, Liverpool*, 1909, 89–91.

To suppose that God can doom any man or number of men to eternal death and destruction, without any fault of theirs and before they have done any good or evil; such a notion is alike shocking to common sense and contrary to the principles of common equity. It is a notion no less dishonourable to God than uncomfortable and confounding to man.[1]

Similar views were being expressed at this time by a younger North Country Presbyterian minister in the Arminian circle, Josiah Owen, who had a highly successful ministry at Rochdale from 1740 to 1752. In 1735 Owen, then only about twenty-four years old, published a pamphlet in which he accused many of the Dissenting laity of 'a blind-zealous attachment to creeds and systems' which made life very difficult for their ministers. In a memorable passage he showed why it was that these creeds and systems were so often unacceptable to those who, like the Arminians, affirmed the absolute and unconditional goodness of God.

'Tis a common mistake for persons that would exalt and aggrandize the love of our Saviour to derogate from the love of the Father. . . . He whose goodness shines throughout all his works has been un-gratefully represented as very severe in his measures, if not arbitrary and cruel.'

His own creed was very simple and very Lockean: there is a God; Jesus is the Messiah; salvation is to be attained in the way that the Messiah has appointed.[2]

## Samuel Bourn's Catechism

The man with whom Benson corresponded most regularly was Samuel Bourn of the New Meeting, Birmingham. It has already been seen how at the outset of his career this sturdy individualist refused to subscribe the Assembly's Catechisms.[3] In 1736 Bourn, who believed that 'sincerity in searching after and in professing religious truth . . . is, as to God, the only acceptable orthodoxy',[4] published An address to Protestant Dissenters in which he made severe criticisms of the Catechisms, and two years later put out

---

[1] H. D. Roberts, Hope Street Church, Liverpool, 1909, 89-91.
[2] The difficulties and discouragements that attend the Dissenting ministry, 1735, 19, 39, 41.
[3] See above, p. 135.                    [4] Sermon on ordination of Job Orton, 1745, 41.

his own revised version of them.[1] At the same time he re-issued the revised catechism that had been quietly put into circulation a few years previously by James Strong of Ilminster.[2] This publication had been bitterly attacked by Guyse, who was particularly critical of Strong's suggestion (upon which the whole Arminian case turned) that it was 'now generally thought that the religious principles set forth in the Bible have been better understood in this present Age . . . than they had been in any since the primitive times' and furthermore that future generations would probably have an even better understanding than they had.[3]

Bourn's catechism was virtually an expanded version of that of Strong (who had recently died). Before publishing it Bourn had sent the manuscript to several leading Presbyterian divines to get their *imprimatur:* the book thus appeared with commendatory prefaces by Benson, Chandler, Grove, Amory and others and became something of an English Arminian 'manifesto'.[4] Nowhere has the essential spirit of rational Dissent been better expressed than in Bourn's introduction:

> Let your children know that religion is a nobler thing than sectarian bigotry, dry opinions and fruitless faith; that it lieth in the image of God on the soul, a likeness to God and Jesus Christ in justice, kindness and charity; that it consisteth in heavenly dispositions, devout affections, in rectitude of spirit, purity of soul and universal goodness.[5]

The work went into three editions, including a special popular one in 1748, and did much to spread Arminian ideas among the Presbyterian laity. To its influence may be attributed the fact that by 1759 the children of the Dissenters' charity school in Gravel Lane, Southwark were no longer instructed in the Westminster Assembly's Shorter Catechism but in 'the principles of common Christianity'.[6]

Most influential of all the Arminian writers was yet another friend and correspondent of Benson's, John Taylor. Taylor, whose

[1] *Lectures to children*, 1738. This catechism represents a more radical departure from orthodox Calvinism than that contained in Ostervald's *Grounds and principles of the Christian religion* (English translation 1704, 6th ed. 1751).

[2] Ibid. 276 ff.; for Strong's catechism see Olive M. Griffiths, *Religion and learning*, 1935, 134–5.

[3] Ibid. 276–7; Cf. [J. Guyse] *Remarks on a catechism*, 1735.     [4] James, 35.

[5] *Religious education begun and carried on in three catechisms*, 1748, p. xv. This was the 3rd ed. of his *Lectures to children*.

[6] Colligan, *Eighteenth-cent. Nonconf.*, 114.

introduction to Arminianism probably came through reading Limborch's works while a student at Whitehaven academy,[1] had settled
at Norwich in 1733 as assistant to the orthodox Peter Finch.
Apparently one of his first actions was to gather together a group of
people for the purpose of studying Clarke's *Scripture-doctrine of the
Trinity*.[2] This book inspired him not so much to preach an Arian
view of Christ as to re-affirm the old Arminian belief in Scripture
sufficiency, a belief that was given very forceful expression in his
own *Scripture-doctrine of Original Sin*, written in 1735 and published
in 1740. Here he made 'a free and candid examination' of what
today would be called the doctrine of Original Guilt. The first two
parts of the book, with their minute analysis of biblical texts and
lengthy footnotes in Hebrew and Greek, are a monument of careful
scholarship, but it is perhaps the third part, where the textual critic
turns moral philosopher and holds up some of the tenets of Calvinism to the light of reason, that made the biggest and most lasting
impression upon contemporary readers.

> What can be more destructive of virtue, than to have a notion
> that you must, in some degree or other, be necessarily vicious? . . . If
> we believe we are in nature worse than the brutes, and this doctrine
> represents it as such, what wonder if we act worse than the brutes?
> The generality of Christians have embraced this persuasion. And what
> wonder if the generality of Christians have been the most wicked, lewd,
> bloody and treacherous of all mankind?[3]

Written in such a vigorous style and in a mood of such strong moral
fervour, what wonder is it that to the generality of readers the book
came as a bombshell? An Irish minister voiced the feelings of many:
'It is a bad book and a dangerous book and an heretical book;
and, what is worse than all, the book is unanswerable.'[4] The effect
of the book, taken in conjunction with the same author's *Key to
the Apostolic writings* (1745) and *Scripture-doctrine of the Atone-
ment* (1751), was to hasten the decline of strict Calvinism as a
religious force not only in England but also in Scotland and
America.

A further effect of this and other Arminian writings was to
hasten the disappearance of the Baxterian Middle Way Men—to

---

[1] McLachlan, *Essays*, 140.    [2] Alex. Gordon in *DNB*.
[3] *Scripture-doctrine*, 1740, 251–2.    [4] Gordon, *Heads*, 37.

make them decide once and for all on which side of the fence they
would come down. By 1740 the Middle Way Men were becoming
fewer in number and rather weaker in influence. Formerly the
leading minister of this persuasion had been Edmund Calamy,
who, though 'a great opposer of narrow souls', preached acceptably
to a congregation that included both Arminians and strict Calvinists
like Sir Richard Ellys.[1] But Calamy had died in 1732.

## Doddridge and the Middle Way

On Calamy's death the leadership of the Middle Way Men may
be said to have devolved upon Doddridge, who, though an Independent, had been 'strongly besieged by Dr Calamy's people' to
succeed to his important Westminster Presbyterian pulpit.[2]
Doddridge, however, preferred to stay at Northampton, where he
had set up an academy, and from which central position he exerted
an unparalleled influence upon English Dissent. His theological
position was as central as his geographical one. He enjoyed the
confidence of men as far apart in doctrine as John Brekell of Liverpool and John Barker of Hackney. Throughout his life he tried with
varying degrees of success to steer a middle course between the
strict orthodoxy of most Baptists and Independents and the heterodoxy which was claiming an ever increasing number of the Presbyterians. He steadfastly refused to throw in his lot with either party.
'Nor will I ever purchase their friendship by running all the lengths
of their party zeal', he wrote of the strictly Calvinistic London
Independents[3]; but he might have said the same of the Arminians.
To the last he exercised the peculiar privilege of the Middle Way
Man, which was to be neither wholly Arminian nor wholly Calvinist
but, as the 1732 report put it, 'sometimes [to] preach one doctrine
and sometimes look toward the other'.[4] In 1734, when preaching in
London, a number of 'orthodox spies' in the congregation accused
him of Arminianism, a charge which he vehemently denied.[5] To the
Arminians on the other hand his preaching and teaching sometimes
appeared to be insufferably orthodox: in 1737 Bourn told Benson

[1] 1732 MS. report, 47. For Calamy, see above, p. 134 ff.
[2] Doddridge, Corresp. iii. 121. (Doddridge to his wife July 17, 1733.)
[3] D.W.L. MS. 38. 96. 28 (Doddridge to Daniel Neal November, 17, 1738).
[4] 1732 MS. report, 87–8.
[5] Doddridge, Corresp. iii. 163 (Doddridge to his wife June 21, 1734).

that he hoped that encouragement would be given to Rotheram's academy because 'we want a man to be a balance to that Northampton tutor'.[1]

Bourn was convinced, however, that Doddridge, Watts and the other Middle Way Men were really crypto-Arminians. 'I can hardly believe', he wrote in 1743, 'that Dr Watts is for absolute, arbitrary Election and Reprobation.'[2] A few months previously he had written to Doddridge in a similar vein and his letter eventually brought forth a 1,500-word reply from the Doctor denying the charge that he was concealing his true opinions. He could not understand why men should suspect him of 'being in what is generally called the Arian scheme'.[3] But it was not Arianism that Doddridge was suspected of; it was Arminianism. He had abandoned strict Calvinism and many felt that such a step must lead inevitably to Arminianism. As Josiah Tucker said to Doddridge in speaking of the Middle Way Men: 'I confess that I am not able to see how they CAN halt between these two opinions.'[4]

Doddridge was much hurt when someone described him as 'a double-dealer and an inconsistent man',[5] yet one feels that there was some truth in the charge. In his first published work he said that ministers ought, for the sake of the peace of the church, to use the 'favourite phrases' beloved of their congregations, even if these phrases were distasteful to them, and strongly commended the motto of St Paul, 'All things to all men'.[6] In one letter he could say that he was 'very happy in the reputation of an orthodox man'[7] and in another use 'orthodox' almost as a term of derision.[8] His adherence to the Middle Way was based upon at least two considerations. In the first place, like other peace-loving ecumenically-minded men (many of whom, incidentally, were Presbyterians), he hated to see the Dissenting interest weakened by theological controversy. In the second place, as the tutor of young men sent to him by orthodox London Independents, he was ever fearful

[1] Benson MSS. (Bourn to Benson March 23, 1737).
[2] Ibid. (Bourn to Watts December 2, 1743.)
[3] Doddridge, Corresp. iv. 137 (Doddridge to Bourn November 12, 1742).
[4] Ibid. 543. (Tucker to Doddridge July 23, 1747); cf. above, p. 135.
[5] Ibid. 423 n. (Doddridge to Wadsworth, c. 1745).
[6] Free thoughts, 27–9.
[7] Doddridge, Corresp. ii. 56 (Doddridge to his brother August 5, 1725).
[8] Ibid. iii. 207 (Doddridge to Barker, c. 1736).

of 'the quick end of my academy [through] the supply turning itself into a different channel'.[1] However, the best verdict on Doddridge (and on other Middle Way Men) is probably that of J. J. Tayler: 'Doddridge's religion consisted so much in feeling that it is not surprising it should have placed him in positions which to everyone but himself seemed inconsistent'.[2]

### The Deist Issue

On one issue, nevertheless, the Middle Way Men were not afraid to stand shoulder to shoulder with the Arminians, and that was in opposition to the Deists.[3] Ever since the appearance of John Toland's *Christianity not mysterious* in 1696 the liberal-minded Dissenters had been defending the Christian revelation against the attacks of Deists. They felt these attacks far more keenly than their orthodox brethren, who, as Bourn informed Benson, were 'more afraid of heresy than Deism'.[4] The heterodox Dissenters feared the Deists because they shared with them their appeal to reason. It was most embarrassing for the Arminian divines to find that reason, which they regarded as complementary to and confirmatory of Scripture, was being used by the Deists to undermine the authority of the sacred books. Toland had been a friend of Locke and it was easy for reactionaries to lump Arminians and Deists together as joint heirs of one master.

The Deistic controversy was greatly stimulated in 1730 by the publication of Matthew Tindal's *Christianity as old as Creation, or the Gospel a republication of the religion of nature*. This work, whose sub-title constituted a summary of many an Arminian sermon, elicited more than thirty replies: among those writing were James Foster and Simon Browne, the scholarly Presbyterian minister at Shepton Mallet.[5] But perhaps the most intense stage of the debate began in about 1739 and lasted until about 1745. At this period the situation was so serious that even Bourn took time off from the work of undermining Calvinism to fire a few shots in the direction of the Deists: 'The Antinomian bigots are a very troublesome and

[1] D.W.L. MS. loc. cit. (November 17, 1738).
[2] J. J. Tayler, *A retrospect of the religious life of England*, 1876, 265.
[3] For the Deistic controversies of this period see John Leland, *A view of the principal Deistical writers*, 1766.    [4] Benson MSS. (Bourn to Benson July 8, 1746).
[5] Browne had been a London minister and one of the leaders on the Non-subscribers at Salters' Hall. He wrote also against Thomas Woolston.

noisy people', he explained, 'but the Deists are more formidable adversaries.'[1] The principal Deistic adversaries at this time were Thomas Chubb, an Anglican disciple of Clarke, and Thomas Morgan, the former Presbyterian minister[2]: they were answered by a distinguished company that included, from the ranks of the Dissenters, Chandler, Watts, Lowman, Caleb Fleming and John Leland of Dublin. The most important single Deistic book at this period, however, was Henry Dodwell's *Christianity not founded on argument* (1741), which was particularly disturbing in that not everyone was quite sure on whose side the author was writing. 'That person best enjoys faith who never asked himself a question about it' was a statement that met with warm approval not only from Deists but also from Methodists—until Wesley warned them that the author was a wolf in sheep's clothing, whose purpose was 'to render the whole of the Christian institution both odious and contemptible'.[3]

Dodwell's pamphlet called forth a weighty reply from Doddridge, who published three Letters affirming *The perspicuity and solidity of those evidences of Christianity to which the generality of its professors among us may attain*. He upheld the place of rational argument in the propagation of Christianity and pointed out that in the Dissenting academies 'the rational evidences of natural and revealed religion, with such a view of the objections against both, are as regularly and as methodically taught as logic or geometry'.[4] In January 1743 he hastened his second Letter through the press because he heard that Benson was writing in the same controversy, 'and I doubt not on principles very different from mine.'[5] The principles underlying Benson's reply to Dodwell, *The Reasonableness of the Christian religion as delivered in the Scriptures*, however, were not so very different from those of Doddridge's Letters, for both men were in some measure disciples of Locke. Doddridge, it is true, did not, like Benson, quote four thousand words from Locke's *Reasonableness*, and he would certainly have shrunk from describing the philosopher as a 'prophet',[6] but the Lockean insistence on rational Christianity runs through both these replies.

[1] Benson MSS. (Bourn to Benson October 27, 1739).
[2] For Morgan, see above, p. 143.  [3] *DNB*, Henry Dodwell (d. 1784).
[4] *Perspicuity*, 1st letter, 47. In teaching Divinity Doddridge used a geometric method.
[5] Doddridge, *Corresp.* iv. 173 (Doddridge to his wife January 7, 1743).
[6] Benson, *Reasonableness*, 342.

The need to defend the authority of Scripture against the Deists provided some of the motive force behind the biblical research undertaken at this period by liberal-minded Presbyterian and Independent scholars.[1] The beginning of Lowman's interest in Old Testament study may be partly attributed to his anxiety to answer Anthony Collins's doubts about the value of Hebrew prophecy. The first of Benson's long series of *Paraphrases of the Epistles*, which carried on the systematic study begun by Locke and continued by Peirce, appeared at the height of the controversy aroused by Tindal's attempt to undermine the authority of the New Testament. The very title of Lardner's mammoth *Credibility of the Gospel history*, the first volume of which was published in 1730, was an assertion of something which the Deists were at that time vehemently denying[2]: Doddridge echoed the feelings of all who looked upon the Deists as the principal enemies of Christianity when, on receipt of Lardner's eighth volume in 1751, he described the work as 'so great a blessing to the Christian world'.[3]

Had Doddridge been able to foresee the eventual consequence of all this close attention to the Bible text he would probably not have been so enthusiastic. For the very books which were buttressing Christianity against Deism were also helping to lay the foundations of an even more dangerous doctrine—that of Socinianism. In detaching the Old Testament from the New, Lowman and Lardner were adopting the rational method of interpreting Scripture used by Socinus.[4] Moreover, as a result of their researches into the New Testament they came to hold a conception of the Logos that led inevitably to a Socinian view of Christ. Priestley became 'what is called a Socinian' after reading Lardner's *Letter on the Logos*, written in 1730 but not published until 1756, the year which also saw the posthumous publication (by Chandler, Lardner and Sandercock) of Lowman's epoch-making *Three tracts*. Lowman, Lardner, Benson and Fleming, the last of the old anti-Deists, were in fact if not in name the first of the new Socinians.

But in the period which saw the break-up of the Old Dissent Socinianism was not yet a force to be reckoned with. Up till the

[1] See above, p. 147 ff, 174.

[2] In 1729 Lardner had defended the historicity of the New Testament miracles against Thomas Woolston.

[3] Lardner, *Memoirs*, 1769, 105.          [4] Colligan, *Arian Movement*, 152.

1760s and beyond, Arminianism remained the prevalent form of heterodoxy among English Presbyterians. It was Arminianism which they preached in their sermons, propagated in their pamphlets and (perhaps most significant of all) taught in their academies.

## Dissenting Academies

The early Dissenting academies had been strictly orthodox in their teaching.[1] Richard Frankland of Rathmell and Timothy Jollie of Attercliffe, the founders of two of the most celebrated academies, had opposed any departure from Calvinist theology: Jollie had even forbidden the teaching of mathematics 'as tending to scepticism and infidelity'.[2] By 1730, however, all the leading academies had been affected by Arminian views. This more moderate outlook owed much to the influence of John Locke. The philosopher's works were read by students in nearly every academy and in some were prescribed reading.[3] In 1736 John Ball, the strictly Calvinistic minister at Honiton, who had been one of the leaders of the orthodox party in the Exeter controversy of 1718, referred disapprovingly to 'such new lights and great masters of reason as Mr Locke', who, he complained, 'is so much admired and recommended to students in divinity'. Locke had become 'a rare light and guide to Dissenting candidates and young divines' and was to be blamed for the widespread disappearance of the fear of Hell.[4]

Ball's diatribe was contained in a pamphlet written against Henry Grove, principal from 1706 to 1738 of the academy at Taunton, in which neighbourhood incidentally many members of the Locke family lived. Grove, who made no secret of the debt he owed to Locke, spoke much of the 'reasonableness of the Christian religion',[5]

[1] The first academies were opened soon after the Ejection, when Oxford and Cambridge were closed to Nonconformists. A number of ejected ministers, in order to supplement their incomes, took students into their homes and gave them the equivalent of a university education in logic, philosophy and divinity. From such modest beginnings there sprang such famous institutions as that of Richard Frankland in Yorkshire: opened at Rathmell in 1670, it moved to Notland in 1674, to Attercliffe in 1688 and back to Rathmell in 1689—where it remained until the founder's death in 1698. Frankland trained more than 300 students, among them Timothy Jollie, who perpetuated the Rathmell tradition at Attercliffe until 1714. McLachlan, *EETA*, 62–70, 106–9.

[2] Ibid. 108.         [3] See above, p. 140.

[4] J. Ball, *Some remarks on a new way of preaching*, 1736, 17, 21–2. Ball's pamphlet, although apparently not printed until 1736, was written in answer to Grove's ordination sermon of 1730.

[5] H. Grove, *Sermon at ordination of Thomas Amory*, 1730, p. i.

and went so far as to affirm that 'whatever religion is rational, in
the propriety of the term, must needs be divine'.[1] His rationalism
was also partly derived from Baxter; in his controversy with Ball
in 1737 he quoted these words from the writings of the great
seventeenth century divine: 'What more can be done to the disgrace and ruin of Christianity than to make the world believe we
have no reason for it?'[2] Under Grove's guidance and that of his
nephew and successor Thomas Amory the academy became
notorious for its unorthodoxy. The 1732 survey specifically blamed
Taunton for the fact that many of the younger generation of Presbyterian ministers 'inclined to the Arminian scheme'[3]: no names were
mentioned but the author probably had in mind men like Sandercock and Strickland Gough, both former pupils of Grove. In 1735
the heterodox element in the congregation at Castle Gate, Nottingham were referred to as 'those who are disposed to send to Taunton
for a minister'.[4] Furthermore, it was doubtless of this academy that
Ball's friend John Walrond was thinking when he said that 'some
of our Academies have ruined many brave young men, who now
do but serve to ruin congregations'.[5] He and Ball had probably
been instrumental in making the affairs of the academy the
subject of a debate at the previous year's meeting of the Exeter
Assembly.[6]

## Latham and Rotheram

The 1732 report, in pointing to Taunton as the principal source
of the supply of Arminian ministers, also observed that a number
came 'from the Peak in the North'.[7] This was a reference to the
academy at Findern near Derby which had been founded in about
1710 by Thomas Hill, who had been succeeded ten years later by
Ebenezer Latham, an ardent disciple of Baxter. In 1725 the Presbyterian Fund named Findern and Taunton as the only two academies
in England where students were to be encouraged,[8] but the northern

[1] H. Grove, *Letter to John Ball*, 1737, 25.
[2] Ibid. 28.                    [3] 1732 MS. report, 90.
[4] Doddridge *Corresp.* iii. 186 (David Jennings to Doddridge, November 11, 1735).
[5] Ibid. 402 (Walrond to Doddridge, November 14, 1739). He was not referring to
numerical decline but to theological ruin.
[6] Brockett, 96. There had been questioning side glances at Taunton heterodoxy in
the Exeter Assembly minutes at an earlier date.
[7] 1732 MS. report, 90.            [8] Presb. Fund mins. iii. 50.

academy had a severe critic in one of the Fund's managers, the orthodox John Barker. In 1729 Barker caused the Fund board to write to
Latham concerning a report that he and his pupils attended worship
in their parish church once a Sunday, but this attempt to discredit
the principal failed, for Latham's reply gave general satisfaction.[1] In
1750 Barker told Doddridge that he had always regarded Latham
as an incompetent tutor whose pupils did no honour to the Dissenting cause.[2] He may have been thinking of men like Paul Cardale,
the radical minister at Evesham who was later responsible for the
spreading of Socinianism in the Midlands. But even Barker could
hardly have failed to approve of Matthew Bradshaw of Kidderminster, another Findern pupil, at whose funeral in 1742 Latham
said: 'He began . . . where the great Mr Baxter ended, with a noble
negligence of all those controversies which take off men's attention
from practical holiness.'[3]

Barker was also strongly critical of the academy founded at
Kendal in 1733 by Caleb Rotheram. Rotheram, like Benson, Winder
and John Taylor, was a former pupil of Thomas Dixon, whose
academy, located first at Whitehaven and later at Bolton, had closed
in 1729. Kendal academy was virtually a continuation of Whitehaven: it too produced a remarkable number of liberal divines,
including the two John Seddons and George Walker. To the influence of its students may be attributed the fact that so many of
the Presbyterian congregations in Lancashire eventually became
Unitarian.[4] In spite of Barker's dislike of Rotheram the academy
enjoyed the regular support of the Presbyterian Fund; this was due
in large measure to Benson, who became one of the managers in
1740 and who, through their mutual friend Bourn, was in constant
touch with Rotheram.

The only other academy regularly supported by the Presbyterian
Fund was the one which had been founded in South Wales not
long after the Ejection and which, after several migrations, eventually became established at Carmarthen. The academy took on a
markedly liberal character after 1743 when Evan Davies, a former
pupil of John Eames, succeeded to the theological tutorship.
Benson apparently kept in close touch with the academy. In 1751 a

[1] Presb. Fund mins. iii. 102, 110.
[2] Doddridge, *Corresp.* v. 158 (Barker to Doddridge, June 5, 1750).
[3] *Sermon on death of Matthew Bradshaw*, 1742, 40.      [4] Halley, ii. 394–5.

N

Welsh correspondent wrote to thank him for certain benefactions to the academy and to assure him of its liberal character: 'Your writings cannot but be very acceptable to young men disposed to a free enquiry after truth, as most of the students are.'[1]

## Congregational Academies

While the four academies supported by the Presbyterian Fund were all decidedly liberal in character, the two supported by the Congregational Fund, at which many Presbyterian ministers were also trained, were not very much less so. The London academy that had been set up in 1701 under the principalship of Daniel Williams's old adversary Isaac Chauncy became less orthodox in outlook after Chauncy's death in 1712. In that year John Eames, an Independent layman and friend of Isaac Newton, joined the staff and proceeded to broaden the curriculum to include anatomy and other scientific subjects. Some indication of this tutor's standing among the liberal Dissenters of his day is given by the fact that it was to him that Grove sent his nephew and star pupil Thomas Amory for further education when he felt that the young man had assimilated all that Taunton had to offer. Eames's influence was at its height between 1734 and 1744, when he occupied the position of theological tutor: Richard Price, who became famous later, was one of the pupils of Eames. When Eames died in 1744 he was succeeded by David Jennings, who was much less inclined to Arminianism: in his letters to Doddridge he referred derisively to 'the gentlemen of the new scheme' and used 'orthodox' as a synonym for 'sound'.[2]

In Doddridge's own academy at Northampton, which flourished from 1729 until his death in 1751, 'orthodox' was a word that was used somewhat disparagingly of those who were 'so devoted to a peculiar set of human phrases . . . that they will hardly entertain a favourable thought of any who scruple the use of them'.[3] Doddridge believed in teaching his students to think for themselves: his method was to present both sides of any theological controversy and then to leave it to their judgment to decide which side to take. In this he may be likened to John Jennings under whom he had studied at Kibworth and of whom he himself said:

[1] Benson MSS. (D. Lloyd to Benson, September 15, 1751).
[2] Doddridge, *Corresp.* iii. 149–50; iv. 258–9.
[3] Doddridge, *Free Thoughts*, 25.

[He] does not follow the doctrines or phrases of any particular party, but is sometimes a Calvinist, sometimes an Arminian and sometimes a Baxterian, as truth and evidence determine him.[1]

To anyone brought up within the narrow bounds of ortho-dox Dissent, as many of his pupils had been, the atmosphere of Doddridge's academy was most refreshing. Samuel Merivale, whose parents were members of Northampton Baptist chapel and had very much wanted him to be educated at the strictly orthodox King's Head academy,[2] thus described his emancipation:

> I left the principles of Calvin, or rather of Crisp and Hussey, for those of Arminius, or Baxter at least; and forsook, at 14, the Baptist meeting for the sake of hearing Dr. Doddridge; and at 16 . . . gained the very difficult point of being brought up at his feet.[3]

Merivale, like so many of Doddridge's students, eventually went not into the Independent but into the Presbyterian ministry, where he was better able to enjoy the freedom of enquiry that he had learned to love at Northampton. It is not without significance that of the fifty-nine former pupils of Doddridge known to be in the Dissenting ministry in 1772 no fewer than fifty-three are found among those liberal-minded men who in that year signed the petition for a relaxation of subscription to the Thirty-Nine Articles: of the remaining six, four did not sign because they were Unitarians of the Priestleyan school who wanted a much more radical reform, while only two remained to champion the cause of Calvinistic and Athanasian orthodoxy. Moreover twenty-nine of the fifty-three petitioners were serving congregations that were later to become Unitarian.[4] It is therefore not surprising that shortly after Doddridge's death Joseph Williams, the leader of the orthodox faction in the congregation at Kidderminster, wrote:

---

[1] Doddridge, *Corresp.* i. 156 (Doddridge to Clark, September 1722).

[2] This had been established in London in 1730 by a number of Independents who were disturbed by the spread of Arminianism.

[3] S. Merivale, *Family Memorials*, 5-6.

[4] The petitioners' names are printed in *CHST*, v. 205-22, 261-77, 372-85. The names of Doddridge's students are in *MR*, x (1815), 686, and their careers (where details are available) have been summarised in Mr Surman's card index in D.W.L. A number of Northampton students conformed to the Church of England.

I don't think even Dr. Doddridge's [academy] was strictly enough governed. . . . It is certain many under his tuition have run into the scheme of the Remonstrants.[1]

It is also fairly certain that the Doctor himself was rather alarmed by this mass defection of his former students. In 1740 he told Watts of the sad fate of two of them. Moses Carter, 'one of the best furnished lads I ever bred' had become 'a pupil of Messrs Emlyn, Taylor, Foster, &c.',[2] while Charles Bulkeley, 'one of the greatest enemies of the gospel that ever came under my care', had turned out to be 'an Arian, a Socinian or a Pelagian'.[3] He could, however, take comfort in the assurance of Nathaniel Neal: 'If your Academy produces none whose sentiments differ from your own, you are a tutor without a parallel'.[4]

## Training at Glasgow

The academies were not the only places where candidates for the Dissenting ministry received their training. From the 1690s onwards a number, like Lardner, Hunt, Chandler and Lowman, had gone to the Low Countries to further their education at Leyden or Utrecht, sometimes (in the case of Utrecht students) with the support of the Presbyterian Fund.[5] From the beginning of the eighteenth century it became more usual for students to go to Scotland, and generally to Glasgow, where Daniel Williams supported many students during his lifetime and by his will founded scholarships tenable there.[6] In many cases students went on there after they had completed a course at one of the academies: Benson, for example, entered the University from Whitehaven.

At Glasgow the theological climate was particularly liberal. John Simson, appointed Professor of Divinity there in 1708, had been suspected of heresy in 1712 and finally suspended for it in 1729, after which date no Divinity was seriously taught for many years.[7] Francis Hutcheson, Professor of Moral Philosophy from

[1] *Extracts from the Diary . . . of Joseph Williams* (ed. Hanbury), 348. Remonstrants was the name by which the Dutch Arminians were known.
[2] Watts, *Posth. Works*, ii. 43 (Doddridge to Watts April 23, 1740).    [3] Ibid. 38–9.
[4] Doddridge, *Corresp.* iv. 387 (Neal to Doddridge March 15, 1745).
[5] O.M. Griffiths, *Religion and Learning*, 178. The Fund did not favour Leyden.
[6] Ibid. 181–2; Univ. of Glasgow MSS. Stirling Correspondence with Daniel Williams.
[7] H. M. B. Reid, *The divinity professors in the University of Glasgow, 1640–1903*, 1923, 234, 243.

1729 to 1746, spent the weekdays propounding a common-sense philosophy which owed much to Locke and on Sunday evenings lectured to packed audiences on the evidences of Christianity, 'taking his views of its doctrines and divine schemes from the original records of the New Testament, and not from the party-tenets or scholastic systems of modern ages.'[1] William Leechman, who occupied the Divinity chair from 1743, resembled Doddridge in his practice of teaching both sides of every theological dispute and urged his students when they left the University to 'retain the character of enquirers and to keep their minds open to new light and evidence from every quarter'.[2] This liberalism soon got him into trouble: in 1744, when the Glasgow presbytery found fault with one of his sermons, he nearly went the way of Simson. But he managed to clear himself of the charge of heresy. As Winder reported to Benson:

> I am glad that Professor Leechman is so far safe, though he certainly crept into the chair by a very strait door . . . which squeezed good old Simson before him.[3]

Leechman had many friends among the English Presbyterians and was instrumental in getting the University authorities to award a D.D. to John Taylor in 1756; but he failed to persuade them to give one to Benson, whom they suspected of Socinianism.[4] Benson's diploma, like that of Doddridge and a great many other Dissenting divines, came eventually from Aberdeen. The Arminian prophet was without honour in his own *alma mater*.

## Congregational Splits

It was inevitable that the heterodoxy engendered in the academies and disseminated by the men that they trained would sooner or later come to affect the local Dissenting congregations. Indeed the repercussions of the new way of thinking were felt in almost every meeting-house in the land. Even remote country congregations were alive to what was happening and were often gravely concerned. In 1733, for example, when there was a vacancy in the

[1] William Leechman in preface to Hutcheson's *System of Moral Philosophy*, 1755, p. xxxvi.
[2] Wodrow, 'Life of Dr. Leechman', prefixed to collected *Sermons*, 1789, i. 34–5.
[3] Benson MSS. (Winder to Benson August 10, 1744).        [4] *DNB*, Benson.

pulpit at Wattisfield, Suffolk, an entry in the church book recorded that

> the faithful labourers in Christ's vineyard are so few, and the deceitful and sophisticated corruptors of the word and doctrine so many, that it appears exceedingly difficult for a church really adhering to the good old Protestant doctrines (the glory of our Reformation) to be again settled with a suitable and agreeable Pastor.[1]

The Wattisfield folk were convinced that it was the ministers who were to blame for the departure from the 'good old Protestant doctrines'. Broadly speaking they were right, but it would be inaccurate to regard heterodoxy as a purely ministerial product. In the cities and large towns, where people were more alive to the world of thought, the man in the pew might be as 'sophisticated' as the man in the pulpit. In London it was possible to find layfolk like the redoubtable Mrs Margaret Shepherd who, not long before his appointment as Calamy's successor at Westminster, wrote thus to Samuel Say:

> I should like to have your scheme of Divinity. I am pleased you differ from the orthodox, for to me 'tis a senseless heap of jargon that I can have no reasonable just ideas of, though for many years I was as orthodox as any. . . . But 'tis some years now since I have had other sentiments of things and more enlarged notions, and I think I've changed for the better. I can't but say I think I was easier then in many points than I have been since, for there is a vast pleasure in enthusiasm. . . . I even now am apt to indulge in it.[2]

Evidently Mrs Shepherd helped to offset the influence of people like Sir Richard Ellys, the principal member of Calamy's congregation. Someone wrote to Say at the time of his call to Westminster to warn him about the worthy baronet, who, he said, was 'very strongly attached to that which is commonly called the Calvinistical scheme'.[3] Ellys, whose spiritual pilgrimage had been in the opposite direction to that of Mrs Shepherd (for he had begun life as an Arminian and had been converted to Calvinism), was evidently unable to stomach Say's unorthodox views; he joined Thomas Bradbury's Independent church at New Court, where he felt more at home.[4]

---

[1] T. J. Hosken, *History of Congregationalism . . . in Suffolk*, 1920, 79.
[2] *MR*, iv. 592.          [3] *CHST*, xix. 86.
[4] D. Bogue and J. Bennett, *History of Dissenters*, 1808–12, ii. 412.

While it was a comparatively easy matter for a dissatisfied member of a congregation in London or other larger centre of population to withdraw to another place of worship where the preaching was more to his liking, the situation was very different in a small town where, apart from the Baptists, there might be only one congregation of Dissenters.[1] If the dissatisfied element was strong enough and vocal enough the congregation might be split in two as a result. Often the unorthodox element consisted of the more prosperous and better educated members, who were probably trustees of the building and principal subscribers to the minister's stipend, while the orthodox element was made up of humbler, less influential folk. Thus, if the division became a permanent one, it was generally the unorthodox party who retained possession of the meeting-house, while the others were obliged to secede and find another building.[2]

By the fifth decade of the century such divisions were becoming increasingly common, except perhaps in Lancashire, Cheshire and one or two other counties where the ideals of united Dissent seem to have been more persistent than elsewhere. In 1744 Bourn, writing from the Midlands, informed Benson that 'in almost every town is there a struggle between Light and Darkness'.[3] A particularly bitter struggle was then taking place at Wolverhampton. As often happened the controversy began over the appointment of a new minister. In 1739, on the death of John Stubbs, an old-style Calvinist who had ministered there since 1697, the congregation began to look around for a successor. A majority were apparently in favour of calling a Scotsman, James Barr, but the appointment was distasteful to a substantial minority who wanted Robert Atkinson of Northampton academy as their pastor. The orthodox party triumphed and Barr was duly installed. But the opposition carried on the fight and did all they could to secure the Scotsman's dismissal. In January

---

[1] The existence of these provincial congregations of united Dissenters, comprising Presbyterians, Independents and others who probably refused to use either label, makes it difficult to be precise about the extent and character of English Presbyterianism outside London and the big towns. The picture becomes clearer as the century progresses and the old combined congregations begin to split—or move as a whole to one side or the other.

[2] It is significant that in the period 1725–40, when Dissent was moving to a new theological phase, many new meeting-houses were built on old sites and new trustees appointed. See Colligan, *Eighteenth Cent. Nonconf.* 64.

[3] Benson MSS. (Bourn to Benson December 29, 1744).

1744 Bourn reported that 'the Dissenters at [Wolver]Hampton are
in a most wretched case. Barr declares he'll not stir a foot, but as
obliged by law. He will convert 'em, willing or unwilling.' The
following month Barr was given official notice to quit but refused
to vacate the pulpit:

> The first Lord's Day after a formal dismission Mr. Barr chained up the
> Court Gates of the Meeting House. The 2d. he caused the vault to be
> emptied and spread before the door. The 3d. he got up into the pulpit,
> was pulled down, and his attorney read a declaration of protest. . . . Is
> he not an original!

In April the case went to Chancery and soon, after five years of
wrangling, Barr acknowledged defeat and departed from Wolverhampton for good.[1]

With some congregational splits it is possible to discover something about the theological issues involved. At Maidstone in 1745,
when the appointment of a former student of the Welsh academy
led to the withdrawal of a substantial minority of the Dissenting
congregation there, the seceders stated that the new minister 'was
not sound in such doctrine as we esteem to be the fundamentals of
Christianity, and upon which we desire to build our hopes of pardon
and salvation'.[2] Similar feelings were doubtless responsible for the
split at Treville Street, Plymouth in the preceding year. Here one
of Grove's pupils was chosen to succeed Nathaniel Harding, a
strict Calvinist who had occupied the pulpit for fifty-four years and
whose preaching, according to one of his regular hearers, 'was
eternally upon such things as election, adoption, sanctification, &c.'[3]
Even the least wide-awake members of the congregation could
detect a difference between Harding's theology and that of his
successor.

From the division that took place at Yarmouth in 1732 it is clear
that fault could be found with a preacher not only for what he said
but for what he left unsaid. In that year Ralph Milner, a former
student of Whitehaven and a close friend of Benson, was invited,
apparently on the recommendation of certain London ministers,

---

[1] Benson MSS. (Bourn to Benson October 27, 1739, September 12, 1740; January 23,
March 9, April 20, 1744). Cf. A. G. Matthews, The Congregational churches of Stafford-
shire, 1924, 152.

[2] T. Timpson, Church history of Kent, 1859, 335.     [3] MR, xvi. 257.

to occupy the pastoral office. The majority of the church, however, who represented a minority of the total body of 'hearers', did not approve of this appointment. At first, from conversations that they had had with Milner, every one had thought that his scheme of preaching would be the 'evangelic one', but later it was discovered that his preaching was deficient in many important respects, such as 'the necessity of the influences of the spirit of the Redeemer, the new birth, the freeness and richness of divine grace in the salvation of the Church of God, the utter impotency of the fallen creature to be its own Saviour, and the like, which in our apprehension are doctrines of great importance, tending to glorify God and humble man'. Some of these doctrines, they complained, 'have either not been at all insisted upon, or so very slightly that it could give us but little satisfaction'. Accordingly, despite Milner's assurances that 'he was no Arminian but a moderate Calvinist', the orthodox party refused to be satisfied and proceeded to withdraw from the meeting-house.[1]

## Old Style on the Defensive

Many congregational divisions, it seems, were deliberately fostered by outsiders. Samuel Bates, the minister at Warminster, affirmed that the split there in 1719 had been engineered by London ministers and that the separatist congregation there would not long survive without support from the metropolis.[2] This last was doubtless a discreet reference to the activities of David Jennings and John Guyse and the other managers of the Congregational Fund. In 1748 Bourn publicly attacked these two men when they were in the Midlands, accusing them of being responsible for the building of an Independent meeting-house in Birmingham in opposition to the Presbyterian Old and New Meetings. Jennings denied that he had assisted in the project but was so displeased by Bourn's words that he said that he would henceforth do the separatists every service he could.[3] Three years later Bourn sent a report to Benson of an ordination at Darwen 'where 3 of your London dons attended, Dr Guyse, Dr Jennings and Mr Goodwin'. Guyse and Jennings

[1] [J. E. Clowes], Chronicles of the Old Congregational Church at Great Yarmouth 1642-1858, 1906, 53-7.
[2] Murch, 90; Doddridge, Corresp. iv. 533 (Bates to Doddridge May 16, 1747).
[3] Benson MSS. (R. Murray to Benson September 21, 1748).

delivered the same discourses that they had given at an earlier ordination. 'What pains do they take to keep up a party! And what public money do they expend to support separations!'[1]

Jennings had probably been fostering such separations for some years. As early as 1735, when the congregation at Castle Gate, Nottingham was divided over the appointment of a minister, he had written to Doddridge to ask:

> whether the congregation at Nottingham be not too far divided already ever to be comfortably united under one minister, and whether they had not better split (as the people have done at Yarmouth and much for their peace), rather than unite, like Jeremy's two figs, one very good and one very bad, which may be squeezed together, but will never incorporate.[2]

Doddridge's reply is not extant but it was almost certainly 'No!' For while he agreed that in a big city like London it was sometimes desirable that 'persons of generous and bigoted sentiments should meet in different places',[3] he hated to see division in provincial congregations. But for all that he could not help getting involved in congregational disputes. In September 1740 Bourn reported that 'Dr. D——ge has sent a young man to [Wolver]Hampton to support the separation in opposition to the orthodox party; I hear a good character of him: his name is Atkinson'. Bourn, however, doubted if Doddridge really wanted to help the heterodox party; 'the Dr. would gladly have fobbed them off with a young bigoted Scotsman named Johnson'.[4] Three years later, when the Kidderminster people were divided over the choice of a successor to Bradshaw, Doddridge recommended Samuel Statham who also had the support of Dr Latham, but he was not orthodox enough for most Kidderminster people.[5] Perhaps the last disputed election that Doddridge became involved in was at Dorchester in 1749. In November of that year Samuel Bates of Warminster wrote to tell him that the Dorchester people were looking for a minister. 'They have been trained up long in principles of moderation and one of such a spirit will please.' Bates had been secretly approached by

[1] Benson MSS. (Bourn to Benson November 9, 1751). 'Public money' may be a reference to the Congregational Fund.
[2] Doddridge, *Corresp.* iii. 185–6 (Jennings to Doddridge March 11, 1735).
[3] *Free Thoughts*, 25.   [4] Benson MSS. (Bourn to Benson September 12, 1740).
[5] Ibid. (October 7, 1743).

some of the principal members with a view to his writing to Northampton. He wondered whether Andrew Kippis was available.
Doddridge was apparently unable to help.[1]

Doddridge's desire to preserve the unity of Dissent was shared by
many of his pupils, some of whom, by the exercise of much wisdom
and tact, succeeded in preventing the break-up of congregations
containing a wide variety of theological viewpoints. These men, like
their master, were invariably liberal in theology, catholic in churchmanship, and inspired by a warm-hearted concern for the welfare
of their people. Such a man was Benjamin Fawcett, a favourite
pupil of Doddridge, minister at Kidderminster from 1745 to 1780.
One who was brought up in that congregation gave a memorable
description of the situation that obtained in Fawcett's day:

> The congregation ... had the Presbyterian discipline, and was very
> much mixed as to doctrinal opinions. A considerable number ... were
> Calvinists; a considerable number ... were Arminians. ... Some of
> the Arminians were likewise Arians, and among these was the minister
> himself, though he managed so far to conceal his opinions as to be very
> popular with his hearers, and these were very numerous.[2]

It was only after Fawcett's death that the congregation split in two,
with the minister's own family going with the latitudinarians.

At least one other old pupil of Doddridge's academy was similarly
successful. William Blake, one of the last students to sit at the great
Doctor's feet and the first of a long line of West Country Presbyterian divines to embrace Arminian views, was the much revered
pastor of the Crewkerne congregation from 1754 to 1799. On his
death the whole town went into mourning and in his funeral sermon
he was likened to Demetrius, one who 'hath good report of all
men'.[3] It is an interesting commentary on his influence that there
is today no Congregational chapel in that town: the Presbyterian
(Unitarian) congregation retains something of the 'catholic' character of the old Dissent.[4] Here, it seems, Jeremy's two figs did incorporate.

[1] New College London, Doddridge MSS. iv, no. 80 (Bates to Doddridge November
11, 1749).
[2] G. Hunsworth, *Memorials of the Old Meeting House, Kidderminster*, 1874, 40–1.
[3] T. Thomas, *The character of Demetrius*, 1799.
[4] William Blake was succeeded by a son of the same name and similar temper. The
present minister at Crewkerne, the Rev. Margaret Dickin, is a great-grand-daughter of
the younger William.

### 'Calvinophobia'

By the middle of the eighteenth century the breach between the two main Dissenting denominations was generally becoming so wide that it could almost be said that the Presbyterians now had more in common with the Church of England (where Arminian views were prevalent) than with the Independents.[1] The two bodies were divided not just on such ecclesiastical matters as the theory and practice of ordination but on fundamental points of belief. This division had not come about because one body had remained true to the faith of their common fathers and the other had been led astray, but because both bodies had changed. Moreover they were continuing to change and, in reacting to each other, exacerbating the changes: the Presbyterians, under the influence of the scientific revolution, were becoming more rationalistic; the Independents, under the influence of the Evangelical Revival, were becoming more dogmatic. Thus a Calvinistic Presbyterian or an Arminian Independent was becoming an increasingly rare bird (if not a contradiction in terms) and the Middle Way man, who had previously done much to bridge the gap between the two denominations, was almost an extinct species.

Some indication of the extent to which things had changed in twenty years can be seen from a comparison of the London situation in 1732 and 1751. Of the nineteen Presbyterian ministers classified as Calvinists in 1732 at least eight had died and their places had been filled by Arminians. William Harris, for example, had been succeeded at Crutched Friars by George Benson: 'How different a man from dear Dr. Harris!' was Barker's despairing comment on the appointment.[2] Barker in fact was now almost the only London minister who continued to regard himself as both a Calvinist and a Presbyterian. The others had for the most part changed either their theology or their denomination. Among those who had recognized the logic of the situation and joined the Independents was Zephaniah Marryat, who made the change soon after he succeeded to Abraham Taylor's tutorship of the King's Head

[1] An indication of the good understanding between left-wing Presbyterians and Arminian Anglicans is provided by the cordial reception given to Samuel Chandler's overtures to Archbishop Herring regarding comprehension in 1748. The Archbishop, it is said, often attended services conducted by Samuel Wright at Carter Lane.

[2] Doddridge, *Corresp.* iv. 180 (Barker to Doddridge January 13, 1743).

Society's academy.[1] One who had succumbed to another kind of
logic and turned Arminian was Philip Gibbs, described by Doddridge in a phrase that reveals much about the characters of both
men, as 'my desperately honest namesake at Hackney'.[2] In 1737
Gibbs resigned his post as Barker's assistant there and published a
letter to the congregation explaining his reasons for so doing.
'When I came to Hackney, Sirs,' he said, 'I had not made my last
understanding in religious matters.' Brought up by 'Calvinistical'
tutors, he had for some years 'read scarce any but Calvinistic books
—being taught that these alone were orthodox and that looking
into others might corrupt me and endanger my soundness in the
Faith'. But at Hackney he had had an opportunity to read freely
and had come to believe that 'Calvinism . . . is a very wrong, bad
scheme: I know not of anything that has more defaced the beauty of
the Christian religion'.[3]

By this date Calvinism had become almost a term of abuse with
many Presbyterians. 'Almost all the Calvinists I have known',
wrote Christopher Wadsworth to Doddridge in 1745, 'are narrow,
sour, bigoted and wrathful', and he underlined the sentence to
show how strongly he felt about it.[4] This anti-Calvinist feeling,
which a later generation dubbed 'Calvinophobia',[5] was accentuated
by Benson's publishing, in the columns of *The Old Whig*, an account
of Calvin's causing Servetus to be burned.[6] Here was further evidence, it seemed to many Arminians, in favour of John Taylor's
contention that bad doctrines and bad men often go together.

But if Calvin and his system were generally discredited among
Presbyterians in London and in most other parts of the country
there was still one place where orthodoxy and Presbyterianism
often went hand in hand. This was in the Exeter Assembly, where
the spirit of John Ball lived on after 1745, in which year the old
zealot went 'mourning to his grave, trembling to think what, in a
short time, would become of the great truths of the Gospel'.[7] These
words were spoken at Ball's funeral by his friend John Walrond,

[1] Three Denoms. Minutes, i. 96 (April 1742).
[2] Doddridge, *Corresp.* iii. 291 (Doddridge to Clark December 15, 1737).
[3] P. Gibbs, *Letter to the congregation . . . at Hackney*, 1737, 4, 28, 30–1.
[4] Doddridge, *Corresp.* iv. 422.       [5] Bogue and Bennett, ii. 210.
[6] *The Old Whig*, nos. 152–4 (February 2, 9, 16, 1738). This was an abridged version
of an account published in 1711 by Hoadly's friend Michel de la Roche in *Memoirs of
literature.*       [7] J. Walrond, *Sermon on death of John Ball*, 1745, 20.

minister at Bow Meeting, Exeter from 1730 to 1754, who, with his co-pastor John Lavington, henceforward became pre-eminent among the orthodox Presbyterians of Devonshire. Their disagreement with their more liberal colleagues came to a head at an historic meeting of the Assembly in May 1753, when by a majority of fourteen votes to ten, with three abstentions, it was in effect agreed no longer to require a declaration of faith from candidates for ordination.[1] The ten were all strict Calvinists and Trinitarians. In addition to Walrond and Lavington there was, for instance, Aaron Pitts of Topsham, who in 1738 had been given a grant by the Congregational Fund after having been 'recommended as to his orthodoxy by Mr. Ball of Honiton, Mr. Walrond and Mr. Enty of Exeter'.[2] Another favourer of subscription was Richard Orchard who had been given an equally clean bill of health by the same Fund in the same year: 'His sentiments are Calvinist; he declared he can heartily subscribe to the doctrine of the Assembly's Catechism.'[3] Such men, finding themselves to be more and more a minority in the Assembly, gradually ceased to attend its meetings: they may have continued to call themselves Presbyterians for old times' sake, but in fact if not in name they were theologically Independents. It is not true to say of 1753 that 'this year marks the end of Presbyterianism in Devonshire and Cornwall',[4] but one can say that it marks the real beginning of Congregationalism; although there are a few Congregational churches in Devonshire with a continuous history from before 1662, the great majority of them are either old Presbyterian causes or else post-1753 foundations.

Two isolated examples of the survival of Calvinistic Presbyterianism may be mentioned. Risdon Darracott of Wellington, Somerset, a favourite pupil of Doddridge, and a minister whom Whitefield dubbed 'the Star in the West' because he was such 'a flaming successful preacher of the Gospel', continued to be known as a Presbyterian minister until his death in 1759[5]: his fellow Presbyterians, however, never had much to do with him and one of them, William

---

[1] Brockett, 108.
[2] Cong. Fund mins. ii. 112. John Enty had been James Peirce's most embittered opponent after the Exeter split in 1719.          [3] Ibid.
[4] Brockett, loc. cit. This statement is correct only if Presbyterianism be equated with some form of quasi-synodical organization: in fact, of course, such an organization was by no means universal. See below, p. 208.
[5] J. Bennett, *The Star of the West*, 1813, 65.

Cornish of Sherborne, a former pupil of Grove, would not even admit him to his pulpit.[1] Jacob Chapman, minister at Staplehurst from 1740 to 1795, who always described himself as 'a minister of Christ of the Presbyterian denomination', gave free use of his meeting-house, which was his own private property, to all kinds of evangelical preachers and in his will directed that the building should be for the use of 'the people called Presbyterians, Independents, Methodists'.[2] But neither of these men can be regarded as a typical mid-century Presbyterian divine; they probably only retained this particular denominational label because they served congregations which were traditionally Presbyterian.

## End of the Middle Way

The disappearance from the Presbyterian ministry of strict Calvinists was accompanied by that of the Middle Way Men. Of the twelve London ministers so described in 1732 at least four were dead in 1751 and their places had been taken by Arminians. Obadiah Hughes, who succeeded Say at Westminster in 1743, died in 1751; his place was taken by Andrew Kippis, who was much more radical in theology, claiming that he had renounced Calvinism at the age of thirteen.[3] Of those still in the ministry two, Lardner and Sandercock, are known to have abandoned the Middle Way in favour of an uncompromising Arminianism.

Outside London, however, the Middle Way Men lingered on a little longer. Samuel Bates, who evidently regarded himself as 'a moderate Calvinist alias Baxterian'[4] and who told Doddridge that he agreed with his view that 'the middle way between both extremes is the only one to keep us from ruin'[5] continued to minister at Warminster until 1761. But it was not always easy for a minister to walk this particular tight-rope; the orthodox Dissenters had a habit of regarding all who were not for them as being against them. Thomas Milway of Haverhill told Benson in 1748 that 'though I

[1] Densham and Ogle, 257.

[2] T. Thatcher, *Staplehurst Independent Church*, 1903, 19–20.

[3] Wilson, *Dissenting churches*, iv. 105. He renounced Calvinism after reading Elisha Cole's supralapsarian Calvinist *Treatise on God's sovereignty*, which had precisely the contrary effect upon him to that which the author had intended.

[4] New College London, Doddridge MSS. iv, no. 78 (Bates to Doddridge, March 20, 1749). Bates was not here using the term to describe himself but it was clearly one that appealed strongly to him.            [5] Doddridge, *Corresp.* iv. 534.

think myself of middling orthodoxy yet [I] am represented by my more orthodox brethren as the arch-heretic of the corner'.[1] The situation became more difficult after 1751 when the death of Doddridge deprived English Dissent of the most influential advocate and practitioner of Baxterian principles. Wadsworth was probably right in telling Doddridge in 1745 that his attempt to bridge the gap between the Calvinists and the rest could never succeed;[2] but Wadsworth would have been the first to admit that, if Doddridge could not succeed, neither could anyone else.

Bridging the gap between Presbyterians and Independents became increasingly difficult not only because the one denomination had lost nearly all its Calvinists but also because the other had lost nearly all its non-Calvinists. From 1730 onwards Arminian and Baxterian Independents, feeling that their true home was with the Presbyterians, had followed the example of Lardner and Sandercock and had changed their denominational allegiance. Henry Miles, for example, a friend of Lardner and a man of scientific outlook, left the Independents in 1737 and became assistant to Chandler at the Old Jewry. By the middle of the century such migrations seem to have become much more common. Two factors contributed to this situation. One, already referred to, was the increasing strictness of the Independents' theological views. The other was the decreasing strictness of the Presbyterians' ecclesiastical notions. Generally speaking, among English (as distinct from Scottish) Presbyterians these notions had never been very strict, but in some areas, notably those covered by the Warrington and Cheshire Classes[3] and by the Exeter Assembly, strong associations of ministers had long claimed a quasi-synodical jurisdiction over member-churches which Independents found distasteful.[4] But in the middle of the century these associations began to relax their hold on congregations. In about 1750 Josiah Owen persuaded the 'provincial meeting' of the 'associated ministers of Lancashire' to discontinue the customary investigations into the internal state of congregations.[5] After 1753, as has been seen, the Exeter Assembly gradually lost its sway over its member-churches.

[1] Benson MSS. (Milway to Benson September 18, 1748).
[2] Doddridge, *Corresp.* iv. 422–3.                    [3] See Gordon, *Cheshire Classis.*
[4] Since these associations contained no lay element they were very different from the Scottish Presbyterian synods. See above, p. 20, 48, 94.          [5] Gordon in *DNB*, Owen.

## Independent Independents

To an Independent like Merivale the interference of the 'Inquisitors' of the Exeter Assembly in the affairs of his church at Tavistock had, on his first settling there in 1744, seemed quite unwarrantable,[1] but he gradually came to feel that this was preferable to the Independent alternative, which often amounted to dictatorship by deacons. In 1759 he refused an invitation from the Independent congregation at Plymouth because he had heard that some of the members wanted a man who would subscribe the Assembly's Catechism: 'I would as soon subscribe the articles of Pope Pius's creed as the answers in that catechism relating to the Trinity, Original Sin, Justification, &c.'[2] In the following year he accepted a call to the chief citadel of Presbyterianism in the West, George's Meeting, Exeter, where he remained happily settled for the rest of his ministerial career. Had he gone to Plymouth he would probably have suffered the fate of the man who went in his stead, John Hanmer, also a former pupil of Doddridge, who in 1762 was forced to resign the appointment on account of his latitudinarian views and who thereafter became an occasional preacher to the Presbyterian congregation in that town.[3] One of the last liberal-minded ministers to occupy an Independent pulpit was John Burnett, pastor of Dagger Lane chapel, Hull. But his career was beset with difficulties. In 1768 a large number of his flock, confessing themselves weary of 'the mournful Baxterian mixtures we had from the pulpit', withdrew and set up a strictly Calvinist church. 'Your countenance to the New Scheme Preachers,' they informed him, 'in going to hear and to preach at their annual association indisputably convinced us that there is something wrong.'[4] There certainly was something wrong with a situation in which an Independent preacher had to join a Presbyterian ministers' fraternal in order to experience that freedom of expression which he could no longer find among his own denominational brethren.

Only in the neighbourhood of London, it seems, could a liberal-minded man feel at home in the Independent ministry. Philip Furneaux, who became Independent minister at Clapham on Lowman's death in 1752, continued to enjoy complete freedom of

[1] Merivale, 10, 11n.   [2] Ibid. 36.   [3] Murch, 504.
[4] W. Whitaker, *One line of the puritan tradition in Hull: Bowl Alley Lane Chapel*, 1910, 113.

o

utterance in that pulpit until his death in 1783.[1] Caleb Fleming, whose scruples prevented him from accepting Presbyterian ordination, but whose Socinianism made him something of a lone wolf among the Independent sheep, was minister of Pinners' Hall Independent church (formerly served by Hunt and Foster) until its extinction in 1777.[2] Hugh Farmer, minister at Walthamstow from 1737 to 1780, was another Independent radical, and he realized that his situation was a peculiarly fortunate one. Not long after his settlement at Walthamstow he refused a call to the Independent congregation at Taunton: 'If they expected to find a Calvinist in me', he wrote to his old tutor Doddridge, 'or one who would use all their phrases . . . I freely declare they would be disappointed.'[3] Farmer's *Dissertation on miracles* (1771), which was frowned upon by his Independent brethren, became a textbook for Rational Dissenters.[4] It is not without significance that his was the only Independent church in the London area to become Unitarian.[5]

In the second half of the century Burnett, Furneaux, Farmer and Fleming were far from being typical Independent ministers. Most Independent ministers were strict Calvinists and many of them had not been bred up in Dissent but had begun their careers as followers of George Whitefield.[6] It was probably from evangelicals of this stamp that the better educated members of the Plymouth Independent congregation hoped that Merivale would come and save them: 'Come and save us, my dear sir,' one wrote in 1759, 'you will do a glorious . . . thing to keep out noise and nonsense and lay preaching amongst us.'[7] Another class of evangelical preacher came from Scotland. As early as 1731 one observer attributed part of the decline of English Dissent to 'the encouragement shewn to strolling Scotch Ministers.'[8] In 1737 another observer reported that unemployed Scots ministers were strolling south in such great

[1] *DNB*.

[2] *DNB*. Fleming ranked as a Presbyterian in 1742 when co-pastor of Bartholomew Close. (Three Denoms. Minutes, i. 94.)

[3] Doddridge, *Corresp*. iii. 252 (Farmer to Doddridge July 14, 1737).

[4] Gordon, *Heads*, 36.

[5] See H. D. Budden, *The story of Marsh Street Congregational Church, Walthamstow*, 1923. Not long after Farmer's death the congregation split.

[6] Whitefield's followers were Calvinistic Methodists, to be distinguished from Wesley's 'Arminian' Methodists. For Wesley's Arminianism, see above, p. 22–3.

[7] Merivale, 35. Cf. the description of 'leather-apron preachers' in *MR*, iv. 65.

[8] *Some observations upon the present state of the dissenting interest*, 1731, 31–2.

numbers that it would be 'an easy task to find not only sufficient supply for all Britain but perhaps for all the Protestant countries of Europe'.[1] These ministers were not generally acceptable to English Presbyterians because their theology was usually too orthodox and their preaching too 'enthusiastic', but rural Independent congregations were often glad enough to be served by them. One of the best known of these wandering divines was James Scott who, after several brief ministries in Lancashire, crossed over to Yorkshire in 1756 and became minister of Heckmondwike Independent chapel and first principal of the Independent academy in that town.[2]

## Denominational Seminaries

Heckmondwike was one of a number of strictly denominational academies that were established in the 1750s. Hitherto the academies had been almost invariably interdenominational: the Congregational Fund academy in London was open to students for the Presbyterian ministry, just as the four academies supported by the Presbyterian Fund were happy to admit Independents; the only denominational academy of any consequence was the one maintained by the King's Head Society, which was exclusively for the education of Independent ministers. Now, however, the situation began to change. The first development came in July 1750 when the managers of the Presbyterian Fund agreed to set up an academy in Dr Williams's Library, London for 'Protestant Dissenters of the Presbyterian denomination'.[3] Barker, one of the managers, had already warned Doddridge that this was likely to happen and had assured him that the new academy was 'not in opposition to yours'.[4] In September Doddridge said that 'the scheme of a Presbyterian Academy at London . . . can answer no end but that of keeping up a party'.[5]

As it happened the scheme came to nothing but the 'party-spirit' that had inspired it remained. Indeed after Doddridge's death in 1751 it grew stronger than ever: the closure of Northampton academy, in spite of the fact that it was continued under Caleb Ashworth at Daventry, meant the disappearance of the outstanding

[1] Colligan, *Eighteenth cent. Nonconf.* 120–1.
[2] B. Nightingale, *Lancs. Nonconformity*, 1890–3, i. 294–5.
[3] Presb. Fund Minutes, iii. 479.
[4] Doddridge, *Corresp.* v. 159 (Barker to Doddridge June 5, 1750).
[5] Ibid. 182 (Doddridge to Fawcett September 13, 1750).

seat of interdenominational learning.[1] In that year, moreover, the
Congregational Fund decided to give its support to a new denominational academy established at Ottery St Mary by the younger John
Lavington.[2] In the following year it set up a committee to 'enquire
into the state of the academy in Wales', as a result of whose findings
it was decided to appoint ministers to keep an eye on the Fund's
students there.[3] One of these ministers was probably the Edmund
Jones about whom Benson had already had a report:

> He is mighty inquisitive into the principles of the students and wants
> to know from some underhand correspondents whether any of them
> read Clarke, Locke, Whitby, Grove or any such authors, with a view
> to inform the gentlemen of the Ind-p-nd-nt F-nd.[4]

The state of the Welsh academy came up on the Fund Board's
agenda again in January 1757 and in the following month it was
agreed to set up a new Independent academy at Abergavenny,[5] at
which, presumably, the works of Locke would be proscribed.

Its opening very nearly coincided with those of two other denominational academies. Heckmondwike, it has been noted, was opened
in 1756: its establishment was the work of a group of London
Independents who were anxious to do something to help dispel 'the
cloud of Socinian darkness' then spreading over northern England.[6]
The cloud was perhaps thickest over Warrington, where in 1757
there was opened the first avowedly Arminian (and hence, at this
date, almost exclusively Presbyterian) academy in England: its
opening, significantly enough, was followed almost immediately
by a migration to it of several Presbyterian Fund students from
Daventry.[7] The founding of such academies within a few years
of the closure of the old 'catholic' institutions like Northampton,
Kendal, Findern and Taunton meant that the academy was fast
ceasing to be the unifying force that it had once been in English
Dissent.[8] Henceforward it was to become an increasingly rare
occurrence for Presbyterian and Independent students to be educated at the same college. It is also to be noted that the new

---

[1] Daventry had numerous Presbyterian Fund students but only a few Congregational
Fund ones.          [2] Cong. Fund Minutes, v. 32.                    [3] Ibid. 40.
[4] Benson MSS. (D. Lloyd to Benson September 15, 1751).
[5] Cong. Fund Minutes, v. entry for February 28, 1757.
[6] McLachlan, *EETA*, 192.                    [7] Presb. Fund Minutes, v. 150.
[8] Kendal closed in 1753, Findern in 1754 and Taunton in 1759.

Independent academies, following the example set by the King's Head Society's academy, broke with the old custom of educating young men both for the ministry and for secular professions.

## The Denominational Funds

The separation of Presbyterian from Independent academies was accompanied by a widening of the gulf between the denominational Funds from which they drew their support. Although there were still old-fashioned Dissenting laymen like William Holt who saw so little to choose between the two Funds that on his death in 1754 he left £1,000 to be divided equally between them,[1] most of those more intimately concerned with the workings of the Funds knew that their aims and purposes were very different indeed. This is clear from the following minute of a meeting of the Presbyterian Fund board held on May 5, 1759:

> Several cases were mentioned by Dr. Chandler in which it appeared that some ministers supported from hence were struck off from the allowances they had usually received from the Independent Fund; at the motion of Dr. Chandler agreed that a deputation of persons be appointed to meet any such deputation as shall be appointed by the other board to consider of what method may most conduce to the general good and credit of the Dissenting interest and to the maintaining of peace & harmony.[2]

Although Chandler was later able to report a 'very friendly' meeting with the Congregational Fund board,[3] it was clear that there could be no real measure of agreement. For many years it had been the custom of the Congregational Fund to make grants only to ministers known to be 'sound in the faith', and this deliberate policy of separating the sheep from the goats had helped to make such phrases as 'the general good of the Dissenting interest' anachronistic and meaningless. The Presbyterian Fund, on the other hand, continued to make grants to ministers on the basis not of creed but of need: orthodox Calvinists, like Risdon Darracott, whose theology was repugnant to all the managers except perhaps Barker, continued to receive grants so long as their financial circumstances warranted them. But because of the increasing strictness of the Independents' grant-making policy it became increasingly rare for a minister

[1] Presb. Fund Minutes, v. 65.   [2] Ibid. 158-9.   [3] Ibid. 161.

to receive a grant from both Funds. Thus the last vestiges of the idea of a 'Common Fund' now disappeared. The partisan zeal of the Independents had removed one more of the links that had formerly helped materially to unite the forces of Dissent.

The widening of the gulf between the two Funds also contributed to the growth of denominational consciousness at the congregational level. Formerly there had been in many of the smaller towns congregations that were not specifically Presbyterian nor Independent but simply 'Protestant Dissenting'. Often they contained elements of both denominational traditions and received financial help from both Funds. After 1738, however, and even more so after about 1750, a number of congregations that had been assisted from both Funds lost their grant from the Independents because their ministers were not sufficiently orthodox; they thus became more readily identifiable as Presbyterian causes. The classic case is that of Needham Market, where Priestley, minister from 1755 to 1758, refused a grant from the Independent Fund because he would not conform to their doctrinal requirements: from that date Needham, which received a grant only from the Presbyterian Fund, may properly be classified as a Presbyterian congregation.[1]

## Denominational Consciousness

Of much greater significance as a factor in the increase of denominational consciousness at the congregational level was the introduction of strictly congregational constitutions in churches that had previously been very haphazardly organized. Congregations whose government had been in the hands of a vague aggregation of trustees and principal subscribers (a typical Presbyterian arrangement) were re-organized in such a way that authority was vested in the 'church' or the whole body of communicants. What happened at Milborne Port, Somerset, furnishes a clear example of this kind of transformation. In 1744 George Lewis Young settled there as pastor and promptly 'induced the church to become Congregational in its form of church order and discipline'. The change-over was marked by the drawing up of a covenant in which the members set forth their bond of union: 'We believe that Christ has appointed particular societies or Churches on earth, for his peculiar glory, and

[1] Anne Holt, *Joseph Priestley*, 1931, 15; Gordon, *Heads*, 107. Needham later became Congregational.

the good and salvation of his people, whom he has called by his grace out of the world'. To be admitted to this closed community of Christ's elect, people had to make application, preferably in writing, stating their experience.[1] More often, however, this kind of constitution-making took place not in old congregations of united Dissenters but in the new causes formed by Calvinist groups breaking away from old congregations. The first action of the people who seceded from the Maidstone congregation in 1745 was the drawing up of a constitution which vested the government of the new congregation in the body of believers: this, they hoped, would ensure that Arminian views were kept out for ever.[2] Thus the covenant, which had been a mark of Congregational churches since the 1640s, began to be used increasingly as a device for excluding undesirables.

This increase in denominational consciousness was also found in the large towns where there were old-established congregations of both Presbyterians and Independents, which, though separated from each other by differences in church government, had for many years enjoyed the most amicable relations with each other. In the middle years of the century relations began to deteriorate. At Nottingham the breach came rather earlier than elsewhere, owing to the strong views of James Sloss, who tended to tar all Presbyterians with the Arian brush.[3] In December 1739 the Castle Gate Independents ruled that 'no person be received from the High Pavement congregation as a member of this congregation without giving in their experience, unless they have been received members of that Church before the Rev. Mr. Hewes left that congregation'; the operative date was 1735, when Obadiah Hughes (not to be confused with the London minister of that name) left High Pavement and was succeeded by a much more radical minister.[4]

In other towns where there was no such attempt to provoke a Trinitarian controversy the deterioration in Presbyterian-Independent relations tended to come later and more gradually. It was evidently only in 1751 that Joseph Ryder, a prominent member of Call Lane Independent chapel, Leeds, came to realize that there

[1] E. R. Pitman, *Memorials of . . . Milborne Port*, 1883, 48–50, 53–5.
[2] T. Timpson, *Church history of Kent*, 1859, 336.        [3] See above, p. 179.
[4] A. R. Henderson, *History of Castle Gate Congregational Church, Nottingham, 1665–1905*, 1905, 148.

was any significant difference between the preaching at the two Leeds meeting houses, Mill Hill and Call Lane, and even then he continued for several years to make a habit of worshipping occasionally at Mill Hill.[1]

While Independents gradually came to regard Presbyterian chapels as theologically out of bounds, the Presbyterians for their part seem to have entertained no such feelings towards the Independents. With them the old tradition of 'catholic' Dissent persisted much longer. The deed of Gateacre chapel near Liverpool drawn up in 1787, which stated that the minister must be 'of the Presbyterian denomination, as distinct from the established Church of England, from the people called Quakers, Anabaptists, Independents, Methodists, and from any other religious sect whatsoever',[2] reflects a denominational consciousness which only came in, and even then not universally, with the militant Unitarianism of Priestley.

Who then was responsible for the break-up of the Old Dissent? One answer is that it was the Presbyterians, whose disloyalty to the doctrines of the Reformation caused the loyal Independents to dissociate themselves from them, as men dissociate themselves from those stricken with a plague. But a case could be made out for the contrary view—that responsibility lay with the Independents: newly-revived evangelical zeal produced a theological exclusiveness which led them to betray the catholic ideals of Baxter and Doddridge to which the Presbyterians alone remained loyal.

After all, the principal creators of disharmony were not the Arminians, who rarely made public attacks upon anyone except Deists and Atheists, but rather those strict Calvinists, the spiritual heirs of Richard Davis of Rothwell, who lost no opportunity of castigating both the principles and persons of those who did not agree with them. Not often in the long history of religious controversy have men spoken as bitterly as did Guyse in his denunciations of the 'Reverend Bookseller' Chandler, or as David Rees in his answer to Strong. The publication of Strong's revised version of the Assembly's catechism (into which he introduced such 'dangerous' notions as the saving 'example' of Christ) persuaded Rees of the urgent need to 'check the violence and rapidity of the progress of the New Scheme': 'Not that I think there is anything properly

[1] *UHST*, iv. 264 f.    [2] B. Nightingale, *Lancs. Nonconf.* vi. 200.

new in it; for 'tis only a crude collection of heathenish notions, framed into a system of stupid and lifeless morality.'[1]

In preaching Christian morality the Arminians cannot be regarded as innovators: they were not so much introducing new notions as emphasizing old ones that men had lost sight of. Rees was right to say that there was nothing very new about the 'New Scheme'. When a discontented Calvinist member of Upper Chapel, Sheffield asked Thomas Haynes, minister there from 1745 to 1758, for the 'old doctrine', he replied: 'the older the better; mine is as old as the Apostles.'[2] This was merely a different way of saying what the Arminians had long been saying—that Scripture, and Scripture alone, provided men with all that was essential for salvation. Josiah Owen was speaking for a great number of Presbyterian ministers when he said that 'doctrines have been fathered on Christianity, which are not of its own propagation, and the simplicity of the Gospel eclipsed'.[3] The real innovators, so the Arminians argued, were those who replaced the Word of God by the words of the fallible men who had gathered at Dort and Westminster to pontificate about what their fellow men should believe.

But the Presbyterians must take their share of the responsibility for the break-up of the Old Dissent. In their anxiety to avoid 'enthusiasm' they tended to go too far in the opposite direction and to ride their rational horse to the detriment of their own cause. Barker had some truth on his side when in 1744 he wrote thus to Doddridge:

One's ears are so dinned with reason, the great law of reason, the eternal law of reason, that it is enough to put one out of conceit with the chief excellency of our nature, because it is idolised and almost deified.[4]

The evidence is that the average Arminian sermon, though its intellectual and moral content was of the highest order, was a pretty boring performance: Job Orton's comment on the radical Paul Cardale of Evesham that he 'ruined a fine congregation by his very learned, dry and critical discourses'[5] was probably capable of

---

[1] David Rees, *Enquiry into Truth*, 1736, pp. vii–viii.
[2] J. E. Manning, *Hist. of Upper Chapel*, 1900, 71.
[3] J. Owen, *Difficulties and Discouragements*, 1735, 37.
[4] Doddridge, *Corresp.* iv. 359 (Barker to Doddridge October 3, 1744).
[5] J. Orton, *Letters to Dissenting ministers*, 1806, i. 154.

much wider application. Benson, whose 'usual method of preaching was critically to explain the scripture and then to inculcate duty', was likewise never a popular preacher: some apparently found his discourses 'dry and tedious'.[1] Little wonder therefore that some of the Arminian divines preached away many of the simpler souls in their congregations, who then went off and listened to more emotional, if less scholarly, evangelists who were busy reviving the fervours of Protestant Dissent. As early as 1744 Bourn told Benson that 'a gentleman of good capacity' had lately observed that one reason why 'the Independent congregations were more numerous, with worse principles, than the Presbyterians with better' was that the Independent ministers 'laboured the art pathetic more'.[2]

Possibly the fairest view to take of the demise of the Old Dissent is to say that both the Presbyterians and the Independents were responsible for it. The Presbyterians generally failed to realize what one of their more conservative ministers, William Prior, pointed out in 1738, that 'Christianity is more the religion of the heart than the head'[3] and thus tended to alienate themselves from the vast majority who could not or did not wish to follow their reasoning. The Independents on the other hand, through their tendency to neglect reason, often alienated themselves from those who did not share their particular psychological make-up and were not emotionally stirred by their particular theological vocabulary.

In the end David Jennings seems to have been proved right and Philip Doddridge wrong. The two parties within Dissent, the rational and the evangelical, could not easily be contained within one denomination: 'like Jeremy's two figs, one very good and one very bad', they could be 'squeezed together' but they could never 'incorporate'. The only quarrel that any fair-minded person could have with Jennings's analogy is his assertion that one group was 'very bad' and the other 'very good'. They were, it seems, very different—and that is where objective historical comment must end.

---

[1] Amory in memoir prefixed to Benson's *History of Jesus Christ*, 1764.
[2] Benson MSS. (Bourn to Benson March 9, 1744).
[3] W. Prior, *Ordination sermon at Bridport*, 1739, 52.

# CHAPTER VI

# PRESBYTERIANS UNDER A NEW NAME

*by* H. L. SHORT

---

## FROM PRESBYTERIAN TO UNITARIAN

### Political and Social Changes

By the middle of the eighteenth century the English Presbyterians (or moderate Dissenters, as they preferred to be called) were facing a new situation, and they themselves changed to meet it. It can be seen even in their faces. The portraits of Presbyterian divines of the early part of the century show men of assured dignity, in formal wigs and clothes of elegant cut. But in the second half of the century the faces have become more individual and calculating, either with natural hair or with less pretentious wigs and much more sober dress. Formerly clients of the Whig magnates and not far from the seats of power, they have now become a segregated middle class.

The climate of both politics and church-life was changing. The period of Whig dominance was coming to an end. Even when the Tories had been in power, as in the last years of Queen Anne, the Whigs had been a powerful alternative government. It is true that the Whigs never granted the Presbyterian hopes of comprehension or even of relaxation of the penal laws; but the Presbyterians continued to support the Whigs, having no alternative. The Whig policy was to let sleeping dogs lie; and that included leaving the Test and Corporation Acts on the statute book, with only minor relief. The leading London Dissenters preferred not to embarrass the Whigs by pressing for repeal; this annoyed their country cousins. England's commerce and colonial power were increasing as a result of successful wars and Dissenting merchants thankfully accepted the situation.

But the Whig era came to an end. In the period of the American revolution, in the early years of George III, there was fluctuation in power between Whigs and Tories. Then came the French Revolution and the balance swung to the Tories, who remained in power almost continuously until the eve of the Reform Bill of 1832. So the Whigs (and Presbyterians) remained protestingly out of office for nearly forty years, becoming more and more idealist and radical in temper. Some of them followed Burke into the Tory camp and lost their former identity. This political downfall of their Whig patrons effected a great change in the temper and numbers of the Presbyterians.

From the middle of the century the climate of church life also changed. Formerly the Presbyterians were the leaders of Dissent, in numbers, wealth and social tone. But they had suffered three defeats: under the Commonwealth they had failed to remodel the state church, and at the Restoration and again at the Revolution they had failed to obtain comprehension within the Church of England. They were therefore compelled to join the Independents and Baptists in a separated nonconformity. Except for some county and district ministers' meetings (which were active early in the century, but steadily dwindled in importance), a central fund and appeals to the London ministers for guidance in local difficulties, they made no attempt to set up a national Presbyterian church; indeed, as there was already an established national church, most Presbyterians would have regarded such an attempt as schismatic. Yet they did not adopt the congregational polity of the Independents and Baptists. There was no rule by church-meeting; the minister, like a Puritan clergyman in relation to his parish, was in theory the head of the congregation. But since he had no state church behind his authority and financial control was in the hands of lay trustees, he became more and more the nominee and employee of the richer members of his congregation. Everything depended on his personal ability and preaching-power—which meant, in London and the larger cities, his reflection of the spirit of the age.

For a time Independents and Baptists, especially in London, tended to follow the same pattern. Emphasis was on the individual minister, prominent by his personal ability and supported by the richer members of his congregation rather than on covenant and church-meeting. The Happy Union of 1691 was made between Presbyterian and Independent ministers, not between congregations[1]; and although in London it was soon broken and separate funds were established, ministers of all three denominations,

1 See above, p. 113 ff.

especially in cities, tended to be of much the same professional type. This is one reason for their common liberality of temper, especially in the academies which they set up for the education of both ministers and laity and which so far had no special denominational colour. Moderates like Doddridge had friends in both camps.[1]

## The Evangelical Revival and Dissent

By the middle of the century all this was changing. Doddridge died in 1751, and Watts in 1748; and with them departed the liberal temper which up till then had united many of the leaders, whatever the denominational label. The evangelical revival, led by Whitefield and Wesley, began in the late 1730s and by 1750 it had set England and America aflame. The response of the older Dissenters was at first various. Some Presbyterians opened their pulpits to Wesley and some Independents condemned him as a fanatic. But soon Independents gravitated to evangelicalism and Presbyterians called themselves 'rational Dissenters' in protest against it. The evangelical movement revitalized lay piety and the kind of fervent preaching that awakened it; and this in turn re-emphasized personal testimonies of religious experience as a qualification for church membership, and the church-meeting rather than the minister as the controlling authority in a congregation. Thus Independency, or Congregationalism, which for a time had tended towards the same ministerial pattern as Presbyterianism, reverted to a former type. Preachers proclaimed man's fallen state and Christ's atoning death as an emotional crisis, so that moral rationalism, which was the other half of Puritan piety, seemed dull and empty.

The Presbyterians were swept aside by this new wave of religious enthusiasm. Moderation was no longer attractive. Yet it was appropriate to the new thought-world founded upon Locke's common-sense psychology and Newton's mathematical cosmology, accepted by progressive minds of the day. The Presbyterians could justifiably feel that they were holding firm to sound sense and were the true 'catholic' party and the natural leaders of Dissent, when others were turning aside into the dangerous enthusiasm of evangelicalism. They again sought friends among the moderates and latitudinarians of the Church of England, followers of Clarke and Hoadly, rather than among their fellow-Dissenters. In Scotland the moderates kept

[1] See above, p. 186 ff.

control of the Presbyterian national church and the evangelicals were thrust out; so Presbyterians in England had friends in Scotland also.

Newtonian cosmology naturally led to an Arian view of Christ. The Author of Nature (the phrase is typically Newtonian) must be one divine person, the maker and ruler of all; Christ is his lieutenant and messenger, subordinate but pre-existent and divine, whom he sent to reveal those truths of existence and morality which the human reason already guessed at in more general terms. The divine authority of Christ is confirmed by his miracles and his resurrection from the dead. Every biblical truth was maintained in this and could most safely be stated in biblical language. The book of Genesis and the Psalms, especially when versified by Isaac Watts, told of God's creating and ruling power. Deuteronomy and the prophets proclaimed the rule of law in human society and the need for political reform. The New Testament enunciated the principles of personal morality. Into all this could be fitted the Whig ideals of civil and religious liberty and the new scientific faith in a mathematically-ordered universe whose laws were most likely to be discovered by free enquiry and open discussion among the enlightened.

In fact it was a process of 'demythologization', a continued use of traditional language, embodying values, to express a new world of thought. Some men, like William Whiston, realized what was happening and urged caution in imparting the new truth, for fear of alienating friends. Others, like Samuel Clarke, thought that the change could be made without disturbing the devout by a few inconspicuous modifications in the language of worship. The Exeter and Salters' Hall controversies of 1719 showed that it could not be done.[1] The orthodox insisted on a showdown and the Newtonian party, whether they understood all they were doing or not, protected themselves by insisting on defining their faith in scripture—language only—which enabled them to be traditional and Newtonian at the same time. Naturally this party was largely made up of the moderate rationalists among the Presbyterians, and it was not yet clear how far their new principles would lead them.

## Presbyterianism and Commerce

Just as the evangelical revival reawakened lay piety, so the new Presbyterianism found lay support. The early part of the eighteenth

[1] See above, p. 155 ff.

century was an age of commercial expansion; indeed, had it not been for the wealth accumulated in the first half of the century there would have been no Industrial Revolution in the second half. Expansion meant opportunity. Ambitious young men from the country districts and from Scotland, Wales and Northern Ireland moved into the towns to seek new openings in trade. They tended to join the old Presbyterian congregations, which provided them with the right opportunities and introductions. If they came from Scotland or Ulster they were usually already Presbyterian; Wales was traditionally Puritan; but if they were English, the first step in founding a new fortune at this date was often taken when a young man deserted a conventional Anglicanism for a self-conscious Nonconformity. Parish churches were Tory, and Methodist and orthodox Dissenting chapels too tightly disciplined and socially inferior. The Presbyterian chapels gave that combination of social stability, freedom and modernity which would encourage a rising young man, and, if they had in fact lost some of their original impetus and numbers, whilst retaining wealth and social status, this was an attraction rather than otherwise, for it left room for new blood. Within a generation these new men had taken the lead in many of the old Presbyterian congregations, marrying the daughters of the leading families, becoming trustees of chapel property and endowments, taking the initiative in calling ministers. Naturally this strengthened the rationalist tendencies in Presbyterianism. The new men had no links with Puritan orthodoxy. They had imbibed modern ways of thinking; they were practical men and valued freedom of thought. They soon set the tone of the rational Dissenters.

It is a great mistake to think that a religious denomination grows by natural increase within existing families, so that the present adherents are the lineal descendants of the founding fathers. This sometimes happens, of course, but even so it cannot be assumed that the children and grandchildren of the founders will hold the faith in exactly the same spirit as their sires, even if they still use the same key-words. A radical movement, whether religious or political, is usually idealist and protesting, and provides an opening for new men of ambition and vigour; and marriage into families which have already established themselves is an obvious gain in status and wealth, especially if those families have daughters and no sons. The new man is likely to be a primary producer, a maker of wealth, a pioneer of new methods; but his children are likely to be administrators rather than creators and, where he was a manufacturer, they will be bankers and lawyers, and their children gentry.

The ministry is another route by which new men of vigour have in the past been able to establish themselves in an environment favourable to their development. It is a common complaint that the old families do not send their sons into the ministry; ministers more often come from outside, from lower levels of society or from other parts of the country. It was often remarked in the eighteenth century how many ministers came from rural Wales and some of them, like Lewis Loyd, passed through the ministry into the world of banking and finance. Marriage into existing families is here also a way to status, and it is noticeable in this connection how many ministers in the nineteenth century had an old Puritan surname (their mother's maiden-name) as a middle name. Such men were ministers' sons; their fathers had married into established families and now the sons entered the ministry, usually at a higher social level and with a more sophisticated theology; their grandsons in turn did not often enter the ministry, but moved on into education, the professions, the scientific world or the civil service.

## Warrington Academy

An event which marked the new spirit of the Presbyterians was the founding of Warrington Academy in 1757. Doddridge's death in 1751 meant the end of his academy at Northampton, where so many young ministers, both Presbyterian and Independent, had imbibed liberal principles. It was transferred to Daventry by Caleb Ashworth, who tried to continue the same tradition, but without Doddridge's warmth. When Caleb Rotheram died in 1752 his academy at Kendal closed; so did Findern academy in 1754 on the death of Dr Latham. Taunton Academy was moribund. In these institutions lay and divinity students, Presbyterian and Independent and not a few Anglicans, had been educated together under the care of ministers of liberal sentiments.[1] That day was coming to an end. The new foundations which would take their place would be distinctively evangelical or rationalist, not both, as Daventry's troubled history would show—though it was supported by Independents, its

[1] For the earlier academies, see above, pp. 191 ff.

principal from 1781, Thomas Belsham, became Unitarian and resigned in 1789.

Warrington Academy was the child of rational Dissent. Of course many of its innovations were foreshadowed by earlier academies, but what they did tentatively, Warrington did with conscious decision. Earlier academies had had lay students, even at times in the majority, but Warrington catered deliberately for them, stressing a utilitarian bias in preparation for a medical, legal or military career, and for 'civil and commercial life'. Divinity still had formal precedence over other studies, the divinity tutor acting as principal of the academy. But a wide choice of subjects of study was allowed, so that many students took no divinity lectures at all, and discipline was in the hands not of the principal but of the *rector academiae*.

There were new features in organization. Formerly an academy was the personal venture of a distinguished minister, who received pupils into his home; even at Warrington the student-body was still known as the family. The meals and morning and evening prayers were after the model of a private household. But at Warrington all this was changed. The new academy was managed by a committee of laymen, who engaged and paid the teaching staff. The students were lodged in a building fitted for the purpose, with a common hall and meals provided by a steward. Soon the committee erected a neat collegiate quadrangle; if any of the tutors received pupils into his home, it was as lodgers to increase his income and not as part of his duty. Warrington was the first redbrick university.

It was in curriculum that Warrington made the biggest innovations. The beginning was conventional enough. Three tutors were engaged for the three traditional elements of education: divinity, classics and mathematics. The divinity tutor was an elderly liberal divine, John Taylor of Norwich, already famous for his *Scripture doctrine of original sin* (1740) and other works whose titles show his desire to express eighteenth-century rationalism in scriptural language, and also of a monumental Hebrew concordance which was praised by both Anglicans and Dissenters.[1] It was an unfortunate choice; he belonged to a generation which was passing and the students were restive. The mathematical tutor was John Holt, competent but colourless, who also met with resistance from

[1] See above, p. 185.

P

students. The post of tutor in classics was first offered to a layman, itself a portent, but was finally given to John Aikin, a remarkable teacher.

*Joseph Priestley*

When Taylor resigned, disappointed, in 1761, Aikin became divinity tutor. To the tutorship in classics, renamed 'languages and belles lettres', was appointed Joseph Priestley, then a young and unknown Presbyterian minister at Nantwich, but soon to be the leader and remodeller of Rational Dissent. He interpreted his sphere of education in the widest and most modern terms. He doubted the value of more than an elementary knowledge of Latin and Greek, and preferred to teach history, biography, politics and self-expression through writing and elocution. In his time at Warrington lectures in practical chemistry were introduced (which started Priestley himself on his scientific career) and soon afterwards modern languages were taught by a succession of Swiss and German teachers, one of whom was J.-P. Marat, later a leading figure in the French Revolution. For financial reasons Priestley resigned in 1767, to become minister of Mill Hill Chapel, Leeds.

George III came to the throne in 1760, and the Seven Years War, the last great effort of the Whigs, ended in victory in 1763 with the acquisition of Canada and India from the French. Then followed a confused period in politics, Whigs and Tories alternating in power. The British conquest of Canada, and the consequent removal of the French threat to the American colonies, led to the American War of Independence; for the Americans now felt able to stand on their own feet. The war, which began in 1775, was mismanaged by the Tories, and peace was made by the Whigs. The Rational Dissenters were almost all on the American side; while fighting was in progress Priestley was in regular correspondence with Benjamin Franklin and rejoicing in American victories. Priestley's friendship with Franklin, a genial common-sense deist, a practical scientist and inventor, and a republican politician, is significant of the direction in which Priestley would lead the Presbyterians. In 1772 Priestley had become librarian and literary companion to Lord Shelburne, the Whig politician who opposed coercion of the American colonists and who eventually led the government which signed the peace.

Warrington Academy was Whig. While Henry Laurens, president

of the American Continental Congress, was a prisoner in the Tower of London, having been captured at sea, his son of the same name was a student at Warrington Academy. Another student was Archibald Hamilton Rowan, later an Irish revolutionary and an exile in America. In theology a similar radicalism soon became manifest. At first it was not noticeable. Priestley said that when he first went to Warrington the only Socinian in the district was John Seddon of Manchester, 'and we all wondered at him'. But the academy soon became known for theological rationalism and before long its divinity students seeking pulpits caused a crisis in some Presbyterian congregations. At Shrewsbury Job Orton, a moderate reconciler and a former student of Doddridge's academy, retired in 1765. The richer members of his congregation wanted to call Benjamin Stapp, fresh from Warrington; the poorer members, encouraged by Orton, seceded, and called Robert Gentleman, a young evangelical from Daventry Academy (who, however, eventually became Unitarian). At Macclesfield (where the Presbyterian congregation was dominated by John Brocklehurst, a newcomer from the country and a rising business man who had married into the congregation) John Palmer from Warrington Academy was called to the pulpit in 1764. By 1772 the congregation split, Brocklehurst and his business partners supporting Palmer and the opponents seceding, first to join the Methodists and then to establish a Congregational church. Palmer later was a friend of Priestley and a contributor to his journals.

## Cambridge and Essex Street Chapel

Few Dissenters other than Presbyterians sent their sons to Warrington; on the other hand a number of Warrington students became Anglican clergy. The old alliance between Presbyterian moderates and Anglican latitudinarians persisted, through a common rationalism and Whig politics. This was cemented by developments at Cambridge. Oxford was firmly Tory and High-church; Methodism itself, which grew out of the 'Holy Club' at Oxford, began from Wesley's High-church idealism and even owed something to the Non-juror William Law. It is not surprising that Methodism in the eighteenth century was Tory. There was never any doubt at Oxford that all teachers and students must sign the Thirty-Nine Articles. But Cambridge, with a Puritan tradition, developed differently. On the one hand there was an evangelical movement, led by Isaac Milner, William Wilberforce and Charles Simeon, which though Anglican had links with evangelical Dissent; on the other there was a radical and rationalist movement, which opposed subscription to the Articles and made alliance with the rational Dissenters. Oxford was the university of Archbishop Laud, Cambridge of Isaac Newton.

A group of Cambridge men wanted to abolish subscription to the Articles, both in the university and in the Church of England at large, as detrimental, they said, to that candour, liberty and progress of thought which was appropriate to the enlightened age in which they lived. In 1766 Francis Blackburne of St Catherine's College wrote *The confessional, or a full and free enquiry into the right, utility and success of establishing confessions of faith and doctrine in Protestant churches*. From this grew an agitation among Anglican clergy for relief from subscription, culminating in the Feathers Tavern Petition to Parliament in 1772, which was rejected by a large majority in the Commons. In the same year a similar effort to abolish subscription on the part of candidates for a degree was defeated in the senate of Cambridge university by a narrow vote. This was part of a large programme of reform, dealing also with examinations and fellowships, which also failed by small majorities in the face of stiffening conservatism.

The reforming party was influential and vigorous. Two at least of its members, Edmund Law and Richard Watson, became bishops. The chancellor of the university, the Duke of Grafton, belonged to the party and wrote a pamphlet criticizing the Book of Common Prayer on Unitarian grounds. But frustration turned most of them into eccentric individualists, each making his own dramatic protest and then retiring into soured exile. Some, notably William Paley, the eminent moral philosopher and economist, conformed to the rising Tory majority.

Many of the defeated Cambridge reformers found their way into alliance with the Rational Dissenters and greatly influenced them. The main link was Essex Street Chapel in London. Having failed to rationalize the Church of England, a small group of the reformers founded in London a rational model of an Anglican place of worship, with a reformed Anglican liturgy (after the model drawn up by the Newtonian Samuel Clarke). The minister was Theophilus Lindsey former fellow of St John's College and chief organizer of the defeated petition to parliament. He was Blackburne's son-in-law. When the petition failed he resigned his Anglican living and opened Essex-street Chapel in 1774. He was supported by other Cambridge men, including the Duke of Grafton; John Jebb of Peterhouse, who resigned his Anglican orders in 1774; John Disney of Peterhouse, another son-in-law of Blackburne, who resigned his living in 1782 and became Lindsey's colleague and successor; Gilbert Wakefield of Jesus College, who resigned his orders in 1780, and others. Also at the opening service of Essex-street Chapel were Priestley and Franklin and two Whig peers, Lord Shelburne and Lord Spencer. In 1779 Gilbert Wakefield became classical tutor at Warrington Academy, bringing T. R. Malthus with him as a student. Wakefield became a friend of William Shepherd, minister at Gateacre near Liverpool, and of other radical Presbyterians.

## The New Name Unitarian

Lindsey was widely known as a 'Unitarian Christian' in spite of the Toleration Act of 1689, which excluded those who denied the doctrine of the Trinity, and the Blasphemy Act of 1698, which exposed them to heavy penalties. His action, and the fact that it went unpunished, caused the Rational Dissenters to reconsider their theological position. Some of them wished to hold on to the old Presbyterian comprehension; others, in particular Priestley, thought that the time had come for a bold advance under a new name. Priestley himself was not of Presbyterian origin, but a dissident Independent. As well as a new lay leadership, a new ministerial leadership was arising among the Presbyterians, on the part of newcomers from other denominations, from humbler levels of society, or from Scotland, Wales or Ulster. It meant a loosening of ties with the past and a new emphasis on radical theology. A feeling that the way was now open for theological advance was encouraged by the action of parliament in 1779, which, while refusing to relax subscription in the Church of England, no longer required from Dissenting ministers assent to the doctrinal Articles, as prescribed by the Toleration Act.[1]

The new name, vigorously proclaimed by Priestley, was the same as that chosen by Lindsey—'Unitarian'. It meant an emphatic

[1] Cf. R. B. Barlow, *Citizenship and conscience*, 1962, 171 ff.

rationalism, completely Newtonian, determinist and materialist. It was individualist; following Hoadly, Priestley believed that Christ's authority was not in a church but in the individual reason and conscience. The story of Christianity, both as institution and as theology, was one of progressive corruption of the original impulse; and the time had come for a rational recovery. Christ was not the second Person of the Trinity, nor (as the Arians taught) the pre-existent Word, but a man, commissioned by God to proclaim those sacred truths of creation and conduct which the unaided human reason might guess at, but could never know with certainty without divine revelation. Christianity was the one true religion; the other religions of the world were superstitious and vicious. This unique authority of the Christian revelation was guaranteed by Christ's miracles and resurrection; his death at the hands of a reactionary priesthood was not an atoning sacrifice for sin, as the evangelicals claimed, but a grim example of the fate of all prophets and reformers.

## Priestley's Unitarianism

In Priestley's eyes this faith was optimistic, benevolent and obviously true:

> The connections that all persons and all things necessarily have, as parts of an immense glorious and happy system (and of which we ourselves are a part, however small and inconsiderable) with the great author of this system, makes us regard every person and every thing in a friendly and pleasing light. The whole is but one family. We have all one God and Father, whose affection for us is intense, impartial and everlasting. He despises nothing that he has made, and, by ways unknown to us, and often by methods the most unpromising, he provides for our greatest good. We are all training up in the same school of moral discipline, and are likewise joint heirs of eternal life, revealed to us in the gospel.[1]

He admitted, however, that it did not arouse much popular support:

> It is too evident to be denied, that the societies of those who are called Rational Dissenters, whether they be properly Unitarian or not, do generally decline; many of them having become actually extinct, and others being in such a condition that they cannot be supported much longer. This is more especially the case in London and in the south of England; but from the same causes it may in time extend to the north.[2]

[1] J. Priestley, *The doctrine of philosophic necessity illustrated*, 1782, 123.
[2] J. Priestley, *Forms of prayer for the use of Unitarian societies*, 1783, 3.

Unitarians (like the Presbyterians before them, but unlike the evangelicals) demanded an educated ministry, but ministerial salaries were insufficient to support men with middle-class standards of living. The answer, Priestley thought, was the founding of small worshipping groups led by laymen, using a provided liturgy and printed sermons. But Unitarians ought not, he urged, to reconcile themselves to the forms of orthodox worship, for the sake of tradition or social peace; they should be definite and aggressive. In spirit and organization this was an echo of the Independency of his youth. It was a break with Presbyterian moderation and was to be a sore point in the future. Priestley defended his Unitarian faith against all comers and indeed provoked attack, for he loved controversy, whilst proclaiming himself a man of peace. He was a voluminous writer, an eminent scientist and a many-sided man; he is the only figure in the *Dictionary of national biography* whose life had to be written in two instalments by two different experts, one for his career as theologian and politician, and one for his career as a scientist. Politically his faith meant aggressive Whiggism, attacking the government on every issue of 'civil and religious liberty', with such vehemence of metaphor that the political cartoonists represented him as 'gunpowder Joe'. He was a radical, but not a socialist. He accepted the individualist utilitarianism of free trade and commercial enterprise, which was becoming the economic creed of the middle classes. But he had little popular support.

*Priestley and the Presbyterians*

His vigorous leadership largely captured that part of the Presbyterian body which had developed into Rational Dissent. It was now much diminished in numbers, partly because of that general decline which affected all Dissent in the first half of the eighteenth century and then because of the sharp division between evangelical and rational Dissenters in the generation which followed. Some Presbyterian congregations split, the seceders, usually the poorer members, joining the Congregationalists or the Methodists. Others, especially in country districts, went over bodily to the evangelicals. In those that remained, the temper of the times made the interests of the members secular and political rather than devout. For a number of reasons—social, economic and political, as much as intellectual—membership and attendance declined. Gilbert Wakefield, on joining the Rational Dissenters, even wrote a pamphlet, which greatly embarrassed his new friends, denying the value of public worship. Mrs Barbauld, daughter of Dr Aikin, principal of Warrington Academy, wrote a reply, and in *Thoughts on devotional taste* (1775) she admitted with sorrow that 'the spirit of devotion is at a low ebb amongst us'. She blamed it on a too philosophical view of religion and urged a greater trust in the religious emotions. Priestley protested that this was to encourage superstition.

Not all the Presbyterians followed Priestley. His friend Dr Richard Price shared his political opinions—it was his sermon welcoming the outbreak of the French Revolution which provoked Burke's celebrated *Reflections*, the Tory textbook—but remained Arian in theology and a believer in free-will. Some London and other Prebyterians continued in the old 'moderate' tradition, preaching a common-sense morality and refusing to be drawn into theological battles. But all were Whigs in politics.

## Other Unitarian Connections

Priestley's vigorous campaigning stimulated a trend which had already begun; the movement into the staid Presbyterian circle of newcomers who, like Priestley himself, had no Presbyterian background. Often they were poor men, not of that merchant class to which the Presbyterians, or at least their leading members, traditionally belonged. When the General Baptist churches divided in 1770, the evangelicals founding the New Connexion, the radical minority gravitated towards the Unitarians and were soon providing leaders for their new fellowship. From time to time, as the eighteenth century drew to a close, we hear of poor religious men who discover themselves to be Unitarians, not only because they share Priestley's humanitarian view of Christ, but also because they accept his materialism and determinism, the advanced thought of that day. Soon they too provided leaders for their new allegiance.

A further complication was the association of the Unitarians with the Cambridge exiles from the Church of England. Traditionally the Presbyterians were unwilling Dissenters, hoping with nostalgia for a broad national church to which they could be reunited; in this they differed from the other Dissenting bodies, who had no such ideal. The ex-Anglicans, in spite of Priestley's polemics against bishops, strengthened this leaning towards the Establishment.

Already in 1762 a group of Rational Dissenters, led by Thomas Bentley, Josiah Wedgwood's partner (and with him a founder of Warrington Academy), had established in Liverpool a chapel with a liturgy, hoping to draw in both Dissenters and dissatisfied Anglicans. They even tried to get John Seddon, secretary of Warrington academy (not the John Seddon of Manchester), as their first minister. John Taylor and other older Presbyterians opposed this venture, saying that liturgies were contrary to the principles of Presbyteriansm. Though the venture failed, the time would come when a love of liturgy would be a distinguishing mark of those who claimed to be the true descendants of the Presbyterians. When Lindsey opened Essex-street Chapel in 1774 with a modified Anglican prayer-book, other ministers and congregations were tempted towards a liturgical form of worship, usually on the Anglican model. Much deference was shown by the Unitarians to the ex-Anglicans. These were distinguished men with university degrees and fellowships and livings which they had abandoned for the sake of conscience. They were learned in political economy, a favourite science of the day, which proved objectively why trade must be free of all control, how prices are fixed by the market alone and why the poor must be poor. And if some of the ex-Anglicans, like Wakefield, Coleridge and Frend, were eccentrics of one sort or another, and all were individualists, this only demonstrated that liberty of thought was the foundation of an enlightened religion.

Thus Unitarianism at the end of the eighteenth century had become a multiform radical religious movement, partly growing out of, and partly grafted upon, the old Presbyterian moderation. Some Presbyterian congregations joined the Congregationalists or even the Methodists under the influence of the evangelical revival; others split. Some former Independent congregations, as in Cheshire, were by now numbered with the Presbyterians and their successors, the Unitarians.

But the movement had run into a crisis. When the French Revolution broke out in 1789 it was at first welcomed by all friends of liberty and constitutional reform. But even before bloodshed had begun in France, the Tory reaction in England against the Revolution had started. Every event in France confirmed the Tories in England more securely in power. Former Whigs crossed over into the Tory camp. When war between England and revolutionary

France broke out, in general the merchant class lined up behind Pitt, and the Presbyterians lost many substantial members; for, without Whig principles there was not much point in Presbyterian moderation. The moderate party was steadily eroded; only the most convinced Whigs remained and they naturally became more shrill. But the Whig party continued to exist, with Charles James Fox, 'that great, good man', as its parliamentary leader. Since it was kept out of power by Tory rotten boroughs, its chief campaign was for parliamentary reform. Since there was coming into existence, because of the Industrial Revolution, a town-bred proletariat, and since the French Revolution was the first time since the Civil War that the bonds of society had been loosened, behind the Whigs was a much more radical force, which was beginning to talk about 'the rights of the people'. Corresponding societies were established up and down the country to direct agitation for the franchise (the name means that they corresponded with one another to plan a common front, but it also implied in many instances correspondence, actual or hoped-for, with revolutionary organizations in France). As in similar situations, intellectuals and some aristocrats joined the plebeians in their agitation and there was a fluctuating combination of moderation and violence, of dreams and serious planning. Earl Stanhope, who employed Jeremiah Joyce, a Presbyterian minister and an extreme Whig, as tutor to his children, called himself 'citizen Stanhope' and actively engaged in plotting.

It was an explosive situation. The government naturally used coercion and there were patriotic mobs. The Unitarians were early among the victims, however much they protested truly or not their moderation in all things. One of the first to suffer was Priestley himself; his chapel and house in Birmingham, with the houses of other Unitarians, were burnt by a mob in 1791, on the second anniversary of the fall of the Bastille, after a commemorative dinner by the Constitutional (i.e. Whig) Society of Birmingham. In 1794 he emigrated to America. Gilbert Wakefield, Jeremiah Joyce and others suffered terms of imprisonment and William Shepherd, already mentioned, sheltered their children. In Scotland Thomas Fysshe Palmer, a Cambridge ex-Anglican turned Unitarian, suffered judicial transportation and never returned. In Ireland the Arian wing of the Presbyterians of Ulster took a prominent part in the rebellion of the United Irishmen in 1798 and some were executed.

How could the Presbyterians or the Unitarians survive such a crisis? In fact they almost collapsed. Warrington Academy had come to an end in 1786, chiefly because its known radicalism was too much for its subscribers and its constituency was shrinking. Funds and students declined, one of the last students being Thomas Malthus, later an eminent political economist and population expert. Immediately its directors founded two colleges out of the ruins, Hackney College in London, which received the scientific apparatus, and Manchester Academy, which inherited the library; each college had half the remaining endowment. But Hackney College was immediately caught up in the political crisis and failed after only ten years. Manchester Academy was more cautiously conducted; it almost collapsed financially in 1799, but was saved by a transfer to York in 1803 on a smaller scale, with Charles Well-beloved as principal. Its enemies said that it had become 'a Unitarian seminary'.

## THEOLOGICAL CONTROVERSIES

At the beginning of the nineteenth century the Unitarian body (as we may now call it) was greatly discouraged. Its political ideals were frustrated by the long war with France and the consequent long Tory rule in England. The determinism and materialism inherited from Priestley gave little scope for the religious emotions. The individualism and inclination towards the Establishment brought by the ex-Anglicans prevented denominational feeling. The prevailing political economy damped down social sympathies. Congregations remained in existence by the continuing power of inertia and by strong family ties—Unitarians intermarried widely and it was said that many of them, among the leading families, were either descendants of Philip Henry, one of the ejected ministers of 1662, or else married to a descendant of his.

One can sense the discouragement just mentioned in the writings of the time. Thomas Belsham, friend of Priestley, tutor at Hackney College and minister of Essex-street Chapel from 1805, confided it to his diary. John Aikin, journalist son of the principal of Warrington Academy, showed it in the editorials of the magazines he edited.

Mrs Barbauld, who had been so enthusiastic for civil and religious liberty, wrote in her poem *1811* her despair of the survival of European civilization. Some kept their radical hopes, but with little foundation; others swung to a disillusioned Toryism. Belsham came to regret 'the mania of the French Revolution', which had resulted in 'a general spirit of insubordination, giving birth to insidious and daring attacks on natural and revealed religion'. Aikin supported Addington, Pitt's ultra-Tory successor.[1]

But revival came. In part inertia itself helped. Some congregations, chiefly in the west of England, ceased to exist, because of the decline of the cloth trade; the Industrial Revolution had shifted the economic focus of England to the midlands and the north, and wealth drained away from the smaller towns of the west. But other congregations survived, if at a low ebb, and waited for a new impulse. Even Arianism was not quite dead. In a number of the larger provincial towns there was a traditional loyalty, on the part of a group of families, to the local meeting house, awaiting leadership and a new voice. In London there was a social stratum, composed largely of people of the professional class, who valued Unitarianism as a banner of enlightenment and who manned the committees, managed the trust funds, entered Parliament and thus kept the institution alive. But numbers attending worship were said to be small and vitality was low. Lant Carpenter in Bristol in 1817 noted a languid congregational life, the gentlemen renting pews in quite good numbers, but usually represented at worship by their wives and children.

## New Leadership

Some leaders came from the old stock, but became more radical: Timothy Kenrick at Exeter scandalized his congregation by praying for the French Revolution. But a new leadership also came from outside the Presbyterian tradition and from sources even more remote from Anglicanism. Already Priestley and Belsham had come from the Independents, and Joshua Toulmin and Robert Robinson from the Baptists. Wellbeloved's background was evangelical. Native Presbyterian leadership seemed to be in eclipse, and after Disney's resignation in 1805 there were no more ex-Anglican clergy

[1] See Ian Sellers, 'The political and social ideas of representative Unitarians, 1795-1850', an unpublished B.Litt. thesis in the Bodleian Library, Oxford.

to take the Essex-street pulpit, so the succession went to the ex-Independent Belsham. But with the new century leadership came from even humbler and more remote origins. William Vidler, a bricklayer's son, was a Baptist who became a Universalist under the preaching of the American, Elhanan Winchester, minister of Parliament-court chapel, London, whom he succeeded in 1794; in 1802 he was converted to Unitarianism, at the age of forty-four, and became the centre of missionary preaching. Robert Aspland, a Baptist, joined the Unitarian wing of the General Baptists, becoming minister in 1801, at the age of nineteen, of the chapel at Newport, in the Isle of Wight. When he was twenty-three he began his forty-year ministry at the Gravel-pit Chapel, Hackney, an old Presbyterian foundation, his immediate predecessors being Priestley and Belsham. William Johnson Fox was the son of an impoverished Sussex farmer; after studying for the Independent ministry he became, in 1812, at the age of twenty-three, minister of the Presbyterian chapel at Chichester. Five years later he succeeded Vidler at Parliament-court Chapel, soon rebuilt as South-place Chapel, Finsbury. Richard Wright was the son of a Norfolk farm-labourer and became minister of a Johnsonian (Sabellian) Baptist congregation at Wisbech, in Cambridgeshire, which he converted to Unitarianism. David Eaton, a shoemaker of York, was inspired by Priestley's necessarianism and offered himself as a Unitarian preacher to the poor; the Presbyterians were wrong, he said, in thinking that the gospel must first be preached to 'the higher and more cultivated ranks of society'.

Such men provided the dispirited Unitarian body with the leadership it needed. Vidler founded *The Universalist's Miscellany*, renamed in 1802 *The Universal Theological Magazine*. Aspland contributed to it and then bought it in 1805, changing it to *The Monthly Repository*, which he made into the leading Unitarian journal. But it was too literary for the humbler readers whom he wished to reach; so in 1815 he started in addition *The Christian Reformer*, which eventually took its place. In 1813 he opened his own house as Hackney Academy (not to be confused with Hackney College, which had long been closed) for training for the ministry students of lesser academic ability than those who went to Manchester College, York. Johnson Fox shared in editing *The Monthly Repository*, taking it over in 1831 as a political and literary journal, for a brief time publishing Unitarian news as a supplement. Aspland enlarged *The Christian Reformer* to take over its specifically Unitarian functions.

## New Propaganda

A new organizing and propagandist spirit was abroad. The influence of the General Baptists is important in this. Unlike the Presbyterians, who prided themselves on their central churchmanship, the General Baptists were a 'sect' in the sixteenth-century sense, i.e. a closed body with strict rules, governed by travelling officials called 'messengers', and holding an annual Assembly of delegates, with disciplinary powers over the congregations. They practised believer's baptism, their theology was scriptural and they were eager to make converts. All this is very different from the loose and aristocratic 'catholicity' of the Presbyterians. In politics it took the form of a disillusioned criticism of the Tory government and agitation for the removal of religious disabilities. In 1813 William Smith, the veteran Unitarian M.P. and supporter of Charles James Fox, persuaded parliament to abolish penalties on those who impugned the doctrine of the Trinity. But Unitarians still had to be married, and often also buried, with the rites of the Church of England. Unlike the Quakers, they mostly acquiesced in this, but unwillingly; to some, accepted legal status in society was more important than religious scruples. Aggressive agitation against it was left to an extremely radical Unitarian body called the Free Thinking Christians, whose religious principles were so strict that they would have neither paid ministers nor public prayer. They quarrelled with other Unitarians. Their founder was Samuel Thompson, a wine-merchant, who seceded with others in 1798 from William Vidler's Universalist congregation at Parliament-court Chapel. From 1813, whenever one of their members was married, he made public protest to the officiating clergyman and in the newspapers against the use of trinitarian forms. But other Unitarians, Charles Lamb, the essayist, amongst them, said that such intemperate agitation hindered their cause, instead of helping it.

The main energy of the new Unitarians went into theological propaganda. In 1800 the Unitarian Fund was founded in London under Aspland's inspiration, with Vidler, Eaton and Wright as eager supporters. Wright became its first travelling missionary, journeying on foot over much of England and Wales, and into Scotland, preaching on village greens and in barns, wherever he could obtain a hearing. Such an appeal to the poor had never been attempted by the Presbyterians and he did not preach in their chapels 'unless expressly requested to do it', although in time such requests became common. At first he was welcomed chiefly by Baptists and Universalists, and founded many new Unitarian congregations composed of working men and women, who struggled to maintain little churches with the help of small grants of money from the Unitarian Fund. In at least one case a new group and its unpaid minister was allowed the use of an almost empty Presbyterian meeting house and revived a dying cause. Wright challenged the common Presbyterian belief that a preacher should confine himself to those religious and moral topics in which all Christians were agreed and should refrain from controversial divinity; he repudiated the suggestion that Priestley's polemical Unitarianism had isolated and ruined the Presbyterian congregations. 'Not doctrinal preaching, but the want of it, and in particular the want of Christian zeal, which doctrinal preaching might have helped to excite', had led to the closing of Presbyterian and General Baptist churches. The reason for doctrinal reticence, he said, was not Christian comprehension but the fear of giving offence, the love of ease and a desire to stand well with their neighbours. He listed a number of Presbyterian chapels which had been closed and had been re-opened by Unitarian preaching. In 1819 the Unitarian Fund brought him to London to supervise the work of missionary preachers, but except for George Harris there were few to follow him.

In addition to the Unitarian Fund there were established a number of local book and tract societies with similar aims, together with district associations for missionary purposes. Aspland, for example, while minister in the Isle of Wight, had helped to found the Southern Unitarian Society; there was another active society in the west of England, founded by Timothy Kenrick; and in 1813 George Harris founded the Scottish Unitarian Association. Many chapels established lending libraries, chiefly stocked with polemical literature. George Harris vigorously attacked evangelical orthodoxy in Scotland (where he was named 'the devil's chaplain') and in Lancashire, but not everyone agreed with his uncompromising methods and 'many of his ministerial brethren, as well as a large and respectable class of the laity, became alienated in feeling from him'. B. R. Davis, minister of the old Presbyterian chapel at Chowbent, wrote a pamphlet against him; and when Harris preached at the Provincial Meeting at Bury, in 1825, the contention was so sharp between his supporters and his critics that they dined at separate inns.

## The British and Foreign Unitarian Association

In 1825 a number of Unitarian missionary societies, headed by the Unitarian Fund, were amalgamated as the British and Foreign Unitarian Association under the leadership of Aspland, with Johnson Fox as foreign secretary. Individuals, congregations and district associations were invited to take up membership and it was intended that the new society should bind the Unitarians, old and new, into an organized denomination on the same model as the Congregationalists and Baptists, who also at this time were acquiring a denominational polity.

Not all Unitarians welcomed this zeal. Already in 1817 a correspondent in the *Monthly Repository*, signing himself 'Old Unitarian', complained of the new propagandists and 'their fondness for assembling together for the purposes of praying, preaching, eating, drinking, toasting, etc., with all the concomitant exhibition of eloquence, whether sacred or convivial', and feared that 'a few controversial coxcombs' would drive away 'some very respectable individuals' and offend Anglican sympathizers. Some of them were still Arians, believing in the pre-existence of Christ and addressing him with adoration; but they were on the defensive, describing themselves as 'Unitarians of the old school'. Belsham had castigated them as temporizing with orthodoxy and wanted them excluded from Unitarian societies. In 1811 Lant Carpenter, then at Exeter, began a campaign against the wording of the constitution of the Western Unitarian Society, which described trinitarianism as 'idolatrous' and so defined Unitarianism as to exclude the Arians; it took him twenty years to get it changed. When the British & Foreign Unitarian Association was founded in 1825, Carpenter succeeded in preventing the followers of Belsham from excluding the Arians. For a time, in 1827-8, the Arians even had their own magazine, *The Christian Moderator*; it is noteworthy that, though published in London, it had strong links with the Non-Subscribing Presbyterians of Northern Ireland, who included many Arians.[1]

But, in addition to these internal changes, there came a sharp reaction from evangelical Dissent. After the fervours of the eighteenth century came consolidation in the nineteenth. Methodism, it is true, split into sects, but each was well-organized. So far as dates can be given to what was a gradual process, the movement towards Baptist Union began in 1813 and towards Congregational Union in 1809, in spite of protests against the alleged threat to congregational autonomy. Nonconformists became accustomed to united action. Evangelicals, both Nonconformist and Anglican, joined in a great campaign against the slave-trade and slavery, which triumphed in 1833; they also combined in support of the Bible Society and foreign missions. Public meetings, popular excitement, propaganda campaigns, 'lobbying' of parliament, became a familiar aspect of Nonconformity. Unitarians from the first supported anti-slavery and the Bible Society and organized their own pamphlet-war on the accepted Nonconformist model, and they established their national denominational society, the British & Foreign Unitarian Association, at the same time as the other Nonconformist bodies were doing the same. But in becoming a denomination they had lost that central, mediating, comprehensive position in the religious life of the nation which the Presbyterians had claimed. And the battle against Unitarian theology would be fought, not with books and ideas, but with legal processes and Acts of Parliament. Since the Unitarians, as well as the evangelicals, were self-conscious, organized and propagandist, conflict was inevitable.

The tide was flowing against the Unitarians. All over Europe, after the French Revolution and the defeat of Napoleon, there was a wave of religious conservatism. The church was regarded as a bulwark of society. The Whig nobility became cautious churchmen.

---

[1] The Non-Subscribing Presbyterians of Ireland, chiefly confined to the counties of Antrim and Down, and the cities of Dublin and Cork, had gathered themselves out of orthodox Irish Presbyterianism in two stages, parallel to developments in England. The first stage was in the first quarter of the eighteenth century, contemporary with the Exeter and Salters' Hall controversies in England, when John Abernethy was the liberal leader in Belfast and Dublin, organizing the same rationalist and libertarian protest against creeds (especially the Westminster Confession) as inspired the 'non-subscribers' at Salters' Hall. The second stage was in 1829, when Henry Montgomery led a new secession from orthodox Presbyterianism. From time to time Irish N.S. Presbyterianism reacted upon English Unitarianism, as will be seen.

Q

The middle classes, now coming into power, became morally serious, much influenced by evangelical ideals. There was also widespread secularism of a serious kind. Scotland was no longer friendly towards English liberals. In the eighteenth century leadership in the Scottish Presbyterian church had been Whig and 'moderate', and the evangelicals seceded; that is why eminent Non-subscribers at Salters' Hall and the tutors of Warrington Academy, even including Marat, received doctorates from Scottish universities, and Priestley's metaphysics had a Scottish foundation. But in the nineteenth century there was an evangelical revival in Scotland, culminating in the Disruption of 1843. George Harris aroused bitter opposition and found support, not among the intellectuals, but in small protesting groups on the fringes of society, like the former Covenanting congregation in Edinburgh (which had become Unitarian) and the Unitarian congregations at Montrose and Glasgow, founded by William Christie, Priestley's friend.

## Unitarians and Parliamentary Reform

However, except for the Wolverhampton case of 1819[1], the showdown was postponed until a more important public question had been decided. The long rule of the Tories was coming to an end in the campaign for parliamentary reform. The Whigs sought the help of the Dissenters, who had been educated in the tactics of political campaigns against the government and had tasted victory in the long battle against the slave-trade. Whig leaders like Lord Holland, Lord John Russell and Lord Lansdowne appeared on Nonconformist platforms at the annual meetings of Bible and missionary societies, and a common interest between Nonconformity and parliamentary reform was cemented. In 1830 Lord Brougham's election expenses were paid for by subscriptions from Dissenters. Local newspapers were founded by Nonconformists, notably *The Manchester Guardian*, by John Edward Taylor, a Unitarian, and *The Leeds Mercury*, by Edward Baines, a Congregationalist; and they were strong promoters of reform.

In this political campaign both rich and poor Unitarians took a part. The new Unitarians, who had come from the poorer classes, brought their propagandist zeal and their proletarian resentment. The older Unitarians, especially the ex-Anglicans, contributed

[1] See below, p. 245-6.

their professional status and philosophic radicalism. A remarkably large number of them were Members of Parliament, led by William Smith, an M.P. since 1784, a follower of Fox and a fighter for all advanced causes in long speeches which embodied 'all the opinions of all the Dissenters'. In 1828 these Unitarians took a prominent part in founding University College, London, 'the godless place in Gower Street' to be a university without religious tests (though the Anglicans countered with King's College, an unfortunate rivalry solved by incorporating both colleges in the university of London in 1836). After an excited campaign and threatened revolution the Reform Bill was passed in 1832. It transferred the balance of power from the gentry to the middle class and in many places from the Anglicans to the richer Dissenters. It did not enfranchise the poor, whose violence had helped to win it; for a generation they continued to strive for power in the Chartist and similar movements, while the middle-class consolidated its victory and enjoyed the spoils, apart from the poor.

The Whigs were now again in power and the Dissenters could hope for the promised relief from their grievances. There was a spurt of radical measures. Then after a very few years the more conservative wing of the Whigs, under Lord John Russell, took control and a period of political reconstruction ensued, out of which emerged the Liberal and Conservative parties. The Dissenters, in general, disappointed in Lord John Russell's resistance to their demands, helped to wreck the Whig party by voting for Radical candidates for Parliament and by vehement campaigns for dis-establishment of the Church of England. The successful Anti-corn-law League canalized left-wing enthusiasm into free-trade and Gladstonian Liberalism, essentially a middle-class party, leaving the new Conservatism, under Disraeli, to aim at winning the support of the poor by paternal legislation and extension of the franchise. This change of political climate caused a change of leader-ship among the Unitarians. Radicalism developed into Liberalism and alienation from the other Dissenters sometimes led them to a more conservative, rather than a more radical, temper of mind.

Two Whig measures in particular benefited the Unitarians. They had long resented the obligation, from which Quakers and Jews alone were exempted, to be married by a clergyman with the trini-tarian rites of the Book of Common Prayer. Several efforts had been made to meet their case. In 1819 and 1822 William Smith introduced bills in the Commons which would authorize clergy to omit references to the Trinity, on request, when marrying Unitarians; the clergy naturally asked why their own consciences should be affronted to relieve the consciences of the Unitarians. In 1823 Lord Lansdowne proposed that all Dissenters should be allowed to be married in their own chapels, with record in the parish registers. In 1827 Smith wished to allow marriage before a magistrate after calling of banns in a parish church. A solution was finally found in 1836, in a Dissenters' Marriage Act which permitted Dissenters to be married in their own chapels in the presence of a civil registrar, a new official charged with the registration of all births, marriages and deaths—a blow to the former monopoly of the Church of England. After long agitation the Test and Corporation Acts, which in intention (but in many places not indeed in practice) limited public office to members of the Church of England, had been finally repealed in 1828; but now the Municipal Corporations Act, abolishing the old oligarchic town and city councils, opened local government, by election, to Dissenters without discrimination. Unitarians were among the first to take advantage of this Act. But many grievances remained: Church rates, burial in parish church-yards, control of education, admission to Oxford and Cambridge, etc.

## The Coming Rift

The Unitarians were increasingly isolated from other Dissenters because the old method of political pressure was giving way to a new one. Formerly action in legal and political matters was chiefly taken by a committee of laymen, called the Protestant Dissenting Deputies, formed in 1732, chiefly consisting of lawyers. It was an offshoot from a ministerial society, the General Body of Ministers of the Three Denominations founded in 1702. Both dated from the early years of the eighteenth century, when Presbyterians, Independents and Baptists worked together to defend their interests against the Tories, and to press the Whigs to repeal the Test Act.[1] In those days the Presbyterians were the most numerous, rich and 'respectable' of the three denominations and naturally took precedence. The Ministers of London formed a so-called 'privileged body' with rights of presentation at court, assuring the Hanoverian

[1] See above, p. 176.

kings of their loyalty. The Deputies were a body of lay delegates, representing the congregations in and around London, with a committee meeting monthly to watch over the legal rights of Dissenters. The Unitarians inherited the Presbyterian precedence, partly by custom and partly because of their legal and commercial pre-eminence and the long chairmanship (from 1805 to 1832) of William Smith.

The Deputies and the General Body of Ministers tended to work without publicity, looking upon their work as delicate and confidential. Much more public excitement was generated by the Protestant Society for the Protection of Religious Liberty, founded in 1811, which developed into the Religious Freedom Society, founded in 1839, and other popular societies aiming at disestablishment. Because these societies were new, and under evangelical leadership, Unitarians could play only a minor part in them and soon they were squeezed out altogether.

In their own eyes Unitarians were inheritors of the status of the Presbyterians as moderate Dissenters, and the Deputies and the ministerial body, under Unitarian leadership, claimed to be acting on behalf of the whole of Protestant Dissent without reference to theology. Consequently they admitted to membership of their representative body a number of ministers and delegates from congregations which were not of the original three denominations. Scottish Presbyterian congregations in London had naturally been admitted as Presbyterian from the start. Parliament-court Chapel, which was Universalist, was admitted as Baptist. And immediately after the passing of William Smith's Act repealing all penalties on denial of the Trinity, Essex-street Chapel was admitted as 'Nonconformist'; the congregation straightway appointed William Smith as its delegate, although as a Presbyterian he had been a deputy since 1791 and chairman since 1805. Unitarians subscribed liberally to the funds and took the lead in discussion and action.

*Internecine Litigation*

But their position was becoming isolated, as controversy grew on theological grounds between them and the orthodox Dissenters. At Wolverhampton the congregation had been divided in 1780, in the days of Warrington Academy,[1] but there was no action at law until

[1] Cf. above, p. 227.

1816 when a minister, appointed a year previously as a Unitarian, announced his conversion to orthodoxy and said that, since the chapel had originally been orthodox, he could not be dismissed. The Unitarians claimed that, since the trust deed was simply for the worship of God without theological definition, the development to Unitarianism was legally permissible. The issue was taken to law and the first decision of the court, in 1818, was against the Unitarians; there was an appeal, and the matter was not finally settled until 1842, when the Unitarians again lost their case. The Deputies tried to stand aloof, but the case was a portent of legal battles to come. Could the Unitarians justly claim to be the heirs, and even the nineteenth century representatives, of the Presbyterians?

The conflict moved nearer to crisis in the Manchester Socinian Controversy, which broke out in 1824. It arose out of a dinner given in the Spread Eagle Inn in Manchester, when a body of 120 gentlemen met to present a silver tea-service to the Rev. John Grundy, who was removing from Cross-street Chapel, Manchester to Paradise-street Chapel, Liverpool. There were many toasts, including one to 'the Rev. George Harris, and may the zeal which he has been instrumental in kindling prove itself to be such as ought to burn in every Christian bosom'. Harris, who was, as we have seen, one of the most uncompromising Unitarian propagandists of the day, replied in a fiery speech, in which he characterized orthodoxy as 'slavish, mean, cruel and vindictive': 'orthodoxy is gloom and darkness and desolation, Unitarianism is light and liberty and joy'. There was prolonged applause. When this was reported in the Manchester press it caused great offence to the orthodox. How little the Unitarians realized the imminence of the crisis, and its cause, is shown by the report of the meeting in *The Monthly Repository*, which merely said that the speeches had been 'extremely interesting' and that the occasion presented 'a pleasing example of congregational harmony and brotherly love'. George Hadfield, a Congregationalist, protested against this 'railing and invective' and challenged the honesty of Unitarians who, casting contempt on orthodoxy, retained chapels and endowments originally of orthodox foundation. He compiled lists of Presbyterian chapels which were, he said, now wrongly in Unitarian hands. The controversy widened and became more intense.

*The Lady Hewley Case*

There was no escape; the issue had to be tried at law. Already the Wolverhampton case was before the courts, and a legal battle was also in progress over the Presbyterian chapel and endowments in Dublin held by Unitarians. But a more decisive test-case could be made of Lady Hewley's Charity. This was a fund, founded by a wealthy Presbyterian lady of York in 1704, for 'poor and godly preachers of Christ's holy gospel', for an almshouse and for the support of students for the ministry. By the normal method of co-option to fill vacancies it had descended, without any break, from Presbyterian to Unitarian trustees, who had never questioned that they were the lawful descendants and representatives of their predecessors. It had been for more than a century the most important fund (in the north of England) for the support of ministers, students and congregations of the denomination at first generally known as Presbyterian and by this time generally known as Unitarian. As with the Presbyterian Fund, which also had descended to the Unitarians, grants were also made to some orthodox ministers and congregations, chiefly to those which formerly had been Presbyterian or in association with the Presbyterians; and the almshouse had been open to the poor of all denominations without question. Indeed, the Unitarian trustees said, and it was not disputed, that less than a quarter of the income had gone to avowed Unitarians. But an annual grant had also been made to the Methodist Unitarians, a body of humble people of Rochdale and Rossendale who had seceded from Methodism in 1809. They had linked themselves with the Unitarians as a result of a visit by Richard Wright and they were polemically anti-orthodox. It was pointed out that they were helped from Lady Hewley's Charity because they were Unitarian and not because they had any descent from the original clients of the fund. A large grant went to Charles Wellbeloved, principal of Manchester College, as minister of St Saviourgate Chapel, York, and to divinity students at the college, and to no other college, although, it was said, Manchester College had become merely a Unitarian seminary.

The case went to law in 1830 and raised complicated legal problems. It was true that Lady Hewley had nowhere defined her religious beliefs in any restrictive terms, except that she had asked that the inmates of her almshouse should be able to repeat the answers in Mr Bowles's Catechism, already fifty years old at the time of her will. Everyone agreed that she was a Presbyterian, but what strictness of orthodoxy did that mean at that date? Contradictory quotations could be given from the sermons and writings of her associates and contemporaries on this point. Everyone agreed that she was not a Unitarian and that the Presbyterians of her day definitely repudiated Unitarian theology; but could Unitarianism be a lawful development out of an undefined and moderate Presbyterianism, as had actually happened? A strong legal point was that, since Unitarianism was illegal until 1813, Unitarians had a doubtful claim to any trust for religious purposes founded before this date. It was even argued that, since 'Christianity is part of the common law of England', the Act of 1813 had merely exempted Unitarians from certain penalties and had not otherwise given them any legal status whatever.

The Unitarian trustees replied that they had acquired control over the fund by legitimate and hitherto unchallenged descent, with no gap at any point where 'Presbyterians' had given place to 'Unitarians'; for these were merely different names for the same religious community at different periods of time. They pointed to a remarkable family continuity: for example, in the grave-yards of Unitarian chapels and on their membership-rolls the same surnames appeared from early times right up to that day.[1] They argued that the Presbyterians at the beginning of the eighteenth century were in process of intellectual change, though this would not necessarily show in the will of Lady Hewley, who was a relic of an earlier day; Calvinism, under the influence of Baxter and others, was becoming more rational and comprehensive. This, they said, was indicated in the open trusts upon which the Charity and most of the chapels were founded, which made no theological stipulations, merely declaring that they were for 'the worship of Almighty God by their Majesties' Protestant subjects dissenting from the Church of England'.

The orthodox reply was that the trusts, Independent as well as Presbyterian, were open because theological orthodoxy was sufficiently guarded by the Toleration Act itself, which imposed the

[1] One opponent asked what had happened to those families whose names appeared at the beginning and then disappeared, and suggested that there had been an exclusion of the orthodox in the second half of the eighteenth century; but this point was not explored.

doctrinal Articles of the Church of England and actually barred in set terms those who denied the doctrine of the Trinity. And they cited Edmund Calamy, Daniel Williams and other Presbyterians of the early eighteenth century, honoured by Unitarians as their forebears, who were claimed to be notoriously opposed to Unitarianism.[1]

## Presbyterian Revival

The Unitarians, in order to assert their historical continuity with the past, revived the name 'Presbyterian', prefixing it with the adjective 'English' to distinguish it from Scottish Presbyterianism, now becoming increasingly evangelical. The name was indeed a revival, for, with a few exceptions of a historical nature, it had disappeared from use since the beginning of the century and was regarded by Unitarians, until the issue was raised, as 'obsolete and irrelevant'. Even before William Smith's Act of 1813, the name 'Unitarian' or, more usually and more correctly, 'Unitarian Christian', was freely used of chapels and ministers. Lindsey's chapel, though not using the name, was known to be Unitarian; but that could be regarded as a special case, not implicating the Presbyterians. Priestley used it freely as the correct name for the Rational Dissenters: for example, he described the members of the congregation of the New Meeting, Birmingham as 'Unitarian Christians' in the preface of a hymn-book he compiled for them. The silver tea-service presented to John Grundy in 1824, from which arose the Lady Hewley crisis, bore an inscription recording his services to Unitarian Christianity, with no mention of Presbyterianism. When Wellbeloved and others gave evidence in the Lady Hewley case they called themselves Presbyterians and refused to define their faith except in the words of scripture; yet, as their opponents pointed out, they had recently belonged to societies like the British & Foreign Unitarian Association and had spoken in public about 'our Unitarian faith' and 'our Unitarian chapels'. As for the Presbyterian name itself, some ministers in the first half of the eighteenth century, usually included among the Presbyterians, like John Taylor of Norwich, followed Baxter in rejecting it as sectarian and

[1] At the end of the nineteenth century Walter Lloyd and other Unitarian historians poured scorn on 'the open trust myth' and abandoned this defence; but in fact it is true that in the time of Calamy and Williams theological issues were changing and the new ideas of Locke and Newton were taking root among the Presbyterians—and would soon become explicit.

inappropriate and preferred to be called simply 'Protestant Dissenters' or even 'catholic Christians'. Nor was it true that all the old Presbyterian chapels had become Unitarian—many had disappeared and some had become Congregational; nor that all the old chapels now Unitarian were originally Presbyterian—for some were originally Independent or Baptist. The situation was very confused, historically, morally and legally.

In 1833 the Vice-Chancellor ruled that the Charity could not legally be held by Unitarian trustees, who were thereupon dispossessed, the costs being paid by the fund. His judgment, which introduced irrelevant issues, was open to criticism on legal grounds and an appeal was made to the Lord Chancellor, Lord Brougham, who seemed ready to reverse the verdict. But before the appeal was decided he was replaced by Lord Lyndhurst, who referred the matter to two judges; they rejected the appeal, leaving each side to pay its own costs. The Independents then, affirming that 'the term Presbyterian is, in a fair, just and honourable sense, and in accordance with its proper signification, capable of being applied to the generality of the English Congregationalists', claimed the whole of the Hewley funds. But this was challenged by two different bodies of orthodox Presbyterians and by Baptists, who even charged the Congregationalists with heresy. Further litigation ensued. Meanwhile, the Unitarians appealed to the House of Lords. For five days in 1839 the case was argued tenaciously before that authority by some of the most eminent lawyers of the day, and then adjourned without decision. Not until 1842 was judgment given, and it went against the Unitarians,[1] with one-third of the costs to be paid by the ejected Unitarian trustees and the remainder by the fund.

Meanwhile, the Dissenting Deputies and the parallel ministerial society had broken up under the strain of the long battle. William Smith, who had so closely co-operated with the evangelical 'Clapham Sect' in the campaign against the slave-trade that he is often reckoned as one of them, resigned from the chairmanship of the Deputies in 1832 on grounds of age. In his farewell message he lamented that 'some of our brethren seem to think differences on controverted points of theology sufficient grounds of separation even as to the common intercourse of life in civil affairs' and urged

[1] On the grounds that Unitarianism was illegal prior to 1813 and that the Act of that year was not retrospective.

that respect for private judgment was a foundation-principle of Dissent. In 1834 the re-election of the secretary of the ministerial body, who was a Unitarian, was opposed and the Unitarians withdrew from the so-called Three Denominations. Under the cumbersome but significant title of 'the Body of Protestant Dissenting Ministers of the Presbyterian Denomination in and about the Cities of London and Westminster' they were granted separate recognition as a privileged body, and as such presented a loyal address to Queen Victoria on her accession in 1837. This right and privilege has continued to be exercised, as at the accession of Queen Elizabeth II, though on this occasion jointly with other Dissenting bodies.[1]

William Smith died in 1835, and in 1836 the Unitarian laymen withdrew from the Deputies with this protest:

> Open challenge has of late been repeatedly and publicly made of the title and identity of the ministers and congregations hitherto invariably recognised as composing the Presbyterian denomination, and legal proceedings have been successfully instituted by Dissenters, founded on the denial of such title and identity, and seeking to inflict the forfeiture and transfer of the endowments now held by the Presbyterians, as the penalty for the exercise of their conscientious privileges as Christians and Protestant Dissenters.

One Unitarian minister and congregation alone remained associated with the ministerial body and the Deputies until 1844, namely William Johnson Fox and his South-place Chapel. He had been secretary of the British & Foreign Unitarian Association, but in 1831 the Unitarians disowned him because of a scandal in his private life. It is ironical that he should have retained fellowship with two linked bodies who had broken fellowship with the Unitarians, for he had been a vigorous Unitarian propagandist and his chapel, originally Universalist, was included as Baptist.[2]

The Unitarians protested that their separation meant the end of the 'Three Denominations' and there was some dispute about invested funds. But the ancient institution continued, the Scottish Presbyterians (and later the Presbyterian Church of England) constituting the third party with the Congregationalists and Baptists.

---

[1] See above, p. 17 n.

[2] The Unitarians continued, however, to be represented as Presbyterians on the Three Denominations Widows' Fund and on the parallel Fund for the relief of aged and infirm ministers.

On the Unitarians the decision of the House of Lords was catastrophic. The Wolverhampton case, which had dragged on since 1819, was now finally decided against them. Other suits were threatened; for example, Dr Williams's Trust and Library, another Presbyterian foundation of the early eighteenth century which was now largely managed by Unitarians, was said to be the next point of attack; so that Joseph Blanco White, the Spanish liberal who had moved from Romanism, through Broad-churchmanship, to Unitarianism, hurriedly withdrew his application for the post of librarian when he heard the news. It looked as though the Unitarians were to lose all their old Presbyterian endowments. A group of Manchester Unitarians even contemplated emigration to Texas. The Attorney-General, however, refused to allow any further cases until Parliament could decide on the general principle.

## THE AGE OF MARTINEAU

Two years later, in 1844, the Tory government of Sir Robert Peel brought in a measure, known as the Dissenters' Chapels Act, to prevent further litigation. It was introduced in the House of Lords by Lord Lyndhurst, who as Lord Chancellor had tried one stage of the appeal. In spite of many petitions from orthodox bodies against it, it passed both houses by large majorities, with speeches in its favour by leading politicians of both parties. The main legal argument in its favour was that undisturbed possession over a long period establishes a lawful title and that no merely presumed intention of a founder, not explicitly stated, can be cited to limit a trust at some future date. But a new principle also affected the debate—the idea of development. It arose from a new conception of history as a process of natural growth. Lord John Russell, in the course of the debate, said that 'changes of opinion and of doctrine must constantly be taking place'. This caused an important alteration of detail in the Bill whilst it was going through the committee stage in the House of Commons. As originally drafted, the Bill granted possession to those who could show that they had held the property for twenty-five years; whilst this would confirm the Unitarian title, it might, if narrowly enforced, have prevented any further change. So the clause was redrafted to ensure that, if possession of a chapel was challenged, the twenty-five-years' usage by the congregation should be calculated from the date of the action, not of the Act of Parliament.[1] This contemplation of future change, perhaps beyond Unitarianism, was to play a large part in the debates within the Unitarian body which soon broke out.

The rejoicing and thankfulness of the Unitarians was naturally great. But the Act deepened the rift between them and the orthodox Nonconformists, who had instituted the suits at law and petitioned against the Bill. Unitarians, who had formerly taken a lead in the campaign for Catholic Emancipation, refused to join in the Nonconformist agitation for disestablishment of the Church of England, which was one of the popular causes of the day, and drew nearer in sympathy to moderate Anglicans, now coming into prominence as Broad-churchmen, and Unitarians themselves often became more Anglican in their outlook and religious practices. And for a time many of them lost their political radicalism. They were returning to a central position, like that of the old Presbyterians.

There was a threatened change of leadership among the Unitarians as a result of this trying experience. Not that the Lady Hewley case and the Dissenters' Chapels Act were the sole cause, for the same kind of change was taking place in other departments of life; but they certainly helped to bring matters to a head. The change was from Priestley to Martineau, and it was not made without bitterness.

## From Priestley to Martineau

In the first quarter of the nineteenth century the influence of Priestley was paramount. It was he who had popularized the Unitarian name. It was his humanitarian view of Christ and his aggressiveness against orthodoxy which had prevailed. His optimistic determinism was the most usual philosophy among the Unitarians, as exemplified by Thomas Southwood Smith's *Illustrations of divine government, tending to show that everything is under the direction of infinite wisdom and goodness, and will terminate in the production of universal purity and happiness* (1816). Priestley's

---

[1] Martineau's criticism of the original clause may have contributed to the change. J. E. Carpenter, *James Martineau*, 1905, 239.

radicalism, of the middle class rather than of the people, had settled down, in his disciples, into an individualist and utilitarian ideal of reform. Political economy, a rigid doctrine of economic necessity, was regarded as an ultimate wisdom. It could be said (though this was an unfair simplification) that his disciples, who directed Unitarian policy, had brought on this crisis, from which only a return to Presbyterian principles, endorsed by a Tory Act of Parliament, had saved them.

But even without this crisis a change of temper was inevitable in a religious body so open to the thought of the day. Eighteenth century rationalism was giving way to nineteenth century romanticism. The wind of German philosophy was blowing. The English Unitarians, unlike their American co-religionists, could not get it through Coleridge. He, a Cambridge ex-Anglican, had joined them for a time and had almost become one of their ministers. But his theology was pantheist rather than rationalist, and he left them to become the sage of the Anglican Broad-church, with bitter criticism of their coldness. But if not through him it was bound to come to them some other way, especially through the American Unitarian, William Ellery Channing.

## James Martineau

The new leader was James Martineau. He was born in Norwich in 1805, of a poorer branch of a merchant family of Huguenot origin, whose ancestors had come into the Presbyterian body in the 'second wave'.[1] It was a large family, widely married. After a period in Lant Carpenter's school in Bristol, Martineau trained for the Unitarian ministry at Manchester College, York. For a brief period he was a Presbyterian (Unitarian) minister in Dublin and then, aged twenty-seven, he went to Paradise-street Chapel, Liverpool as colleague and successor to John Grundy, whose departure from Manchester to Liverpool in 1824 had had such momentous consequences.

In Liverpool he found an unusual social and religious situation. There had been a radical Unitarian element. William Shepherd, minister of Gateacre Chapel, was a friend of the Whig politicians of the end of the eighteenth century; he took charge of Gilbert Wakefield's children when he was in prison and adopted the daughter of

[1] See above, p 223-4.

Jeremiah Joyce. In 1817 Richard Wright's brother John, a printer, was prosecuted for holding Unitarian services; they were held to be blasphemous, even though denial of the Trinity was no longer illegal. But the leading Unitarian families held an unusually high social position and developed a civic idealism. William Roscoe, a Unitarian layman, wrote a life of Lorenzo the Magnificent, the merchant-prince of Renaissance Florence, and was the first man in England to collect Italian primitive paintings. To Liverpool in 1835 came Blanco White, a former Roman Catholic and Broad-churchman, now Unitarian, a melancholy poet with a stoic faith, who believed that religious truth was known intuitively, by the heart, and not on the authority of a church or of miracles known only through ancient records.

The three Unitarian ministers, who served old chapels of Presbyterian or similar foundation, were all young men, less than thirty years of age. Martineau's close friend was John Hamilton Thom, born in Northern Ireland, Arian rather than Unitarian in his theology. Here were all the ingredients of a romantic rather than a rationalist approach to theology.

In 1839 the Anglican clergy of Liverpool preached a series of anti-Unitarian sermons, to which Martineau and his two colleagues replied. Already a break can be seen with the Priestleyan methods of controversy. Miracles are no longer cited as the main proofs of Christ's authority: 'it is as the type of God, the human image of the everlasting Mind, that Christ becomes the object of our faith.' Man is himself, in his moral nature, the image of God. Martineau explicitly rejected Priestley's favourite doctrine of philosophic necessity, which reduced God, he said, to 'the ultimate-happiness maker, by no means fastidious in his application of means, but secure of producing the end', and which stressed too much in morality the merely prudential motives.

Already he was feeling dissatisfaction with Priestley's type of piety, which, he said in a sermon preached in 1836, 'never prays without hinting at the highly rational nature of its worship'.[1] In 1835, in a review of Priestley's collected works in *The Monthly*

[1] Unitarian hymn-books of the period usually bore on their title-pages the text 'Sing ye praises with understanding' (Ps. 47.7) or 'I will pray with the spirit and I will pray with the understanding also; I will sing with the spirit and I will sing with the understanding also' (I Cor. xiv.15), and sometimes in a preface defined traditional religious words in rationalist and moral terms.

*Repository*, he remarked that Priestley lacked 'sensibility' and that his mind was 'not necessarily devotional'; the review, intended otherwise to convey praise, caused offence. In 1838 an 'aggregate meeting of ministers' was held in Essex-street Chapel, London to consider the state of the denomination and the methods needed to counter the orthodox attack. Better organization and propaganda were suggested by various speakers—and greater zeal. Martineau made a speech, probably unpremeditated, harshly opposing any organization on denominational lines. 'Many of us', he said, 'entirely object to calling Unitarian congregations by that name, and any attempt at sectarian or theological union must in all respects signally fail.' When George Harris proposed 'a closer and more effective union', on the basis of the British & Foreign Unitarian Association, Martineau nearly wrecked it with an amendment stressing 'that spirit of deep and vital religion which may exist under various forms of theological sentiment'. In a speech punctuated with cries of disapprobation, and also some applause, he said: 'I cannot but lament that Unitarianism had a sceptical origin. . . . We grow by men's lapses from their previous convictions; and thus a critical, cold and untrusting temper becomes silently diffused, unfavourable to high enterprise and deep affection.' In a letter to Channing in 1840, after acknowledging his debt to Priestley's writings, 'to which I attribute not only my first call to the pursuit of religious philosophy, but the first personal struggles after the religious life', he went on to say that he had come to believe that 'his metaphysical system is incompatible with any true and operative sentiments of religion, that it is at variance with the characteristic ideas of Christianity, and will spontaneously vanish whenever our churches become really worshipping assemblies, instead of simply moral, polemical or dissenting societies'. Great changes, he said, were silently going on in the Unitarian body, which might even lead to its dissolution and re-emergence in a new form. There had been an increase of both theological doubt and devotional affection: 'there is far less belief, yet far more faith, than there was twenty years ago.'

Two new schools, he considered, were arising among the Unitarians, to challenge the old scriptural and rationalist Unitarianism of the party of Priestley and Belsham. One was anti-supernatural, hostile to miracles and to the uniqueness of Christianity, much influenced by recent German biblical criticism which threw doubt on the authenticity of the gospels, stressing more the religiousness of man than the reality of God—and inclined, he might have added, to political radicalism. Of this school William Johnson Fox was the most conspicuous figure, and Martineau thought that it had no truly religious future.[1] The other school was that of Martineau himself and his friends J. H. Thom, J. J. Tayler and Charles Wicksteed. They were a mediating group. They did not reject miracles out of hand, nor directly attack the idea of a supernatural revelation, but they based their faith on 'the intrinsically divine character of Christianity, a more penetrating appreciation of the mind of Christ and a more trustful faith in him for his own sake'. Its belief was intuitive rather than narrowly rational and its danger (Martineau admitted) was mysticism, 'which, however, the practical turn of the English mind will probably check'. His critics said that this was nebulous and irrational and probably pantheist.

## A Change in Hymnology

To further this type of piety Martineau published a new hymn-book in 1840 called *Hymns for the Christian church and home*. Nine years earlier he had prepared a collection of hymns for his Dublin congregation, which, because of his resignation there, never came into use. In its preface he had said that 'no one, who appreciates the part which the imagination and the affections perform in true worship, will doubt the propriety of bringing all the resources of lyric poetry, the poetry of the affections, into the services of religion', and he praised the hymns of Bishop Heber as 'the unfettered compositions of a deeply moved soul'. (In his review of Priestley's works in 1835 he had praised Heber at the expense of

[1] As has been said, Fox was repudiated by the Unitarians in 1831, because of a domestic scandal; Martineau and his friend J. J. Tayler were among the few who protested against Fox's expulsion, though they made clear that they did not agree with his theology or his views on divorce. He left the Unitarian body, taking his South-place congregation with him. He became a vigorous radical journalist, Member of Parliament and leading orator for the Anti-Corn Law League. In his chapel the music was of high quality, the sermons became lectures and the prayers non-petitionary. South-place Chapel eventually became South-place Ethical Society. A minor member of the same school was William Linwood, whose sermons were so politically radical and anti-supernatural that the leading members of his congregation, themselves mostly incoming Baptists of a generation earlier, ejected him from his pulpit at Mansfield in 1848; for a time he joined Fox and then disappeared from history. To this extent Martineau's prophecy was fulfilled, but anti-supernaturalism grew among Unitarians and in time prevailed over Martineau's type of piety.

R

Priestley.) Now in the preface to the book of 1840 he attacked the moralizing, rationalist hymns of his day as 'rhymed theology, versified precepts, or biblical descriptions capable of being sung'. Puritanism, he said, had killed devotion: 'the minster beheld the rise of the conventicle, and the solemn anthem was exchanged for the rude and shouting psalm.' A hymn should express a strong religious emotion, not merely a 'metaphysical accuracy'; if it had fervour, imagination and grandeur, a general truth of impression should prevail over a precise truth of theological detail. Consequently he felt compelled to choose for his book hymns which were 'for the most part the productions of periods or of churches least affected by the intrusion of the rationalist spirit into their devotions', even though this meant occasional alteration of phrases for theological reasons. So the book included more than fifty hymns by the Wesleys, and others by Anglicans and evangelicals, by German pietists and by metaphysical poets of the seventeenth century. It was a manifesto for comprehension and against propaganda and, though at first it aroused opposition, some of it bitter, it gradually was taken up widely by Unitarians.

Martineau gathered a party, the core of which was the 'quaternion', consisting of himself, Thom, Tayler and Wicksteed; Tayler was in Manchester, the other three in Liverpool, Wicksteed moving to Leeds in 1835. To express their views and combat 'the revived and dogged allegiance of our other periodicals to the system of Priestley and Belsham', they bought in 1839 *The Christian Teacher*, which had been since 1835 an organ of the Priestleyan party in the north of England. Significantly, one of the earliest articles in the new series was by Thom on 'How is life to be maintained in our Unitarian churches?', in which he appealed for less polemical preaching and more faith based on 'moral union with Christ'.

## Changes in Architecture

Even architecture was made to signify a change in religious outlook. The Presbyterian and other Dissenting meeting houses had been consciously different from parish churches in the shape and inner arrangement. They owed their box-like form to the Calvinist desire to put the communion-table in the midst of the people, with the pulpit behind it and the people sitting round; they became mere boxes for preaching in, deliberately plain. Some opulent

Dissenting congregations, like that of Lewin's-mead, Bristol (1791), built chapels in a more ornate style, palladian or georgian; and Stamford-street Chapel, London (1829) was an experiment in the style of the classical revival. Gothic architecture, revived in England in the late eighteenth century, was taken up for church-building first by the Anglicans, a few Dissenters dabbling in it merely for decorative reasons. Romantics and antiquarians made it the appropriate style for churches, its 'dim religious light' giving the right background and arousing the right emotions. It was Martineau and his friends who, first among all the Dissenters, consciously adopted gothic as the truly devotional architecture. In 1839, J. J. Tayler and his Manchester congregation engaged Sir Charles Barry, the fashionable architect of the new houses of parliament, to design a handsome gothic chapel, which however still kept to the Dissenting pattern (modified by Methodist practice) of placing the pulpit in the middle of an end wall, with the table in front of it, so that it faced the congregation sitting in rows. Then followed a number of chapels —Hyde, Cheshire (1848), Mill-hill, Leeds (1848), Hope-street, Liverpool (1849), Banbury (1850)—each of which had a chancel containing an altar, after the Anglican and medieval pattern, the pulpit being to one side; and use was made of stained glass, a spire or pinnacles, and other medieval details. Each new building was usually opened by one of the quarternion, who used the occasion to proclaim the new emotional and aesthetic ideals of worship. In opposition the Priestleyan party also built Unitarian chapels in gothic, but they emphasized a central pulpit, not an altar, and some of these Unitarians brought Dr Montgomery from Ireland to preach the opening sermon.[1] Such were the chapels at Stockport (1842), Upper Chapel, Sheffield (1848, but palladian, not gothic) and Newcastle-on-Tyne (1854), all opened by Montgomery.

### Renewed Baxterian Catholicism

There were thus now two main parties among the Unitarians,

[1] Montgomery, leader of the Non-Subscribers who were ejected from orthodox Irish Presbyterianism in 1828 and who joined the older Non-Subscribing group founded by Abernethy, was a hero to the older school of English Unitarians, who overlooked the Arianism of many of the Non-Subscribers. In the twentieth century, however, some Irish Non-Subscribers tended to take up Martineau's mediating position, or something like it, against the anti-supernaturalism and non-Christian universalism which, in their view, had come to prevail among the English Unitarians. Like Martineau, they were dissatisfied with the Unitarian name and tended to lean towards orthodoxy.

the followers of Priestley and Belsham, and the followers of Martineau and his friends. The former were scriptural and rational, and they tended to radicalism or individualism in politics. They were eager for propaganda and organization and definite theology. They founded missionary societies and new congregations, often composed of members of the working class, and they exalted the Unitarian name. The other party was not interested in propaganda and often repudiated the Unitarian name as a badge of sectarianism. They wished to cultivate a piety of the heart and looked beyond Priestley to an idealized Puritanism, even to an idealized Anglicanism and an idealized Middle Ages. They revived Baxter's use of the word 'catholic', meaning both comprehensive and devout. Tradition meant much to them, and so did social acceptance, rather than newness and social protest—though many of them gave heroic service to unpopular causes for human welfare. They again sighed for comprehension within an enlarged Church of England and found friends among Anglican Broad-churchmen. It was far easier for the new school than for the school of Priestley to claim continuity with the old Presbyterians; indeed they used this in debate against the followers of Priestley and Belsham.

An important question was: which party would the children of the Cambridge ex-Anglicans join? They had formerly supported the school of Priestley, sharing his rationalist and protesting outlook, and they had worked manfully throughout the long struggle of the Unitarians to maintain their Presbyterian inheritance, using their social position and their professional legal skill to avert the threatened disaster. But the British & Foreign Unitarian Association, in order to fight the battle on historical rather than on theological grounds, had created 'the English Presbyterian Association'. Many of them, as a result of this experience, moved over to Martineau's anti-sectarian camp and helped to finance the building of the new gothic churches. But some would move on to that other school which Martineau said had no truly religious future—the anti-supernaturalist school. This had more religious vitality than Martineau guessed.

## Social Aspects

It must not be overlooked that the rise of the school of Martineau was related to social and political trends outside the Unitarian body, but reflected within it. Romanticism was in fashion and middle-class liberalism had taken the place of proletarian radicalism. The decade from 1840 may have been the hungry forties for the poor, but it was also the period of middle-class prosperity and consolidation and of the rise of the Liberal party. That decade marked the last despairing efforts of the Chartists; physical force failed, and moral force, which some Unitarians actively supported, ended in words.[1] When it came to the battle for the Ten Hours Bill, limiting the hours of labour, influential Unitarians opposed it on middle-class political and economic grounds. John Taylor of *The Manchester Guardian* and Mark Philips of Manchester were Unitarian opponents of the Bill, along with the Congregationalist Edward Baines of *The Leeds Mercury* and the Quaker John Bright. The Bill was carried in 1847, largely by Anglican evangelicals, assisted by John Fielden, a Methodist Unitarian.

It was not that Unitarians of the school of Martineau were without concern for the poor; indeed, the contrary is true. But the political radicalism of the early part of the century gave place in them to an aristocratic and paternal attitude to social questions which was not unlike that of Baxter and the old Presbyterians. In 1833 Joseph Tuckerman, founder of 'domestic missions' in Boston, Massachusetts, visited Liverpool and was welcomed by the Unitarians there. Here was prepared ground, in the civic idealism of Liverpool Unitarianism. William Roscoe failed as a merchant, but shone brightly as a radical idealist. William Rathbone became a Unitarian in 1805 on being disowned by the Society of Friends for latitudinarian opinions; his son of the same name took the lead in many philanthropic enterprises and is honoured as the founder of District Nursing. These were examples of a group of mercantile and professional men who applied their Whig zeal to social welfare in their native town, where Unitarians had a secure status. Martineau and Thom were young ministers who were ready for a new field of endeavour.

## Domestic Missions

Domestic missions were established by Unitarians in many towns. The stated object was to help the poor to help themselves,

---

[1] The Methodist Unitarians, adherents of the Belsham school of theology, were also Chartists.

without pauperizing them. The missioner visited the derelict poor in their hovels and cellars, and by means of personal friendship and advice and the provision of opportunities for self-culture (penny-banks, reading rooms, allotments, etc.), he tried to enable them by their own efforts to rise out of destitution. At first no provision was made for public worship; on principle there was to be no proselytization and nothing resembling Methodist evangelism. But eventually most domestic missions developed simple forms of public worship, partly because the poor themselves expected it. All this was in accordance with the principles of political economy, the prime theory of the early nineteenth century, based on materialist, individual and competitive self-help, with religion merely pointing to the rules of life and counselling obedience to them. But when Martineau became Professor of Mental and Moral Philosophy and Political Economy at Manchester College in 1840, he urged that society should be guided by motives of benevolence as well as by strict economic law. This was a serious breach in the pure theory, but who was to exercise the benevolence? Obviously it was the middle class, who were to act with paternal generosity towards those below them in the economic scale. So we find sermons at this period on the obligations of wealth and much philanthropic activity.

However, in London and most other large towns where domestic missions were set up, they tended to be continuations of the former missionary activities of the Unitarian Fund. It was argued that a poor man would be more likely than an educated man to be able to speak to the poor; so John Ashworth, a Methodist Unitarian and formerly a weaver, was appointed domestic missioner in Manchester and R. K. Philp, a former Methodist, similarly served in London. The pattern was soon established of a popular Sunday-evening service, a Sunday school and a number of social and benevolent clubs, in a building of unecclesiastical appearance. But in Liverpool the aristocratic and paternal element was more strongly marked. Instead of engaging a poor and unlettered man as missioner, the Liverpool committee appointed John Johns, a poet and an intellectual, at a high salary. It was an inspired choice; not only was Johns a devoted visitor to the poor in their derelict homes, but soon he began to urge, in his annual reports and in the pages of *The Christian Teacher*, that personal service was not enough, but must be backed by municipal housing, sanitation, police and public parks. This was an even more serious breach in classical political economy and it was taken up with vigour by Unitarians in Liverpool and other cities, as a kind of municipal socialism. Johns died heroically in a typhoid epidemic in 1847. He wrote one fine hymn ('Come, kingdom of our God'), much mediocre Wordsworthian poetry, some hard-hitting and highly-coloured reports on his work and a number of mawkish religious tracts for distribution to the poor.

## The Institutional Church

By the middle of the century the institutional church had arrived. Ministers no longer preached only on Sunday and spent the rest of the week in the conduct of a school in order to supplement an inadequate stipend; in any case, there was by 1850 less opportunity for school-mastering, now that the great national voluntary school-societies were at work. Instead the minister was urged to take up a double task: on Sunday mornings to preach to his middle-class congregation and for the rest of Sunday and during the week to conduct a variety of philanthropic activities, centred in the Sunday school, for a quite different body of people, of the poorer classes. These latter activities were financed by the wealthier members of the congregation and some help was given by the ladies and young people, but there was a social gap between the two which was hard to cross. John Wright of Macclesfield, addressing the Manchester Sunday-school Association in 1850, said: 'The very best way for the more educated class to elevate the less educated, for the virtuous to reform the erring, for the refined to act on the uncivilized, is to associate with them.' And he gave a detailed list (of impressive length) of the educational and philanthropic institutions connected with his chapel. The sentiment was excellent, but its terms, and the fact that he said it, shows the gulf that existed.

Martineau and his friends rose to prominence within Unitarianism in the 1840s and soon their point of view became dominant, though never unopposed. It was hostile to sectarianism and the Unitarian name and claimed to be 'catholic' in religious sympathy after the pattern of the old Presbyterians. Manchester College, sharply criticized as a Unitarian seminary during the Lady Hewley proceedings, was moved back from York to Manchester in 1840 and was refounded on a more general and comprehensive plan, reminiscent of Warrington Academy. It was to be a miniature university college for all branches of study from theology to civil engineering, affiliated to the University of London. A royal 'Letter in Council' authorizing this higher status was obtained; a new name, 'Queen's College', in honour of Queen Victoria, was even suggested, but not adopted. Martineau and Tayler were on the enlarged teaching staff. *The Inquirer*, a Unitarian weekly newspaper founded in 1842, soon moved from criticism of Martineau to support.

But the opposition was severe. Martineau's first volume of sermons, *Endeavours after the Christian life* (1843), and his hymn-book of 1840 were savagely reviewed in *The Christian Reformer* as opening the door to mysticism and virtual infidelity. In 1845 there was a painful breach with his sister Harriet, who had moved from rationalist Unitarianism to non-religious political economy. Unitarians had an awed respect for Martineau's intellectual powers, but suspected his cloudy theology and his opposition to denominational organization. But anyone who crossed swords with him was silenced with cutting rhetoric.

## New Ingredients

The situation was made more complex, but possibly saved from sterility, by a new accession to the Unitarians in 1841. Joseph Barker was expelled from the Methodist New Connexion for heresy and founded a popular religious movement, scattered over the north of England from the Potteries to Tyneside, called the Christian Brethren, which he brought into association with the Unitarians. He had been reading John Taylor's *Scripture doctrine of original sin* and the writings of the Methodist Unitarians, so his approach was biblical. But it also had an element of radical quietism with Quaker features; indeed it bears out that theory of the origin of religions according to which they arise in periods of political frustration, in this case the failure of Chartism. Since he rejected the Unitarian name as sectarian,[1] this seemed to confirm Martineau's principle. But it was a poor man's church of protest and so tended to be rationalist and radical, in biblical terms. The older type of Unitarians rallied to Barker's support. In 1845 they raised a fund to present him with a printing press, on which he printed tracts for his own churches and for the British & Foreign Unitarian Associa-

---

[1] The Christian Brethren church at Mossley near Manchester, now Unitarian, must by its foundation-deed never bear any other name than 'Christian'. Barker's motto was the text 'One is your master, even Christ, and all ye are brethren' (Matt. xxiii.8).

tion. In 1846 there were about 200 Christian Brethren congregations, a welcome accession to the Unitarians. But Barker plunged
still deeper into radical politics and into secularism, and his movement collapsed—the last religious tremor of Chartism, which also
collapsed in 1849. Soon the Unitarians were distressed to find him
using their press for attacks on the Queen; but finally Barker, after
adventures in England and America and in many fields of radicalism,
found his way back to Methodism.

To the Unitarians he left a handful of new proletarian congregations and a new impetus towards Unitarian popular evangelism.
For these and similar congregations a new kind of Unitarian minister was needed. Manchester College trained men for the ministry
in educated congregations; who was to serve these poorer groups?
A new effort was made, on the lines of Aspland's short-lived
Hackney College of 1813 (not to be confused with Hackney College
of 1786–96, a successor to Warrington Academy). The need was met
by John Relly Beard, a Hampshire carpenter's son who since 1825
had been a Unitarian minister in Manchester, of the Belsham
school.[1] In 1854 he founded the Unitarian Home Missionary
Board and opened, over a stable, a humble college in which working
men of poor education were trained for the Unitarian ministry in
these lesser churches. A new rival to Martineau's influence was
born. Contrary to his wishes, it was likely to be propagandist and
denominational in spirit and it had no links with the old Presbyterianism.[2]

[1] His middle name was given in honour of James Relly, the eighteenth century Universalist preacher, and his surname may be of Anabaptist origin. He was the founder
of a remarkable family, devoted to progressive causes. His son, Charles Beard, moved
over to support of Martineau and was secretary of Manchester College.

[2] How cross-currents caused conflict is shown by what happened at Macclesfield.
From 1846 to 1853 John Wright, grandson of Richard Wright, had a very successful
ministry there. He drew many new adherents from the Christian Brethren movement.
On his departure to Bury, Lancashire, an old Presbyterian foundation, the wealthy
Brocklehurst family, who, as already described, had dominated the Macclesfield congregation since the middle of the eighteenth century (so much so that it had become their
private property and was called 'Brocklehurst Chapel'), appointed a safe man of old-
fashioned views. The Christian Brethren seceded and founded a new congregation.
One of their leaders, Adam Rushton, entered the Unitarian ministry through the Unitarian Home Missionary Board and served a Methodist Unitarian church, a domestic
mission and finally a Spiritualist Free Church, which he founded. The church of the
seceding Christian Brethren in Macclesfield rejoined the old chapel, which was Presbyterian, in 1888 and saved it from extinction; just as the Methodist Unitarians in Rochdale joined the old Presbyterian congregation there in 1890 with the same result.

*Mid-Century Dissension*

During the 1850s there was conflict between the two parties. Martineau's opponents were led by Samuel Bache, his brother-in-law, who from 1832 to 1868 was minister of the New Meeting, Birmingham, Priestley's old congregation. In 1862 they built for him a new gothic church (but with a central pulpit, not an altar), which was given the Priestleyan title of 'Church of the Messiah'—Priestley followed Locke in affirming that the only fundamental article of Christian belief was acceptance of Jesus as messiah. When Bache resigned his pulpit in 1868 he sent a circular letter to every member of his congregation, urging them to remain faithful to scriptural Unitarianism, especially to belief in the miracles and resurrection of Christ, but they chose for their new minister a man from the other camp, H. W. Crosskey.

In 1852 Bache tried to persuade the trustees of Manchester College, which was facing a financial crisis, to keep the college in Manchester and associate it with the newly-founded Owens College, which was later to become the University of Manchester. But Martineau and Tayler were among those who wanted to move the college to London, to closer affiliation with University College, and their view prevailed. It was argued in favour of London that it would provide a better scientific and literary education; those on the other side replied that Manchester furnished better training for 'usefulness to the poor'. The college moved to London in 1853. In 1857 Tayler was appointed principal, with Martineau as the only other full-time member of the staff. There was immediate protest by a large number of trustees that the two men belonged to one school of religious thought, which had not the confidence of the majority of Unitarians. At an excited meeting of trustees Bache spoke against the appointment and R. B. Aspland, son of Robert Aspland, accused Martineau of intellectual vacillation, of subordinating scripture to philosophy and of being so eager to see the truth in every form of theological error that he encouraged Unitarians to turn Anglican and Anglicans to refrain from becoming Unitarian. Another storm arose the same year when Martineau's son was appointed Hebrew lecturer in the college.

In 1858 S. F. Macdonald, minister at Chester, wrote a letter to *The Christian Reformer* in which he expressed wonder that some of 'our leading minds' (i.e. Martineau and his friends) appeared to think that 'it is of the essence of the Unitarian church to have no clearly-defined opinions'. In reply, Martineau wrote a powerful letter, entitled 'Church-life? or sect-life?', in which he gave the clearest statement of his ecclesiastical position, making the same distinction between 'church' (comprehension) and 'sect' (separation) which Troeltsch was to make more than fifty years later. Individuals, he said, might correctly describe themselves as Unitarians, but to describe congregations as such was to repudiate the past and compromise the future. He urged that the British & Foreign Unitarian Association was a mere propagandist body, with no representative functions, and in protest he refused to take the chair at its annual meetings that year. In order to defend their old endowments the Unitarians had revived the name 'English Presbyterian', claiming an undogmatic basis; they ought now to drop the name 'Unitarian' and take another, more expressive of their historical origin or their principle of free development. But what was it to be?

## The Free Christian Union

The matter came to a head in 1865. Samuel Bache proposed that the term 'Unitarian Christianity' in the constitution of the British & Foreign Unitarian Association should be more strictly defined, to rule out the 'theological juggling' of 'the new and (as they style themselves) advanced school of Unitarians'. His motion was defeated, but the situation obviously could not stand there. P. W. Clayden of Nottingham urged Martineau to take the lead in founding a new fellowship of churches on a free basis with a new name. Seventy ministers joined in planning a new 'Free Christian Union', which should take over from the British & Foreign Unitarian Association all its representative functions.

Next year, at the annual meetings of the British & Foreign Unitarian Association, Bache renewed his motion, which was again defeated amid even stronger displays of feeling. But, when the meeting turned to discuss the proposed new Union and its relation to the Association, there were bitter recriminations. Tayler and Martineau succeeded in confining membership of the Association to individuals, with no congregational or district representation; but this in fact was the situation that virtually existed already, for the Unitarians had always tended to join such bodies as individuals and had little organic denominational sentiment. The proposed

Free Christian Union lasted only a couple of years. Tayler wrote an eloquent pamphlet, *A catholic Christian church the want of our time*, and it was proposed to establish a new central London church where undogmatic Christian preaching and worship could be maintained. Invitations to membership were made to non-Unitarians who might accept the free basis, and a few joined. Francis W. Newman, brother of the Cardinal, protested that even the word 'Christian' was a restriction on religious freedom. In 1870 Martineau himself proposed that the Free Christian Union, having achieved little, should be disbanded.

How is this to be explained? From a theological point of view it looks like a painful step from an old-fashioned scriptural rationalism to a new intuitional piety; and it may be mentioned that the same transition, amid similar scenes of crisis, was taking place among American Unitarians—first in 1838, over Emerson's Divinity School Address, and then after the Civil War, in the Middle West, exactly contemporary with the events just described. But why did nothing concrete emerge?

In addition to the theological aspect, there is a significant relation to social change. The older radical Unitarianism was linked with a political radicalism, partly proletarian and partly 'philosophic' (i.e. individual), which was appropriate to the period of attack on entrenched Tory rule. But now, in the middle of the century, that situation no longer existed. The mercantile and professional class was now socially dominant. To this class the new Unitarian leadership belonged, and the leading churches were no longer the newly-established propagandist outposts, but the old Presbyterian chapels with their substantial families. Martineau frequently warned his readers that sectarianism would lose for the Unitarian churches their hold on 'the spiritual and intellectual sympathies of their own best members and of the most promising elements in English society'. In the 1860s the General Baptists, who fifty years earlier had provided leaders for the Unitarian churches, were repeatedly rebuked in *The Inquirer* for their low ministerial standards and restrictive membership. To a propagandist movement a denominational name and a statement of belief is a necessity, but to a group of ancient congregations, securely established in history, wealth and social status, the lack is less important. Their main task was not to spread Unitarian tenets, but to conserve the traditions,

Presbyterian, moderate and libertarian, and to claim the place in society and public affairs to which their intellect and property entitled them. It was important to be in the main stream of life and not to erect unnecessary barriers. To be 'a mere sect' was to lose touch with the effective forces of the age.

## Victorian Liberalism

For a generation from about 1870 Unitarians played a considerable part in public life, which to some extent recaptured the old substantial, aristocratic Presbyterian ideal. The faces in the portraits again become assured and solid—except G. F. Watts's portrait of Martineau in 1874, which Martineau's friends said was 'not a successful likeness', because it showed the troubled soul underneath.

A foretaste had been given in the life of Lant Carpenter, who died in 1840 but who reveals many of the traits of these later men. When he went from Exeter to Bristol in 1817, as minister of Lewin's-mead Meeting, he was not content merely to undertake Unitarian propaganda under the auspices of the Western Unitarian Society. He was eager for comprehension; as has been said, he persuaded the Priestleyan Unitarians to remove from the constitution of the Society a declaration that Arian views of Christ were superstitious. At Bristol he worked hard to win back the confidence of the merchants and professional men, whose membership of his chapel had become merely nominal. He made friends with the Anglican clergy and took a leading part in philanthropic work in the town. His school (for merchants' sons paying high fees) was famous and he was a noted educational theorist; but Harriet Martineau said that his teaching was so nebulously romantic that his pupils landed anywhere between catholicism and atheism. Martineau served for a time as assistant in this school and other Unitarians who were prominent after the middle of the century, like Samuel Greg, were pupils there.

Such men were radicals until the Reform Bill was achieved; after that they were liberals. By the middle of the nineteenth century the Whig party, whose leadership was aristocratic (traditionally in a small group of titled families), gave place to the Liberal party, whose leadership was middle-class. Most leading Nonconformists, whether Congregationalist, Baptist, Quaker or Unitarian, belonged to this party and consequently were social and political allies. In the second half of the nineteenth century Unitarians won back some of the social esteem they had lost—so much so that by 1907 the eminent Congregationalist R. W. Dale, in his *History of English Congregationalism*, could regret the Lady Hewley case and praise the wisdom of the Dissenters' Chapels Act. Eminent Unitarian preachers, like H. W. Crosskey of Birmingham, P. W. Clayden and R. A. Armstrong of Nottingham and H. E. Dowson of Hyde, Cheshire, were powerful advocates of Liberal political ideals, both in the pulpit and on the public platform.

Unitarians also valued their links with the world of literature and science. From Carlyle and Dickens to Browning and Darwin most of the literary figures of the mid-century had connections with Unitarianism in some respect. In 1869 Martineau joined the Metaphysical Society and rubbed shoulders in discussion with Tennyson, Browning, Gladstone, Ruskin, Tyndall, Huxley, Cardinal Manning and others of the contemporary great; such intellectual acceptance seemed far more valuable than any success won by polemical preaching. In 1845 the quaternion (Martineau, Thom, Tayler and Wicksteed) turned *The Christian Teacher* into *The Prospective Review* and entered the wider world of literature and public affairs. There were of course limits to this acceptance: in 1866 Martineau, already a reputable philosopher, was a candidate for the Chair of Mental Philosophy and Logic at University College, London and was rejected—by an odd combination of circumstances, including the scruples of Unitarian electors, who did not wish to appear to be seeking a denominational advantage.

But this movement to the centre of the stage had another side: by removing the polemical barriers Unitarians made it more easy for some of their valued members to pass out of Unitarianism, either into the Church of England or into secular life. P. W. Clayden and R. H. Hutton, like Hazlitt and others earlier, passed from the ministry into political journalism. Thomas Madge's son Travers, Lant Carpenter's son Philip and F. D. Maurice, also a Unitarian minister's son, and many others found their way into Anglicanism, often emphatically so. The notable Beard family followed a common pattern of development: John Relly Beard was a scriptural Unitarian, his son Charles a disciple of Martineau, and his grandchildren eminent in science and philanthropy.[1] During this period the

---

[1] See H. McLachlan, *Records of a Family*, 1935.

Unitarian denomination, largely rejecting the Unitarian name, achieved status and acceptance in general society on the basis of the old Presbyterian foundations, a libertarian religious outlook and Liberal politics. Martineau was unusual, or perhaps (in view of Joseph Chamberlain's Liberal Unionism) only prescient, in being a Conservative.

## Changing Piety

For these influential congregations of old foundation a new service-book was compiled in 1862 by Thomas Sadler, minister of the old Presbyterian congregation at Hampstead. It was deliberately modelled on the Book of Common Prayer, even to the rubrics, sung responses and penitential opening prayers; the title itself, *Common prayer for Christian worship*, is significant, and the word Unitarian nowhere appears. Martineau was invited to share in editing it; but he was an individualist and preferred to contribute two services of his own. He revealed himself as not quite in step with Unitarian piety of that day, for his prayers and canticles are more full of personal feeling and dramatic imagery than the rest of the book. Where the other services in the book were rational and traditionally devout, his were existential cries from the heart, owing something to Luther, Tauler and Augustine. But he was always somewhat reckless and emotional in his use of words and Watts's troubled portrait came nearer to the inner truth of his life than his friends liked to think.

In fact another temper, not altogether compatible with Martineau's outlook, was becoming prominent among Unitarians. Martineau himself had recognized in 1840 that, in addition to the old scriptural rationalism and his own intuitional school, there was a third party, the anti-supernatural; but he did not think that it had any future as a religious force. He was wrong. Indeed he himself helped to break up the mediating traditional position which he tried to establish, as his enemies said he would. Martineau had not denied miracles or scriptural revelation; he had only refused to accept them as primary evidence for faith. Truth is inward, but this can also be taken to mean that all outward expressions of truth, in symbol, creed or scripture, especially if traditional, will convey truth, even if imperfectly. In his earlier sermons he exalted Christ as image of God and type of humanity. Through Christ we know

God and in Christ's life and in the whole biblical story from Eden to Gethsemane we see the journey of every man's soul. Some of his language sounded, in the ears of his older Unitarian critics, almost orthodox. In many respects Martineau was an English Schleiermacher and, like him, eager to commend Christianity to the cultured through traditional symbols, apprehended psychologically rather than argumentatively. Broad-churchmen like F. W. Robertson read him with delight and used his images in their own sermons.

But some of his followers said that if the seat of authority in religion lies in an inward intuition and an inward moral impulse, why limit this to Christianity? Surely the true religion is a pure theism, of which Christianity is only a local and temporal form. One should concentrate on a generalized moral idealism or seek a fellowship of all the faiths, Christian and non-Christian alike. It may even be that Buddhism or Idealist metaphysics or mysticism is more fundamentally religious than any form of Christianity.

*Anti-Supernaturalism*

Martineau himself, it was said, prayed and preached like a Christian and taught philosophy like a pure rationalist. In 1873 he compiled a new hymn-book, *Hymns of praise and prayer*, in which he admitted that many people had given up belief in 'ecclesiastical mythology' (i.e. scriptural history and symbolism) for 'the poetry of the inner life'; God is known by immediate experience and so scripture is sacred only 'by consent of sympathy and reverence'. But he wondered whether this had not gone too far: 'For myself, both conviction and feeling keep me close to the poetry and piety of Christendom.' He doubted, with some sarcasm, whether much religious value could be found in the other world-faiths: 'If there be any who can waft their souls to God on Vedic hymns or toil upwards by the steps of Gentile metaphysics, far be it from me to question the exercise.' But in fact this was the step that many contemporary Unitarians in both England and America were taking. Ram Mohun Roy, the founder of the reformed Hindu movement called Brahmo Samaj, was welcomed by English Unitarians in 1831 (he died in Bristol in 1833) because he approached agreement with them as Christians; his successor, Keshub Chunder Sen, was welcomed by English Unitarians in 1870 because he was non-Christian, so that fellowship with him was a token of a more

universal religion. Some theists, like F. W. Newman and Frances
Power Cobbe, were almost aggressively neutral towards Christianity.
R. A. Armstrong, who succeeded P. W. Clayden at High-pavement
Chapel, Nottingham, in 1869 (and in 1883 moved to Martineau's
former pulpit in Liverpool), preached a cosmic theism which 'placed
Jesus among the other men of history'. To Martineau's arguments
for the existence of God from causality and conscience Armstrong
added a faith, which he called Wordsworthian, in an overarching
divine love, known by sympathy rather than by reason. Such a faith
rejected supernaturalism, whether in the crude form of miracle or
the more subtle form of any doctrine which dualistically separated
the soul from immediate union with God. This was in tune with
contemporary developments in German theology, particularly that
of Ritschl, who declared that man's relation with God is 'practical',
in loving trust and an actively good life. Armstrong drew such large
congregations by a combination of this theology with an earnestly-
moral Gladstonian Liberalism that his Nottingham chapel was
rebuilt in 1876 on a huge gothic scale, seating more than 1000
hearers. When in 1883 he moved to Liverpool, however, his
popularity fell off. In 1899 he wrote *Back to Jesus: an appeal to
evangelical Christians*, in which he took a more positive attitude in
favour of Christianity.

A further complication was that this anti-supernaturalism also
appealed to some polemically-minded Unitarians, who made it a
rationalist campaign against evangelical orthodoxy and so rejected
Martineau's mediating efforts. The communion service, which
Martineau and his friends had cherished just as much as the scriptural Unitarians had done, withered away, some ministers even
making its abolition a condition of their acceptance of a pulpit.
Some of them, like John Page Hopps, moved towards spiritualism.
So Martineau found uncongenial allies and protested, but he was
now too old to influence developments.

This was the pattern of Unitarianism in the last thirty years of
the nineteenth century. The old Presbyterian congregations in
the larger towns flourished under enlightened and actively-political
ministers, supported by a body of substantial laymen of the same
views. H. W. Crosskey had a brilliant ministry of this type at
Birmingham from 1869 to 1893, to which he added eminence as a
geologist; and there were many like him. Martineau became an

s

elder statesman (he lived until 1900) producing, after his retirement from Manchester College in 1885, a series of theological and ethical works which really belonged to an earlier generation, being in fact the three-year cycle of his former lectures at Manchester New College. He continued to insist that 'Unitarian' could only be the name of the belief of individuals (including Martineau himself) and should never be adopted as the restrictive title of a denomination or a congregation, and that in fact the persons called Unitarians were of very mixed unorthodoxy, united only by the principle of freedom. In this he was supported by most of those ministers and laymen in control of the older and wealthier congregations, who when challenged appealed to the open trusts and comprehensive ideals of 'our Presbyterian ancestors'.

## THE LATER STORY

### Changing Organization

This Presbyterian ideal did not go unchallenged. There were many who cherished the old Unitarian faith, even if modified, based upon scripture and reason, and meant to be preached to all men, in opposition to orthodoxy. They tended to gather round the British & Foreign Unitarian Association, which in 1886 acquired Essex-street Chapel as denominational headquarters on the removal of the congregation to Kensington. The British & Foreign Unitarian Association, though its membership was now limited to individual subscribers, administered many of the funds which supported the smaller congregations in many parts of the country, the so-called 'aided churches', which were to be distinguished in this from the well-endowed and well-supported congregations, mostly of Presbyterian origin, which were called 'self-supporting'. The aided churches of course included many of those founded by missionary preaching, whose membership was often of the poorer classes and which did not share in the renewed social status of the old Presbyterian chapels in the larger towns. An increasing number of ministers was trained at John Relly Beard's foundation in Manchester, the Unitarian Home Missionary Board, which in 1889 changed its

name to the Unitarian Home Missionary College and raised its
academic status by closer association with Owen's College (which
in 1903 became the Victoria University of Manchester). Here was
trained the Unitarian Association's indefatigable secretary (from
1891), W. Copeland Bowie. Since *The Inquirer* supported
Martineau's position, a rival paper, *The Christian Life*, was founded
in 1876 to promote denominational advance. An important figure of
this party was Brooke Herford, minister of Upper Chapel, Sheffield
and later of Manchester and Hampstead, who organized missionary
activity, published pamphlets and a magazine called *The Christian
Freeman* and tried to stop what he considered a dangerous drift
towards a non-Christian anti-supernaturalism.[1] As a preacher
Herford was a great contrast to Martineau; where Martineau was
metaphysical and mystical, Herford was warmly human.

In 1886 Martineau was joining with Broad-churchmen in an
abortive effort to widen the Church of England to include liberal
Dissenters, which was Thomas Arnold's ideal. *The Christian Reformer*, in its later years edited by Aspland's son, had come to an
end in 1863, still battling against the school of Martineau; in 1886–7
it was revived, this time in the hands of Martineau's followers, to
promote the ideal of 'a truly national church'. Liberal Anglicans
like Canon S. A. Barnett and Stopford Brooke were among the
contributors and much space was given to ecclesiastical news,
nearly all Anglican. But it came to nothing.

Next year, though now over eighty years of age, Martineau was
busily occupied, in the words of his biographers, with 'an endeavour
to organise the old English Presbyterian congregations, in such a way
as at once to emphasise their catholic principle and to secure for
them that corporate strength which was needed for the maintenance
of the weaker societies'. In his view the British & Foreign Unitarian
Association, which had just moved into its new headquarters,
'stood in the way', since it was 'doctrinally organized'. He hoped
for a new Presbyterian national church, in which the separate
'presbyteries' (congregations), without the intervention of district
associations (which were mostly 'for missionary purposes'), should be
related directly to a representative General Assembly; this assembly

[1] Though of English origin, he was a Unitarian minister in Chicago, at the Church
of the Messiah, from 1876 to 1881 and led the conservative Unitarians against the new
'ethical-basis' school which grew out of Transcendentalism.

should administer a fund, obtained by a tax upon the congregations, for the payment of ministers and the support of weaker churches. 'There is some difficulty', he admitted, 'in resuming the name "English Presbyterian" after having allowed it to fall into disuse. But every suggested alternative is attended, I think, with more serious difficulty. The links have never been broken, and we are entitled, as I think, to take them up and secure them.' But in spite of manful efforts the venture came to nothing.

Instead, those who agreed with Martineau had to be content to continue with a loose association of individuals and congregations, founded four years previously, with the long title of 'The National Conference of Unitarian, Liberal Christian, Free Christian, Presbyterian, and other Non-Subscribing or Kindred Congregations', associated with the British & Foreign Unitarian Association and meeting triennially. It undertook certain denominational activities—a fund for the augmentation of ministers' salaries, a ministers' pension and insurance fund—and there was some overlapping of function with the Unitarian Association. Martineau hoped to turn this indefinite body into a new English Presbyterian denomination, but he failed, as did others who tried again later. He spoke vigorously: 'If anyone, being a Unitarian, shrinks on fitting occasion from plainly calling himself so, he is a sneak and a coward; if, being of our catholic communion, he calls his chapel or its congregation Unitarian, he is a traitor to his spiritual ancestry and a deserter to the camp of its persecutors.' He even accused 'foreign influences', seceders from orthodox churches, of responsibility for 'attaching doctrinal names to societies which had hitherto rigorously avoided them'. Of course he was partly right, if by 'foreign influences' he meant Priestley and Belsham, Aspland and Fox; but there were 'foreign influences' on his own side too.

*Manchester College, Oxford*

In 1888 Manchester College was moved from London to Oxford, with the large aim of establishing it there as a college of liberal religion without denominational ties. Martineau in fact opposed the move, but it was generously supported by wealthy Unitarians and others, including Broad-churchmen, who had been influenced by him. Handsome buildings were erected in 1893; but Mrs Humphry Ward, grand-daughter of Thomas Arnold, wrote to *The Manchester*

*Guardian* after attending the opening, to protest that a Nonconformist type of service in the college chapel would make no impression
on Oxford. A marble statue of Martineau was placed in the library,
backed by a window containing portraits and coats-of-arms of
founders and worthies of Warrington Academy.

The Hibbert Trust, founded in 1853 (the founder wanted to
call it the Anti-Trinitarian Fund), now devoted its income to
promoting public lectures on comparative religion and similar
subjects, and (from 1901) to supporting a journal of liberal theology
(*The Hibbert Journal*). J. Estlin Carpenter, grandson of Lant
Carpenter, taught comparative religion at Manchester College and
became a pioneer scholar in this field. P. H. Wicksteed,[1] son of
one of the quaternion, gave up the ministry to become a celebrated
economist and an expositor of Dante and Aquinas; he inspired the
founding at Manchester College of a lectureship in 'social studies',
a reminder of the social concern of the Martineau group. When in
1904 W. E. Addis, tutor in the Old Testament, resumed the status
of an Anglican clergyman, a majority of the trustees of the college
resisted an effort to compel him to resign; his place was later taken
by another Anglican, Canon D. C. Simpson, who served for
thirty-nine years. Here, at least in intention, was no sect, but a
comprehensive effort to take the lead on a broad front of life and
religion. Here, its promoters unhesitatingly claimed, was the English
Presbyterian ideal of catholicism, liberty and moral idealism.

## The Turn of the Century

As the century drew to a close the political temper of the younger
Liberals changed. Gladstone's 'Little England' idealism, stressing
free trade and wanting to grant home-rule to Ireland, gave place
to an imperial fervour. The Conservatives under Disraeli, in addition to encouraging a sense of Britain's imperial destiny, were in
many respects a party of paternal socialism, in opposition to the
middle-class individualism of the Liberals. In extension of the
franchise, in education, in labour legislation, it looked as though
'they had caught the Whigs bathing and run off with their clothes'.
Because of competition with Germany, there was a feeling in the
nation that it must become scientifically up-to-date and accept its

[1] Philip Henry Wicksteed, as his name shows, was a direct descendant, like so many
leading Unitarians, of the ejected minister Philip Henry (1631–96).

colonial responsibilities and its status as a great power. This fitted in well with the civic idealism of the middle-class Unitarians who followed Martineau, and even more with the more secular idealism of his anti-supernaturalist successors. Joseph Chamberlain was a member of Priestley's former congregation in Birmingham, which built the Church of the Messiah in 1862, and was from 1869 to 1893 under Crosskey's vigorous leadership. In 1873–5 Chamberlain was mayor of Birmingham, as a municipal reformer, improving housing and sanitation. In 1870 he became a Liberal Member of Parliament, but soon took an imperialist line unwelcome to his colleagues. In 1886 he broke with Gladstone over Irish home-rule and led a group of Liberal-Unionists into the Conservative camp. He was Colonial Secretary in the Conservative government at the outbreak of the Boer War, for which he must bear some responsibility. The war split the leading Unitarians. The older men remained faithful to the old Liberal ideals and were 'pro-Boer'; some of the younger men were more inclined to support the government. Particularly in Liverpool the division within the Unitarian body was acute. It looked as though there was an element in the Unitarian body which might become even more conservative.

But the war was followed by the 'Liberal landslide' of 1905, when the Liberals came to power with an overwhelming majority. Under their rule the first steps were taken towards social insurance and the welfare state, with other radical measures. This, like previous political changes, was reflected in changes in the Unitarian body. It gave great encouragement to all radically-minded people and there was an almost immediate influx of young men from Methodism and other denominations into the Unitarian ministry. In 1905 the Unitarian Home Missionary College moved into larger premises and advanced its academic status still further, and in the same year it sponsored the Van Mission, which toured the market-places of northern England. In 1912 the Pioneer Preachers, a body of open-air evangelists founded by R. J. Campbell, a liberal Congregationalist, was transferred to the care of the British & Foreign Unitarian Association, and most of its young men sought training for the Unitarian ministry at the Home Missionary College. It was the age of the social gospel and what Campbell called the New Theology, based on an evolutionary anti-supernaturalism and expressing itself in socialist politics. Campbell was accused of being 'no better than a Unitarian', though he said that official Unitarianism was rationalist and unspiritual; many Unitarians, however, shared his views.

The swing to a more radical Unitarianism, and against the traditional moderatism of the school of Martineau, was so strong that in 1909 an attempt was made by C. J. Street and W. C. Bowie of the British & Foreign Unitarian Association so to organize the election of officers of the National Conference that the Conference would virtually pass into the control of the Association. A list of favoured candidates was circulated to voters believed to be sympathetic and when by mishap it fell into the hands of the other party there were angry and bitter recriminations and a threatened split in the denomination—and this in spite of the fact that many Unitarians belonged to both organizations. A matter of principle plainly was involved; the denomination seemed to consist of two overlapping circles, one labelled 'Unitarian' and eager for organization and propaganda, the other rejecting labels and treasuring comprehension. Each side had its own college, newspaper, assembly and hymn-book[1]—and many Unitarians cheerfully patronized both.

This burst of denominational fervour was very unwelcome to some of those who so recently had been celebrating the re-establishment of the Presbyterian ideal and repudiating the Unitarian name. How strong the feeling could be against 'Essex Hall' can be seen from a pamphlet published in 1898 by E. I. Fripp, minister of the Second Non-subscribing Presbyterian congregation, Belfast, which he had inspired to build a new gothic church with chancel and altar (unlike anything else in Irish Non-Subscribing Presbyterianism), which he called All Souls. The pamphlet was entitled *Two opposing tendencies*. He bitterly attacked the British & Foreign Unitarian Association, which, he said, 'has grown to be a dangerous ecclesiastical power', especially as it has control of the distribution of funds, so that 'it has become a pecuniary interest to ministers and congregations to adopt and keep Unitarian views'. The Association had in fact made a grant towards the erection of All Souls' Church, at Fripp's request, but he hastily sent it back and resigned his membership. He appealed to the authority of Richard Baxter, who was 'for

---

[1] On the Unitarian side, the Home Missionary College, *The Christian Life* (and other papers), the B. & F.U.A. and *The Essex-hall hymnal* (1890, revised 1902): on the other side, Manchester College, *The Inquirer* (and other journals), the National Conference and *The new hymnal* (1905).

catholicism against parties', and made much of what he declared to be the undogmatic comprehensiveness of the old Presbyterians, with their open trusts and their devotion to religion rather than doctrine. He urged that the National Conference should be made into a representative Free Church national assembly, to which 'all our Free Church institutions, such as Manchester College, the Sunday School Association, Ministers' Augmentation Fund, Dr. Williams's Library and so forth' should belong, but to which the British & Foreign Unitarian Association should have no more right of entry than the London Society for Promoting Christianity among the Jews. From John Taylor of Norwich he quoted: 'We are Christians and only Christians and disown all connection, excepting that of love and good-will, with any sect or party whatever.' Dr Martineau, then aged ninety-two, wrote him two approving letters, which he printed.

The retort of the editor of *The Christian Life* was: 'Let us be done with this cant about freedom. We are no more free than other churches. Nor are any of our churches "Presbyterian"—not one of them.' At the same time the editor protested against grants being made by the National Conference's sustentation fund to ministers and churches which declared themselves to be theistic rather than Unitarian, or doubted the resurrection of Christ. But E. I. Fripp continued his war with the British & Foreign Unitarian Association. As minister of the Old Meeting House, Mansfield, a Presbyterian foundation, he introduced a service-book closely based on the Book of Common Prayer and officiated in cassock and surplice. At the chapel's bicentenary in 1901 he rejoiced that it was not founded by nineteenth century Unitarians but by 'broad-minded Trinitarians of 1701 or earlier', he thought the best title for the chapel would be 'Reformed Church of England' and he looked 'with passionate yearning' for the expansion of the Anglican church into 'a genuinely national fellowship'. Joseph Bull Bristowe, during whose ministry from 1800 to 1811 the chapel was first called Unitarian, he referred to as a 'mad Bull'; but he had a good word for William Linwood, whose popular radical preaching had led to the crisis of 1848. At the same bicentenary J. Estlin Carpenter read a paper tracing the history of all such chapels to the Presbyterians and Richard Baxter, and maintaining that they were therefore dedicated to 'the widest liberty'.

*The Free Catholic Movement*

Leadership in this anti-sectarian movement was taken up by J. M. Lloyd Thomas, minister of High-pavement Chapel, Nottingham from 1900 to 1912, and from 1912 of the Old Meeting, Birmingham.[1] In 1907 he published *A Free Catholic Church*, inspired by Roman Catholic modernism. Religion, he said, cannot be defined: 'It is as elusive as the beauty of a picture, the emotion of music, the breath of poetry.' It must therefore be widely catholic, not even limited to Christianity; and it withers under a dogmatic system of organization. He looked for a new comprehensive church, emphasizing common worship rather than agreement in belief, using 'symbols that devotionally unite, not creeds that theologically separate'. 'And this church will be an organ of justice and mercy to rebuke the greed and cruelty of modern society. Being constitutionally democratic, she will make the cause of the people her own cause; seeing the multitudes she will be moved with compassion and seek to live like the Son of Man, to minister and not to be ministered unto.' He appealed much to Baxter, of whose autobiography he published an abridgement in 1925 to show him as a 'moderate episcopalian' and 'never a Presbyterian'.

This was of course closely related to similar developments in other churches at this time. Roman Catholic modernism came to an end in 1907 with the Papal Bull *Pascendi gregis*, but there were men in all denominations who wanted to combine modernism (acceptance of the scientific outlook and of the new historical view of the Bible), immanentism (God not apart from the world, but indwelling in the time-process and in man's heart), catholicism (traditional symbols of devotion and inter-denominational comprehension) and socialism. It was a new kind of high-churchmanship, aesthetic, and warmly socialist, rather than creedal, sacramental and Tory. Percy Dearmer published *The Parson's Handbook* in 1899 and *The English Hymnal* in 1906 and inspired many in the Church of England; *Songs of Praise*, which followed in 1925, was more secular. There were unexpected liturgical movements among Congregationalists and Scottish Presbyterians. Among the Unitarians it was the Free Catholic Movement.

[1] The Old Meeting, founded in 1687, seems to have always been more conservative than the New Meeting, founded in 1692, and Joseph Wood, minister from 1884 to 1912, was a strong advocate of the catholic ideal and of liturgical forms of worship. For the ultimate fate of the Old Meeting, see below, p. 285.

It was an attempt to apply Lloyd Thomas's book. He had made no practical suggestions for bringing his ideal church into existence, but a number of fellow-Unitarian ministers, moved by his devotional ideals, began to meet from time to time in 'retreats' for the cultivation of the devout life by prayer and discussion. Different motives brought them together: socialism, mysticism, poetry, liturgy (both traditional and experimental, expressive of new social ideals). In 1916 the group, which was never large, organized themselves as the Society of Free Catholics and began to publish a monthly magazine, *The Free Catholic*. 'Unitarianism', wrote Lloyd Thomas, who was editor, 'interests me less and less', though he admitted that there was no other denomination he could join. Other members of the group contributed articles about liturgy, prayer, catholic comprehensiveness and social ideals. For a brief time a Free Catholic friar, Brother Douglas, tramped the roads in monastic habit and sandals. The original group of Unitarians who founded the society were very faithful; they included some of the most idealist and devout ministers in the denomination. But not many other Unitarians were interested, and from time to time there was exasperated controversy in the denominational press.

Merely to appeal to Unitarians, however, was not the aim of the Society of Free Catholics; they were delighted when Conrad Noel, the socialist vicar of Thaxted, showed interest, and even more so when W. E. Orchard, minister of the King's Weigh-house, a Congregational chapel in London, became an active member. Orchard was an extremist in 'catholicism', in every meaning of the word; he cultivated liturgy and comprehensiveness to the extent of performing what was virtually a Roman Catholic Mass in a Congregational church, while wearing John Wesley's silver shoe-buckles. But he diverted the Society of Free Catholics from an ideal of devout freedom to a desire for reunion with the One Holy Catholic Church, and he himself was eventually received into the Church of Rome in 1932.

Indirectly the Society of Free Catholics had a beneficent influence on the Unitarians, in stimulating a concern both for dignity and depth of worship and for community service. J. S. Burgess of Flowery Field, Hyde not only built up a sacramental worship in his church (in which he used Dearmer's *Songs of Praise*), but linked it with many interests in the local community, himself becoming mayor of Hyde. F. Heming Vaughan of Hyde Chapel, Gee Cross, developed experimental methods of worship and also was associated with the British Film Council and other artistic enterprises of that day, which were concerned to relate art and life. Dr Stanley A. Mellor of Hope-street, Liverpool drew a large congregation by his modernist and socialist preaching. Socialism, indeed, became popular with the Free Catholics, as it was with the contemporary Anglo-catholics. It was no longer necessary for a socialist minister to leave the church, as John Trevor had done in 1891 when he resigned from Upper Brook Street, Manchester to found the Labour Church—or be dismissed, like J. Bellamy Higham of Park-lane Chapel, near Wigan in 1912. There was protest from some Unitarian subscribers to Manchester College when Graham Wallas and R. H. Tawney, prominent socialists, successively occupied the lectureship in social studies which P. H. Wicksteed had helped to found, but it was without effect. All these developments took place in old Presbyterian foundations which had come under Martineau's influence.[1]

But for all their good qualities the Free Catholics hindered rather than fostered an organic fellowship among the churches. They regarded the British & Foreign Unitarian Association as the enemy of a truly comprehensive, free and spiritual church and frequently objected in print to 'the Unitarian name'. The Society of Free Catholics had in fact begun to decline by 1922, largely because of the diversion of aim introduced by Orchard, but also because of their own individualism. Membership seriously fell off; its contribution was almost over, though it did not officially disband until 1929.

## The General Assembly

There was need for statesmanship. Most of the key-positions in the denomination were held by 'Unitarians'. *The Inquirer*, formerly pro-Martineau, was now edited by W. G. Tarrant, trained at the Unitarian Home Missionary College. In 1925 the centenary of the British & Foreign Unitarian Association was celebrated—in the same year as the centenary of its American counterpart, which had much more executive power. The president of the National

[1] To be accurate, Upper Brook-street, Manchester, was founded in 1789; but all the others were Presbyterian. Other members of the Society of Free Catholics were W. Whitaker, of Platt Chapel, Manchester, whose chief concern was the deepening of personal piety, and H. H. Johnson, of Evesham, a poet and liturgiologist.

Conference, for so long the stronghold of the 'anti-dogmatic' party, was C. J. Street, recently retired from a long ministry at Upper Chapel, Sheffield (and so successor to Brooke Herford, who had opposed Martineau), and the secretary was Dendy Agate, both of whose names go far back into General Baptist history. At the Triennial Conference in 1926 Mrs Sydney Martineau, a distant relative by marriage of James Martineau (her own background was the Birmingham congregation formerly led by Priestley and Bache, and the London congregation of which Lindsey and Belsham had been ministers), boldly proposed, in an official speech, an amalgamation of the National Conference and the B. & F. U. A. 'Mr Pepys', the witty reporter of *The Inquirer* (he was Mr Ronald P. Jones), writing as usual in the style of the famous diary, commented: 'This all very clear and bold with no sliding over matters of dispute, so that I do greatly marvel that so much should here be spoken openly which but a few years back had been like to provoke an instant uproar.' The matter was put in the hands of negotiating committees and for two years it was discussed, sometimes with heat, in print and on platform. The most vigorous opponent was Dr L. P. Jacks, principal of Manchester College, who revered the devotional, libertarian and social ideals of Martineau and the Free Catholics.[1] Lloyd Thomas, declaring himself a Trinitarian, also opposed; and so did a number of others who, though not at all of the Martineau school, feared some loss of liberty and treasured the old Presbyterian principle of catholicity and non-subscription.

The matter was finally put to the vote at meetings of the two bodies in 1928. Wisely the name chosen was a double one—'the General Assembly of Unitarian and Free Christian Churches'—and it was claimed that the combination of two names made the new body wider than either name taken separately. Membership was made up of individuals, congregations and district associations, on equal terms and not as a hierarchy. The British & Foreign Unitarian Association remained legally in existence as custodian of funds only. Already the two competing hymn-books had been superseded by a

---

[1] Jacks was a novelist and a popular philosopher of a pragmatic and Bergsonian temper. He had recently fulfilled a social and educational ideal of the Free Catholics by introducing lay students, chosen from the Workers' Educational Association, into Manchester College; and he had compiled a service-book for the college chapel, and established a surpliced choir of men and boys, as was done in some other churches influenced by Martineau and the Free Catholics.

new book, *Hymns of Worship* (1927), and in 1932 a service-book, *Orders of Worship*, was added, both bearing on their title-pages the statement that they were for use in Unitarian and Free Christian churches. In 1929 *The Inquirer* and *The Christian Life* were amalgamated, for a short time under a double title and then as *The Inquirer* only. The two colleges however remained separate. In 1926 the Home Missionary College changed its name to the Unitarian College, Manchester and took equal place with Manchester College, Oxford in the training of ministers. After a long and devious history a distinct and organized denomination had been born and the decision in the end was taken with surprising unanimity.

There were objectors, heartfelt in their opposition, but they were few. For some years Dr L. P. Jacks refused to allow Manchester College, of which he was principal, to be officially represented on the Council of the General Assembly. J. M. Lloyd Thomas and his Old Meeting congregation at Birmingham refused to join. He quoted Baxter: 'Thus have I found the old saying true, that reconcilers are hated on both sides, and put their hand in the cleft, which closeth upon them and finisheth them.' (But Baxter had given the Happy Union his blessing.) The comparison of himself with Baxter was perhaps more just than he realized, for Baxter also was a man who believed he was striving for comprehension, yet was a centre of dissension, and who preached a universal church, of which he seemed to be the only member. Lloyd Thomas repudiated Orchard and said that the Society of Free Catholics would continue; but in fact it quickly came to an end. For his lonely congregation he compiled a lavish and scholarly *Free Church Book of Common Prayer* (1929), traditional in many details, and with contributions drawn from Anglicanism, Nonconformity, Judaism and, of course, Martineau. He also compiled a supplement to *The New Hymnal*, containing hymns of invocation to the Virgin Mary and the saints. His congregation dwindled and finally disappeared in the 'blitz' of an air-raid on Birmingham in 1941.[1]

Dr Jacks too refused to join the General Assembly and under his influence Manchester College refused representation on the Council of the Assembly until 1943, though of course most of its students

---

[1] Some of its endowment went to the General Assembly and the Birmingham district churches and some to the Chapel of Unity of Coventry cathedral, after a legal enquiry, in 1955–60. See *UHST*, xii. 53–68.

went into the ministry of churches of the Assembly. The annual report of the college has carried on its title-page since 1885 the legend, 'The College adheres to its original principle of freely imparting Theological knowledge without insisting on the adoption of particular Theological Doctrines'. This is at least in the tradition of the Rational Dissenters and Warrington Academy, foreshadowed by Doddridge and by the Presbyterians. This liberty of conscience was not the whole of Presbyterianism, but it was an important part.

There is a direct line of inheritance, not merely of institutions but also of outlook, from the Presbyterians ejected in 1662 to the General Assembly of Unitarian and Free Christian Churches. They are not identical; 300 years of development, in themselves and in the world, have made a considerable difference. And the story has not been a simple unfolding from the original impulse, but a complex interaction of many forces. It cannot be said that in any particular generation the descendants have completely fulfilled the promise of their forefathers, but usually, where one generation has fallen short, the next generation has done something to redress the balance. In one age it has been religious freedom which has been stressed, in another a polemical message, in another a deeper piety, in another a social idealism. At different times different names have been adopted: Presbyterian, Catholic Christian, Rational Dissenter or Rational Christian, Unitarian, Free Christian, Liberal Christian, Non-Subscriber, Free Catholic, Universalist, Theist—each representing one facet of a many-sided tradition and each leaving something out. No doubt the present representatives of this many-sided tradition fall short, in this respect and that, of the possibilities of their heritage. But what shall emerge from the present situation will be decided by interaction between the tradition, the current faith and the historical circumstances. The story continues.

# INDEX OF NAMES AND A SELECTION OF OTHER MATTERS

## 296

# INDEX

Thomas Aquinas, *Saint*, 277
Thomas, J. M. Lloyd, 281 f., 284 f.
Thomason, G., 69
Thompson, Samuel, 238
Three Denominations:
  Committee, 126, 167, 171
  Deputies, 176, 242 f., 244 f., 250 f.
  General Body, 17, 125, 162, 242 f., 251
Tillotson, John, *Archbishop of Canterbury*, 84, 101, 103, 109 f., 129, 139
Tindal, Matthew, 141, 188
Toland, John, 131, 144, 188, 154
Tomkins, Martin, 173
Tomlyns, John, 136
Tong, William, 157, 161
Toulmin, Joshua, 236
Traill, Robert, 90
Travers, Walter, 31 f., 72
Trevor, John, 283
Troeltsch, Ernst, 267
Trosse, George, 86
Tucker, Josiah, *Dean of Gloucester*, 187
Tuckerman, Joseph, 261
Turner, John, 86, 107
Twisse, William, 39
Tyndall, John, 270

Udall, John, 33
Unitarian Home Missionary Board (College), 274 f., 283
Unitarians, 17 f., 28, 229 ff., 234 ff., 238–86
*Universal Theological Magazine*, 237
*Universalist's Miscellany*, 237
Universalists, 237
Ussher, James, *Archbishop of Armagh*, 36 ff., 42, 60 ff., 69 f.

Vaughan, F. Heming, 283
Victoria, *Queen of England*, 265
Vidler, William, 237
Vincent, Thomas, 86 f.

Wadsworth, Christopher, 187, 205, 208
Wakefield, Gilbert, 229, 231, 233 f., 254
Walker, George, 193
Wallas, Graham, 283
Wallis, John, 84
Walrond, John, 192, 205 f.
Walpole, *Sir* Robert, 176
Ward, Mary A., *Mrs* T. Humphry, 276
Warrington Academy, 212, 224 f., 242 f., 277
Watson, Richard, *Bishop of Llandaff*, 228
Watson, Thomas, 87
Watts, George Frederic, 269, 271
Watts, Isaac, 96, 131, 135, 142, 146, 169 f., 172, 178 ff., 187, 189, 196, 221
Wedgwood, Josiah, 233
Wellbeloved, Charles, 235 ff., 249
Wells, Edward, 148
Wesley, John, 189, 221, 282
Westminster Assembly, 27, 38 ff., 44, 56, 135, 152, 184
Wharton, Philip, *Lord*, 79
Wharton Bequest, 159
Whiston, William, 140, 149 f., 155 f., 161, 222
Whitaker, William, 18, 283
Whitby, Daniel, 147, 212
White, Joseph Blanco, 252, 255
Whitefield, George, 206, 210, 221
Whiteman, Anne, 65
Whitlock, John, 85, 89
Wicksteed, Charles, 257 f., 270
Wicksteed, Philip Henry, 277, 283
Wilberforce, William, 228
Wilbur, E. M., 18
Wilcox, Daniel, 152, 161
Wilcox, Thomas, 31
William III, *King of England*, 91 f., 101 f., 124, 133
Williams, Daniel, 102 f., 117–23, 125, 127 f., 130, 142, 194, 196, 249
Williams, John, *Archbishop of York*, 37

Williams, Joseph, 195
Williamson, *Sir* Joseph, 87, 98
Wilson, Samuel, 181
Winchester, Elhanan, 237
Winder, Henry, 182, 193, 197
Withers, John, 157
Wodrow, Robert, 133, 160, 168, 172
Wood, Joseph, 281
Woolston, Thomas, 188, 190
Worcester House Declaration, 76 ff.
Worcestershire Association, 52 f., 60, 62, 68

Wordsworth, William, 263
Wright, John, *brother of Richard Wright*, 255
Wright, John, *grandson of Richard Wright*, 263, 265
Wright, Richard, 237, 247, 255, 265
Wright, Samuel, 155, 204

Young, George Lewis, 214
Young, Thomas, 34 f. *See also* Smectymnuus

# GEORGE ALLEN & UNWIN LTD

*London: 40 Museum Street, W.C.1.*

*Auckland: P.O. Box 36013, Northcote Central. N.4*
*Bombay: 15 Graham Road, Ballard Estate, Bombay 1*
*Barbados: P.O. Box 222, Bridgetown*
*Buenos Aires: Escritorio 454–459, Florida 165*
*Calcutta: 17 Chittaranjan Avenue, Calcutta 13*
*Cape Town: 68 Shortmarket Street*
*Hong Kong: 105 Wing On Mansion, 26 Hancow Road, Kowloon*
*Ibadan: P.O. Box 62*
*Karachi: Karachi Chambers, McLeod Road*
*Madras: Mohan Mansions, 38c Mount Road, Madras 6*
*Mexico: Villalongin 32–10, Piso, Mexico 5, D.F.*
*Nairobi: P.O. Box 4536*
*New Delhi: 13–14 Asaf Ali Road, New Delhi 1*
*Ontario: 81 Curlew Drive, Don Mills*
*Rio de Janeiro: Caixa Postal 2537–Zc–00*
*Sao Paulo: Caixa Postal 8675*
*Singapore: 36c Prinsep Street, Singapore 7*
*Sydney, N.S.W.: Bradbury House, 55 York Street*
*Tokyo: P.O. Box 26, Kamata*

# FAITH AND LOGIC

## OXFORD ESSAYS IN PHILOSOPHICAL THEOLOGY

### *Edited by* BASIL MITCHELL

There have been lively debates on the air and in the Press, about the bearing of modern philosophy upon Christianity, but there has been relatively little sustained discussion of the subject. This book of essays is the product of a small group of Oxford philosophers and theologians, who had met and talked informally for some years before they decided to write it. It is not a piece of systematic philosophical theology in the old style, but an attempt to discuss with care and candour some of the problems raised for Christian belief by contemporary analytical philosophy.

The questions raised are not altogether new; what is new is the rigour and precision with which they have been formulated. They cannot, therefore, be lightly dismissed as the product of a philosophical fashion. Nor are they of merely academic interest. In asking them philosophers are making articulate the perplexities of many intelligent people, both believers and unbelievers.

Philosophical criticism and defence of theology often takes the form of asserting or denying some very general theory of meaning. The contributors to this book think it more useful to concentrate on the way such concepts as God, Revelation, the Soul, Grace are actually used. In this way they hope to make some positive contribution to the understanding of them.

# THE CONCEPT OF HOLINESS

### O. R. JONES

It is Dr. Jones' conviction that a detailed analysis of particular religious concepts is necessary if the structure and meaning of religious language is to be properly displayed. He has chosen to examine one of the most distinctively religious concepts—the concept of holiness—and he considers its role in the sphere of Hebrew and Christian belief. The intimate connections between this concept and the associate notions of fear, power, separatedness, wholeness and goodness are carefully unfolded, and the analysis shows that in none of its connections can holiness be fairly understood unless reference is made to the key-concept of divine personality.

After giving a suggestive philosophical account of this key-concept by linking it with the notion of a 'perfect vision', the author shows how the concept of holiness in its manifold connections is thereby illuminated. The book should interest both theologians and philosophers since it is concerned with the area where both sides should meet, but where far too often they are separated by what appears to be an unbridgeable gulf.

# WE BELIEVE IN GOD

### Edited by RUPERT E. DAVIS

That belief in God is no longer held by intelligent people is the impression given in some circles. Here are eleven writers—two Anglicans, two Methodists, one Orthodox, one Roman Catholic, two Presbyterians, one Congregational, one Baptist and one Quaker, but none of them speak officially for his or her denomination—who firmly believe in God and are prepared to give grounds for their belief. They plainly indicate that religion for them is not a matter of convention or superstition, or 'something which is good for the children, but not needed by intelligent adults'. On the contrary, it comes out of deep conviction, grounded both in sound reason and personal experience. The writers come from very different educational and social backgrounds, as well as from different Christian traditions; but they show a remarkable harmony in their central affirmations, while their emphases and formulations vary considerably. It is a book for the open-minded enquirer, non-Christian and Christian alike.

# DYNAMICS OF FAITH

### PAUL TILLICH

The *New York Times* has described Dr. Tillich as 'a prophetic voice speaking with compelling power to our generation'. In this volume he makes an eloquent and convincing case for a renewal of faith—"the central phenomenon in man's personal life."

Drawing on a vast knowledge of human history and varied religions, Dr. Tillich reveals a number of intellectual distortions of the concept of faith. He reveals why there should be no conflict between the demands of science and of religion.

Beyond this, he has inspiring advice on the meaning of myths and symbols, the true nature of faith's healing powers, the role of faith in the community, and the role of doubt. More than almost any other work, these wise words by a great man of the church demonstrate the supreme importance of faith to all of us.

# FAITH IN A CHANGING CULTURE

## THE REVEREND A. D. GALLOWAY

Christendom is our heritage. What is to become of it? Everyone knows that the church must change with the times. But where should we set the limits of change? When is a Christian not a Christian? How can we be both faithful to the past and honest with the present?

Too many definite answers have already been given to these questions. This book does not attempt to add still more. It tries rather to find ground on which we can stand to begin answering such questions responsibly for ourselves.

This calls for a penetrating analysis of the whole relationship between religious faith and secular culture. In conflict they destroy each other. In union they devour each other. But in situations of true social growth they exist for each other. The Judao-Christian tradition is pre-eminent as an expression of this creative tension between religious faith and secular culture.

# FAITH AND CULTURE

## BY BERNARD MELAND

Dr. Meland draws upon cultural anthropology and modern metaphysics to show why Christian faith, in a profound sense, is indispensable to Western culture as well as ineradicable. Arguing that faith is a form of psychic energy which arises from individuals and social groups as they respond to the ultimate demands of living, he sees faith, in the history of any culture, as forming a pattern of sensibilities which gives incentive and direction to the human psyche. Thus in any culture a structure of experience arises to provide the emotional context of the people and give character and motif to all that is expressive of the human spirit. He is convinced that we must look to the liberal tradition to effect a recovery of Christian faith in Western culture. Hence he turns from his analysis to expound a renascent theological liberalism based upon the realism of our cultural situation. *Faith and Culture* is a valuable contribution to contemporary thought about the nature of faith, man, the church, and about the relation between religion and culture.

# PILGRIM IN THE MODERN WORLD

## L. J. BAGGOTT

The author of this book has had long experience in the ministry of the Church of England, from work in the slums to that of Abbey, Minster, and Cathedral; from a chaplaincy of the Tower of London to the vicariate of large industrial parishes; from a visiting Lecturership at a Theological College to the parochial tasks peculiar to four great seaports; from the supervision of Ordinands to the archdeaconship of a hundred peaceful Norfolk villages.

Throughout, it has become increasingly clear to him that, whether in the docks or in the professional chair, man is indeed the 'Eternal Pilgrim of the Infinite'. For twentieth century man, his pilgrimage is set in the most challenging era that man has ever known, a scientific era and a temporal order in which his most important problems take their rise and shape his life.

Christianity is an historical religion of which the 'redemption of man' is the central and ruling thought. The question at once arises: in the light of new knowledge and discovery, particularly of the new cosmology and the emergence of dialectical materialism and logical positivism—the most influential forces in modern scepticism—does the Christian faith meet the intellectual, moral, and spiritual needs of the contemporary situation; or is it like the irreducible surd in a mathematical problem—present as a fact but to be ignored in use?

This book offers what the author believes to be the only valid and satisfying answer.


# THE LIFE OF JESUS

## MAURICE GOGUEL

M. Maurice Goguel, one of the most distinguished New Testament Scholars of today, completed his great triology *Jesus et les Origines du Christianisme* in 1947. The first volume, *The life of Jesus*, was first published in 1933 but has been out-of-print for some time. Following the excellent reception accorded to the second volume, *The Birth of Christianity* (42s.), we have reprinted volume one. Volume three, *L'Eglise Primitive*, has yet to be translated.

*The Life of Jesus* is an important historical book based upon a long, detailed and profound study of the sources of the Gospel story, both Christian and non-Christian. It is a reverent and critical work which won a richly deserved recognition as a major contribution to the subject.

# HISTORY OF THE MORAVIAN CHURCH

EDWARD LANGTON

In the tiny village of Kunwald in Moravia began a fine religious movement which celebrated in 1957 the five hundredth anniversary of its birth. Fierce persecution dispersed the tiny community and forced them to practise their religion in secret. A small group were given a place of refuge in Germany by Count Zinzendorf and at Herrnhut began one of the most interesting experiments ever known in communal religious life.

Most people know something of the influence of the Moravian leaders upon John Wesley; how God used them to illumine his mind and to teach him the secret of having faith. But few know how ancient and honourable had been the witness of this Church to that type of religion which was to find its largest embodiment in the world-wide Methodist Church. Here the story of this unique community is told lucidly, and with appreciation, though not uncritically, for the first time by a nonmember of the Church.

Famous personalities find a place in the story: John Huss, John Amos Comenius, Count Zinzendorf, Bishop Spangenberg, Peter Boehler, Christian David, John Wesley, and many more. The Moravian Church, greatest of all Missionary Churches in proportion to its numbers is still devotedly carrying on its ministries in many parts of the world.

# JESUS—KING MOST WONDERFUL

A. E. GOULD

'. . . an important book by the Chairman of the Congregational Union of England and Wales. It makes its own unique contribution to the body of knowledge and adds something to our understanding of the New Testament and the person and work of Jesus . . . Preachers will find it invaluable as a source-book, of starting-points and useful outlines for sermons.'

*Methodist Recorder*

'No preacher, teacher or witnessing Christian could read this book without gaining a great deal.'

*Baptist Times*

## GEORGE ALLEN & UNWIN LTD